Imperialism and Development

The East African Groundnut Scheme
and its legacy

NICHOLAS WESTCOTT

James Currey
is an imprint of Boydell & Brewer Ltd
PO Box 9, Woodbridge, Suffolk IP12 3DF (GB)
www.jamescurrey.com

and of

Boydell & Brewer Inc.
668 Mt Hope Avenue, Rochester, NY 14620-2731 (US)
www.boydellandbrewer.com

© Nicholas Westcott 2020

First published 2020
Paperback edition 2022

The right of Nicholas Westcott to be identified as
the author of this work has been asserted in accordance with
sections 77 and 78 of the Copyright, Designs and Patents Act 1988

All Rights Reserved. Except as permitted under current legislation
no part of this work may be photocopied, stored in a retrieval system,
published, performed in public, adapted, broadcast, transmitted,
recorded or reproduced in any form or by any means, without the
prior permission of the copyright owner

The publisher has no responsibility for the continued existence or accuracy
of URLs for external or third-party internet websites referred to in this book,
and does not guarantee that any content on such websites is, or will remain,
accurate or appropriate

British Library Cataloguing in Publication Data
A catalogue record for this book is available from the British Library

ISBN 978-1-84701-259-3 (James Currey hardback)
ISBN 978-1-84701-345-3 (James Currey paperback)

Typeset in 10 on 12pt Cordale with Gill Sans MT display
by Avocet Typeset, Bideford, Devon, EX39 2BP

An exemplary study of how politicians and planners can get development so wildly wrong, wasting everyone's money in the process. Of real relevance to anyone interested in British politics or African development.

Sir David Cannadine, Dodge Professor of History, Princeton University

Paced like a thriller, this wonderfully-told account of 'How Not To Do It' of 70 years ago is also a cautionary tale for today: how political urgency overcame expert doubt and did not stop to consider local African knowledge, how imperial hubris cast aside colonial caution – and, at the end, how little independent Africa has learned from imperial farce. How difficult it is for modern states to acknowledge that little peasant steps are more sure than great leaps forward.

Professor John Lonsdale, Emeritus Professor of African History and Fellow of Trinity College, University of Cambridge

an important contribution to the study of an infamous episode in the history of late colonialism and top-down development in Africa. ... As a case study in the mismanagement of development it is unique.

Professor Martin Walsh, Adjunct Professor in the School of Business Studies and Humanities, Nelson Mandela African Institution of Science and Technology, Arusha, Tanzania

The iconic story of government overreach – confident technocracy incapable of learning from local knowledge. This is the definitive account.

Sir Paul Collier, Professor of Economics and Public Policy, Blavatnik School of Government, University of Oxford

a very readable story, well researched, wittily told, with many lessons on how to avoid such tragedies, lessons that have never been properly learned in the meantime but badly need to be learned for the future.

Emeritus Professor Peter Lawrence, Keele University

for Miriam

Contents

List of Illustrations   viii
List of Abbreviations   ix
Preface and Acknowledgements   xii

Introduction   1

1 Austerity   25

2 A Scheme is Born   37

3 'The Poison of the Official Pen...'   56

4 The Groundnut Army   78

5 Beating about the Bush   99

6. The Overseas Food Corporation   114

7 1949: The Crisis   132

8 The Last Chance   154

9 A Sudden Death   171

10 Legacy and Lessons   189

Bibliography   221
Index   231

List of Illustrations

DRAWING

Spike Milligan's cartoon on Concorde, 1975   xi

MAP

Map of Tanganyika in 1948, showing provinces and Groundnut Scheme areas   xvi

PHOTOGRAPHS

1.1	John Strachey, as Minister of Food, 28 May 1946	30
2.1	Arthur Wakefield, author of the Plan for the Mechanised Cultivation of Groundnuts in East Africa	49
4.1	Unloading a bulldozer onto a lighter, Dar es Salaam port, 1948	86
5.1	Bulldozer clearing bush at Kongwa	100
5.2	Mtwara deep-water quay under construction, 1950	108
6.1	John Strachey visiting Kongwa 1948, accompanied by Dick Plummer, David Martin, Adam Noble and Major-General Harrison	126
6.2	Ploughing the experimental plot at Kongwa	131
7.1	Aerial view of Unit 1 farm at Kongwa	135
8.1	Chain-clearing of bush by bulldozers and Shervicks in Southern Province, near Nachingwea	169
9.1	Groundnut field at Kongwa with baobab, 1949	188

Abbreviations

ACET	African Centre for Economic Transformation
BDEE	British Documents on the End of Empire
CAB	Cabinet Office
CDC	Colonial Development Corporation
CD&W	Colonial Development and Welfare
CEDC	Colonial Economic Development Council
CO	Colonial Office
CUP	Cambridge University Press
DAR	District Annual Report
DEVCO	Directorate for Development Cooperation, European Commission
DFID	Department for International Development
DO	District Officer
EARH	East African Railways and Harbours
FCB	Fabian Colonial Bureau
FCO	Foreign and Commonwealth Office
HMG	Her Majesty's Government
HMSO	Her Majesty's Stationery Office
HMT	Her Majesty's Treasury
IMF	International Monetary Fund
IT	Information Technology
JICH	Journal of Imperial and Commonwealth History
LSE	London School of Economics
MAF	Ministry of Agriculture and Fisheries
MoF	Ministry of Food
MP	Member of Parliament
OFC	Overseas Food Corporation
ORD	Overseas Resources Development (Bill and Act)
OUP	Oxford University Press
PC	Provincial Commissioner
PM	Prime Minister
RAF	Royal Air Force

SILABU	Sisal Labour Bureau
TAC	Tanganyika Agricultural Corporation
TNA	Tanzania National Archives
TNR	Tanzania Notes and Records
UAC	United Africa Company
UMCA	Universities Mission to Central Africa
US	United States

Spike Milligan's cartoon on Concorde, 1975 (courtesy of Spike Milligan Productions Ltd)

Preface and Acknowledgements

In July 1982, I visited Kongwa.

It is a small stop along the Dar es Salaam–Dodoma bus route in Tanzania. There were a few market stalls, a scattering of dwellings separated by dusty pathways and an occasional modest *hoteli* (local bar-cum-guest house). It was very dry. The pump for the new well was broken, so the people relied on dribbles of water from a large storage tank for their supply.

Nobody had heard of the Groundnut Scheme. I tried to explain what it was in my broken Swahili, but a boy eventually took me to see Mzee Mbogo, who spoke English. 'Ah,' he said, 'you mean "The Overseas"...'. He used to work for 'The Overseas' as an accounts clerk, and was most amused that anyone wanted to write about it. I explained that I wanted to see what was left of the scheme. This led immediately into a bureaucratic morass over whether I had the necessary permits to do so, and whether the local Party officials would let me wander around on my own. A part of the nearby area had been given by President Nyerere to the ANC as a training camp. In those days a white face in these parts looked suspicious unless accompanied by a dog collar or a cassock.

Eventually, the next day, I was taken by two young lads to walk around the area the locals referred to as 'Half London'. Two miles from the village, the old site of the Overseas Food Corporation (OFC) headquarters was like a ghost town. Empty concrete platforms lay among the thorn bush, steps leading up to emptiness, where a long-vanished veranda used to stand. A waterless washbasin stood alone on one. A small overgrown roundabout in the middle of nowhere had one or two barely legible road signs: 'Piccadilly', 'The Strand' ... and a small stretch of tarmac ran 30 yards from each of the turnings until it petered out into sandy track. A ruined, roofless church stood on the hillside above, looking forlornly over the scene.

The only extant buildings belonged to the local hospital. 'It used to be three times the size', said the old doctor, 'but they took the other buildings away to South Africa.' Nearby was a building still labelled

'Upper Mess'. The wreck of an ancient Austin Seven rotted away, a pile of long-perished tractor tyres leaned perilously, and the last broken down Massey-Ferguson tractor in Kongwa had become a plaything for the children.

In Britain and elsewhere the Groundnut Scheme is almost equally forgotten, unless you are over 70 or studied development economics. It was one of the first major failures of agricultural development in Africa – the prototype of many a large-scale, government-run, high-cost development project that failed to deliver what it promised. Along with the *Office du Niger* in West Africa and similar schemes in Belgian and Portuguese African colonies, it was among the first but probably the greatest economic white elephant in Africa.

This book is a study in failure. Not just agricultural or imperial failure, but commercial, organisational, political and bureaucratic failure. That it has left little physical legacy in Tanzania was clear from my visit nearly 40 years ago. But failures are as significant historically as successes, their impact as profound, and the lessons they teach as, if not more, useful. In some ways the most important thing about the Groundnut Scheme is that it failed. But if we fail to understand *why* it failed, similar agricultural schemes and in fact megaprojects of every stripe, will simply be condemned to repeat that failure again and again.

I first encountered the story in the 1970s when researching a doctorate on Tanzanian history. In the British National Archives in leafy Kew (in those days still the Public Record Office), I found file after file on the scheme, almost untouched since they were first written. The more I read, the more I was struck by a sense of disbelief that such a scheme was ever launched, and a profound feeling of *déja vu*. The story seemed so familiar, so resonant of other great national projects that began with ambitious visions and high hopes but ended in disaster. So vast was its scale, so eloquent its advocates, so trenchant its critics, so disastrous its implementation, that it seemed the very prototype of every other government failure in my own lifetime (and there have been plenty).

In writing this book, as explained more fully in the Introduction, I wanted to address three particular questions: Why have so many megaprojects of this kind failed, despite the inspiration and the effort poured into them? Secondly, how can African agriculture be transformed: by mechanisation or by other means? And thirdly, what does it tell us about the British Empire and how it worked in Africa in the mid-20th century?

This book has had a long gestation. Following the historical research undertaken in the 1970s and '80s, my life took an unplanned 35-year detour into diplomacy, during which I worked for a number of years in Tanzania and Ghana, as well as visiting many other African countries.

Returning to the book when I became Director of the Royal African Society in 2017, I hope the text has benefited from my greater understanding of the ways of government, as well as from the advances in scholarship on the history of colonialism and development (as described in the Introduction), while inevitably suffering from the fact that many of the participants and protagonists had passed away and could no longer provide oral evidence. Nevertheless, I believe the intervening years have shown that the lessons of the book are even more relevant now than they were then. I set out this context in the Introduction, and draw the lessons for our own times in the final chapter.

Over these years I have accumulated many debts. First and foremost, I owe to John Iliffe, that outstanding scholar of Africa who supervised the original thesis, as well as to John Lonsdale and many friends, Fellows, supervisors and students in Cambridge my training as a historian. For that I am eternally grateful. I was lucky to be taught and inspired by a generation of imperial historians that included Jack Gallagher, Ronald Robinson, Eric Stokes, Anil Seal and Chris Bayly. I am also grateful to Sidney Sussex College for its support throughout my eight years as a student there, and particularly to Derek Beales, Tim Blanning and Otto Smail as supervisors, and to the Smuts Memorial Fund for financial support. The University of Dar es Salaam welcomed me as a Research Associate for a year in 1979, where I am particularly grateful to Professors Isaria Kimambo and Fred Kaijage and Head Librarian Mrs Mascarenhas for their help and friendship. That veteran of the nationalist movement Ally Sykes, and the former Mayor of Dar es Salaam Manu Devani and his wife Sushila also showed me much kindness and generosity as well as insights into African views on the colonial period. I owe to my time and many colleagues in the Foreign and Commonwealth Office (FCO), the Treasury, Whitehall and Brussels, the understanding of how governments work in practice, the relationship between ministers and officials and the relationship between government and Parliament, especially when a great political project is embarked upon. To colleagues in the British Department for International Development (DFID), the Directorate for Development Cooperation (DEVCO), the World Bank and the International Monetary Fund (IMF) as well as to Professors Paul Collier and Stefan Dercon in Oxford, and K.Y. Amoako in Ghana, who were generous with their time and views, I owe an understanding of development in practice as well as theory. I offer my thanks to all my academic, diplomatic and bureaucratic companions, colleagues and sparring partners for their friendship, support and challenge over the years.

For access to the necessary archives I am very grateful to the directors and staff, past and present, of The National Archives in Kew, the Tanzania National Archives (TNA) in Dar es Salaam, the Bodleian Libraries in Oxford (especially the former Rhodes House archives and the ever helpful Lucy McCann), the University Library, the African Studies Centre and Churchill College Archives in Cambridge, the London School of Economics Library and the School of Oriental and African Studies Library in London; and especially to Elizabeth El Qadhi and the family of John Strachey for permission to quote from his archives, to Edward Bunting and his family for access to Dr Hugh Bunting's papers and photographs of the scheme, and to Vicky Unwin for permission to use some photographs and quote from her mother's letters from Kongwa. Peter Le Mare, one of the last surviving 'groundnutters', gave invaluable information, local colour and comments on the manuscript before he sadly passed away in 2017. The BBC kindly permitted me to refer to their 1982 radio documentary on the scheme. To the late Mike Cowen I also owe many ideas and much encouragement.

For comments on the ideas for or drafts of this book, I am particularly grateful to John Iliffe, John Lonsdale, Dave Anderson, Sarah Stockwell, Matteo Rizzo, Tim Lankester, Anthony Barker and Alex Plant (whose original suggestion for the title of this book, 'Nuts: The story of the Groundnut Scheme', had to be put aside for marketing reasons). I am especially grateful to John Gilkes who drew the map. To the admirable and invaluable James Currey I owe the fact that this book appears in print at all, and to Jaqueline Mitchell and the editors and readers at Boydell & Brewer I owe a considerable debt for their help, care, attention and suggestions on the manuscript.

But my greatest debt is to my family: my parents, my brother and sister, my children Anna and Finn, and above all to my wife Miriam, the light of my life, who lived for years with the Groundnut Scheme as well as with me, but sadly did not live to see it bear fruit as a book. It is dedicated to her memory.

Putney, London
January 2020

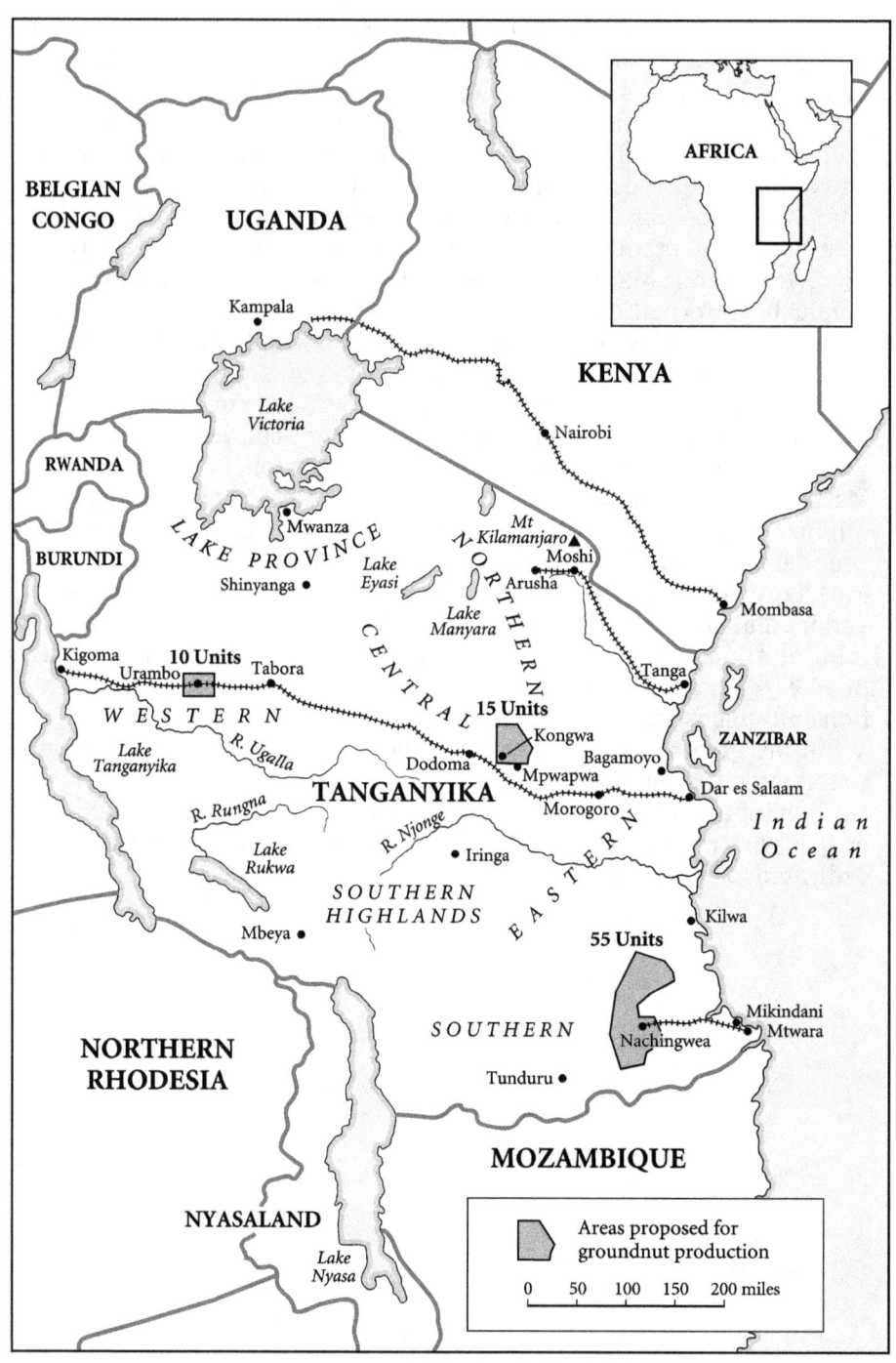

Map of Tanganyika in 1948, showing provinces and Groundnut Scheme areas
(John Gilkes MapArt)

Introduction

In the 1940s and '50s, the East African Groundnut Scheme was infamous to the British public, and to the wider world, as both a development and financial disaster and a political scandal. It was brought into being by the post-war Labour Government at almost the same time as the National Health Service. But while the one became an outstanding success, widely admired throughout the world, the other was a disastrous failure. Today, the extraordinary story of the conception, initiation and failure of the scheme lies buried, lost and forgotten, another failed legacy of colonialism. Yet there are good reasons to dig it up and tell this story again, for a new audience.

First, the Groundnut Scheme was the most ambitious development project ever undertaken by the British Government in any of its colonies. It was launched in the new dawn of colonial development that followed the Second World War, and was intended as a flagship enterprise to show how African agriculture could be transformed, a core objective of British colonial development thinking at the time. Given the scale and importance of the scheme, a detailed study is fully justified to understand the intellectual and practical context that gave rise to it, the development thinking that drove it, and the reasons it proved such a spectacular failure.

But the history of the scheme also illuminates a number of wider issues. For one thing, it exposes to plain sight the workings of British imperialism in its final, declining phase. What indeed was the purpose of the empire after the Second World War? The war itself had demonstrated that one of its fundamental purposes was to support the metropolis in its hour of need. This continued into the post-war period. But both periods also reveal the domestic and international constraints on colonial rule. The Groundnut Scheme, as a study of British imperialism in operation, therefore also helps us understand how the mind and the sinews of empire worked.

It also casts an interesting, almost contemporary, light on British politics in the 1940s. The post-war Labour Government of Clement Attlee has taken on a hallowed, almost mythic status in the public imagination. Yet, as other studies have shown, it was riven by deep rivalries and challenged by the most difficult of circumstances. Attlee, as much as Lincoln, led a team of rivals through dark days. The Groundnut Scheme was the Labour Government's most spectacular failure, and has tended to be air-brushed from the political memory of the period despite the fact that it played a not insignificant part in Labour's eventual defeat by the Conservatives in 1951. It is worth explaining in more detail why a government that achieved so much on this occasion fell so spectacularly flat on its face.

There are equally lessons from this fiasco not just for development, the study of imperialism or the analysis of politics, but for all ambitious government schemes – 'megaprojects' as they are now known, *'grands projets'* in the French tradition. From decision-making to implementation and accountability, there is great contemporary relevance in this story. Anyone who has followed the fate of disastrous megaprojects, from the US 'Desertron', the Superconducting Super Collider in Texas, to the British NHS IT system or HS2 railway project, or, in Africa, Tanzania's Dodoma capital project, Nigeria's Abeokuta steel mill, South Africa's Medupi and Project Bravo coal-fired power stations, and Zairean President Mobutu's ill-fated nuclear programme, will recognise many of the failings that have driven these projects to disaster. The final chapter therefore explores in depth how we should better learn the lessons of the Groundnut Scheme if we are to avoid the same mixture of wishful thinking, hubris, mendacity, haste and incompetence giving us one Groundnut Scheme after another.

Finally, the full story has never been told. While there are many references to the scheme in secondary literature, only two detailed studies of the scheme have ever been published. In 1950, Alan Wood's book *The Groundnut Affair* revealed to the world the scandalous mess the scheme had become. It is a great work of contemporary investigative journalism by someone who, as head of its information department, saw the scheme in operation from close quarters; but Wood had no access to the official records of his day. Thirty years later, Volume II of D.J. Morgan's *Official History of Colonial Development* provided a detailed account drawn from those official British Government papers, but does not cover the local African or British political contexts.[1] A

---

[1] Alan Wood, *The Groundnut Affair* (London, The Bodley Head, 1950); D.J. Morgan, *The Official History of Colonial Development, Vol. II: Developing British Colonial Resources* (London, HMSO and Macmillan, 1980), ch. 5. The five best short summaries are in Ronald Hyam, *Britain's Declining Empire: The road to decolonisation 1918–1968* (Cambridge, Cambridge University Press (CUP), 2006), pp. 131–6; Joseph Morgan Hodge, *Triumph of the Expert: Agrarian doctrines of development and the legacies of British colonialism* (Athens, Ohio University Press, 2007), ch. 7; Michael Havinden and David Meredith,

full account, drawing together the political, public, official, imperial and local elements is long overdue, and only such an account can fully explain the nature and scale of the failure.

This bulk of this study takes the form of a conventional narrative account of the scheme, drawing primarily on British and Tanzanian archives. It seeks to explain why things happened as they did, drawing on the widest possible range of contemporary sources, to understand the motives, the thinking, the experience and the practical constraints influencing the decision-makers and actors who made it happen. Only in the context of the time can we understand all these things. In that sense it is a case study in what Joseph Hodge has dubbed the 'historicist' approach to development.[2] But it is equally important to draw out the themes and trends that we can see in retrospect but which may not have been apparent to those engaged in the enterprise at the time. It is therefore a history with a purpose, to understand better what happened and to learn lessons for the future, a message that is underlined in the final chapter of the book.

A word about terminology and sources. The world of the 1940s was one still dominated by men. Women's voices are few and far between and their perspective on the scheme is under-reported, though I have included it where sources do exist. I have occasionally used terms such as 'housewife' that were in common usage at the time where it is appropriate in the historical context. I have also used other contemporary terms such as 'groundnutter', a self-description used by and for all those working on the scheme, and 'native' (in quotations) which at the time was deemed by the colonial administration the acceptable term for the original inhabitants of the African colonies. I have equally retained the name 'Tanganyika' rather than Tanzania to avoid dissonance with contemporary sources. As explained in the Preface, the accidents of life meant that by the time I took up this study most of the protagonists had died, so very little oral evidence was available, and it was hard for me to undertake field research in Tanzania. In particular, this has made it difficult to fully reflect the African perspective on the scheme, and has made me almost entirely

---

Colonialism and Development: Britain and its tropical colonies, 1850–1960 (London, Routledge, 1993), ch. 12; Jan S. Hogendorn and K.M. Scott, 'Very large-scale agricultural projects: The lessons of the East African Groundnut Scheme', in Robert I. Rotberg (ed.) *Imperialism, Colonialism and Hunger: East and Central Africa* (Lexington, The Lexington Press, 1983); and the most recent interpretation in Stefan Esselborn, 'Environment, Memory, and the Groundnut Scheme: Britain's largest colonial agricultural development project and its global legacy', *Global Environment,* 11 (2013), pp. 58–93.

[2] Joseph M. Hodge, Gerald Hödl and Martina Kopf (eds), *Developing Africa: Concepts and practices in 20th century colonialism* (Manchester, Manchester University Press, 2014), p. 22.

dependent on imperial sources, both in the UK and in Tanzania. This inevitably skews the perspective and, though I have tried to redress the balance as best I can, makes it a less fully rounded picture than is desirable. The more research you do, the larger the gaps you find, and there remains great scope for bottom-up research on the African perspective on the scheme that must await future historians. Another gap was in the commercial records. No archives of the OFC could be traced, and the records available from Unilever reveal very little that is not in the official public record.[3] But all remaining factual or judgemental errors in this work are entirely my own.

Development and empire

A great deal has been written on the origins and meaning of 'development' as a concept and as practice in the colonial empires, highlighting in particular the distinction to be drawn between development as a process and development as an objective.[4] This section explains the main themes that have been identified and the debates that have taken place, both to put the Groundnut Scheme in context and understand the impetus behind it.

The theological and administrative origins of the concept of development in Victorian England and 19th-century India were applied at an early stage to the imperial possessions acquired in Africa in the late 19th century. The great liberal conservative Joseph Chamberlain was passionately attached to the economic potential of the empire, and appealed to reluctant Tory parliamentarians by comparing the development of Britain's newly acquired African territories to the need for investment in 'great estates' to make them economically rewarding for both the owner and the inhabitants. This resulted in the Colonial Loans Act of 1899, allowing the British Treasury to lend to colonial administrations in Africa. But this approach was overtaken by Lord Lugard's concept of the 'Dual Mandate' in the early 20th century,

---

[3] D.K. Fieldhouse, *Merchant Capital and Economic Decolonization: The United Africa Company, 1929–1987* (Oxford, Oxford University Press (OUP), 1994), trawled their archives extensively and found 'virtually nothing in the UAC or Unilever archives which could add significantly to the story told by Morgan' (p. 216). New perspectives on the business history of Africa can be found in Veronique Dimier and Sarah Stockwell (eds), *The Business of Development in Postcolonial Africa* (London, Palgrave Macmillan, forthcoming 2020).

[4] M.P. Cowen and R.W. Shenton, *Doctrines of Development* (London, Routledge, 1996); Stephen Constantine, *The Making of British Colonial Development Policy, 1914–1940* (London, Cass, 1984); Hodge, *Triumph of the Expert*; Havinden and Meredith, *Colonialism and Development*; Morgan, *Colonial Development, Vol. I: The Origins of British aid policy, 1924–1945*.

which presaged a less interventionist form of laissez-faire development.[5]

There is always a risk that we read back into the past the assumptions and preoccupations of the present. For many of the early missionaries and colonials in Africa, as well as for some of the Africans they ruled, what the imperial powers claimed to bring was 'civilisation'.[6] In economic terms, most colonial officials were brought up on a version of British history that underlined the private ownership of property and individual initiative that led, firstly, to a commercialisation of agriculture and then to the industrial revolution. For most of them, this was the trajectory along which the (to their eyes) undeveloped regions of Africa would evolve. They firmly believed that integration into the world economy would bring to these territories the benefits they had brought in the past to Britain itself. In terms of the role of the colonial administration in these early years, it was not so much 'development', which tended to be understood in terms of welfare, but a cash revenue which was sought, to generate income that would enable Africans to pay a poll tax to help cover the costs of the colonial administration itself.[7]

So, despite Chamberlain's vision, the dominant philosophy of colonial authorities was that they should act as the guardian, not developer of the empire, and that growth would occur naturally through the provision of law and order, infrastructure and education, though preferably not so fast as to disrupt the native way of life.[8] It was no accident that the Colonial Office had no formal economic department until 1935, as the Treasury liked to maintain a firm grip on colonial financial and economic policy. It remained a bastion of fiscal rectitude, insisting that colonies should be self-sufficient, pay their way and not become a burden on the imperial exchequer. Africa's inherent poverty combined with the shortage of external capital meant that colonial administrations had no option but to be economical; using indirect rule, which was cheap, was in part a response to this constraint.[9] In the 1920s this led to there being no love lost between the proponents of colonial development, like Sir William Ormsby-Gore, who opined that 'the Treasury continuously and by tradition do everything they can to make Colonial Development difficult'; and the Treasury who regarded the kind

---

[5] Constantine, *British Colonial Development*, pp. 11–16; Hodge, *Triumph of the Expert*, pp. 21–4.
[6] For a contemporary African perspective on this, see N.J. Westcott, 'An East African Radical: The life of Erica Fiah', *Journal of African History*, 1981,22:i, pp. 94–6.
[7] Havinden and Meredith, *Colonialism and Development*, chs 2–5.
[8] Constantine, *British Colonial Development*, pp. 9–24.
[9] P.J. Cain and A.G. Hopkins, *British Imperialism: Crisis and deconstruction, 1914–1990* (Harlow, Longman, 1993), p. 218.

of development schemes involving Treasury guarantees put forward by Ormsby-Gore's friend Leo Amery as, 'sheer financial immorality, a temptation to the Colonial Governments to embark on premature and ill-conceived enterprises by financial inducements which blind them to the ultimate risk.'[10]

But this model of non-interventionism came under extreme stress during the Depression. Almost the only source of cash revenue that most Africans could access was from the production of primary products for export, or from working as manual labour on European-owned farms or mines that themselves produced for export. The slump in raw material prices therefore had an immediate and drastic effect on colonial revenues. Several colonies struggled to pay the interest on Treasury loans they had taken out to build basic infrastructure such as railways. Throughout Britain's African colonies retrenchment was imposed, staff reduced, building and research stalled and colonial administration put on pretty much a care-and-maintenance basis. The consequences were twofold: an increase in the production of peasant crops, as farmers sought to sustain income levels by growing more to compensate for lower prices; and a serious decline in the health, nutrition and welfare of the population at large and those Africans working for European enterprises in particular. Scandals, both of neglected famines in rural backwaters and appalling working conditions on estates and in towns, began to multiply.[11]

Tanganyika, where the Groundnut Scheme was to be based, was a classic case of this imperial lassitude, and the legacy of the Depression was to play an important part in the scheme's future. Taken from the Germans after one of the longest and most debilitating campaigns of the First World War, Tanganyika was thereafter administered by Britain under a League of Nations Mandate, though in practice it was treated exactly the same as any other colonial territory. Its assets were modest and its European population small, so it became during the 1930s something of an imperial Cinderella. The government's budget fell from £2.1 million in 1929 to £1.7 million in 1933, and nearly 20% of that was spent on servicing the territory's £8 million debt.[12] In consequence the

---

[10] Ormsby-Gore minute, Dec 1923, CO 536/128/Treas 55494, and Hopkins minute, 21 Jan 1929, T161/291/S.33978, quoted in Constantine, *British Colonial Development*, pp. 128, 169.

[11] See ch. 2, 'Aspects of economic history' by C.C. Wrigley, and ch. 13, 'East Africa' by Andrew Roberts (esp. pp. 687–701) in A.D. Roberts (ed.), *The Cambridge History of Africa, Vol. 7: 1905–1940* (Cambridge, CUP, 1986).

[12] Tanganyika Territory, *Estimates* and *Blue Books* for 1929-1935, in Tanzania National Archives, Dar es Salaam (TNA); minute by Lee, 2 Mar 1936, CO 691/147/42011/3, Colonial Office papers in the (British) National Archives, Kew. See generally for this paragraph John Iliffe, *A Modern History of Tanganyika* (Cambridge, CUP, 1979), ch. 11.

colonial administration shrank: the Native Affairs and Labour Departments were scrapped altogether and their duties handed to overworked provincial officials, while spending on medical, educational and technical departments was severely cut. Officials were overburdened with work, and so tied to their desks that a severe famine in Bugufi district went undiscovered for months.[13] Development spending stopped dead. The administration responded to the revenue shortfall by launching in 1931 a 'Plant More Crops' campaign aimed at African producers: 'Whatever the price, a tonnage for export is to be aimed at as a duty', district officers (DOs) were ordered in 1931, and from 1933 the energetic new Director of Agriculture, John Wakefield, threw himself into encouraging cotton cultivation wherever possible.[14] But by 1937–38, it was clear that there was only so much that could be done without a more significant financial investment to facilitate faster economic growth. In 1938 the Governor set up a Development Committee in Dar es Salaam and requested increased financial aid from London to accelerate the territory's growth – part of the pressure that was building on the British Government to change its overall approach to colonial development.[15]

At the imperial level, the crisis brought on by the Depression led to two significant shifts.

Firstly, what had been perceived in the early years of colonial rule as a problem of underpopulation in Africa was replaced by a rising fear of demographic growth. Officials became concerned that colonial populations were growing faster than the land could support them. The evidence seemed clear: from increased competition for the most fertile land, to the degradation of soil in many areas either as a consequence of over-cultivation, over-grazing, drought or all three combined, it resulted in an increased supply of unemployed African labour seeking jobs on European farms and mines or in towns in order to earn a little cash. Of course, the challenge was greatest where alienation of large areas of the best land to European settlers had pushed Africans onto the more marginal lands. But it also reflected the difficulty of trying to raise African agricultural productivity without trained agricultural staff or budgets for research and innovation. This consciousness of environmental fragility gave rise to a strain of neo-Malthusian thinking in discussions about Africa's economic future which pushed the question of agricultural reform swiftly up the agenda.[16] When this concern

[13] *Report by Sir S. Armitage-Smith on a Financial Mission to Tanganyika*, Cmd 1428 (London, HMSO, 1932); correspondence in CO 691/142/42026 and TNA 13252/I.
[14] McElderry to Provincial Commissioners, 14 Oct 1931, TNA 215/155/8.
[15] 'Note of a meeting at the Treasury', 1 Jul 1938 (attended by Colonial Office and Tanganyika officials), and Governor (Young) to Colonial Secretary (Macdonald), 31 Dec 1938, CO 691/157/42154.
[16] Hodge, *Triumph of the Expert*, pp. 166–78; Karl Ittmann, 'The Colonial Office

was linked with a serious global food shortage in the aftermath of the Second World War, Malthusian warnings seemed to be coming to pass. Alan Wood's book on the Groundnut Scheme begins with a chapter devoted to 'The Monster Malthus', setting the context clearly in terms of worry about an impending population disaster as the number of people outstripped the available food.[17]

Secondly, it became a priority to head off the growing discontent that was stimulated by the deteriorating living conditions in many colonies. Colonial rule always felt more precarious to the imperial administrators themselves than it did to their subjects (or indeed to many later commentators), and they had a deep-seated fear of unrest. Across much of Africa the thin red line was very thin indeed, worn threadbare by the retrenchment of the 1930s. The spate of disturbances that broke out late that decade, especially in the West Indies but also stretching across much of Africa, even reached Dar es Salaam, Tanganyika's sleepy capital, where dockworkers went on strike for a week in July 1939.[18] It became increasingly clear that the economic and social grievances driving this unrest needed to be addressed more swiftly than the fullness of time and the action of the market would ever do. The outbreak of war merely accentuated this argument.[19]

The Colonial Office concluded that it was imperative to find ways to ameliorate living conditions for its African subjects, and that additional resources would be needed to achieve this. As Secretary of State for the Colonies, Malcolm Macdonald championed this approach, leading directly to the adoption in July 1940 of the Colonial Development and Welfare Act. Macdonald's rationale was clear:

> if we are not going to do something fairly good for the Colonies, and something which helps them to get proper social services, we shall deserve to lose the Colonies, and it will be only a matter of time before we get what we deserve.[20]

It was an Act not to prepare the colonies for independence, but to keep them peaceful and so preserve colonial rule. The Treasury was for once accommodating and, though the financial provision was halved from the proposed £10 million to £5 million in response to the war effort, the

---

and the Population Question in the British Empire 1918–1962', *Journal of Imperial and Commonwealth Affairs*, 27:3 (1999); David M. Anderson, 'Depression, Dust Bowl, Demography and Drought: The colonial state and soil conservation in East Africa during the 1930s', *African Affairs*, 83:332 (Jul 1984), pp. 325–39;
[17] Wood, *Groundnut Affair*, ch. 1.
[18] John Iliffe, 'A History of the Dockworkers of Dar es Salaam', *Tanzania Notes and Records*, 71 (1970), pp. 119–48.
[19] Constantine, *British Colonial Development*, ch. 9.
[20] Macdonald minute, 14 Jan 1940, CO 859/19/7475, quoted in Morgan, *Colonial Development, Vol. I*, p. 75.

Treasury also wrote off £11 million in loans to colonial governments that were never likely to be repaid. It marked a major ideological shift that the concept of 'trusteeship' for colonial subjects included some assurance of a reasonable condition of life, and overruled the requirement of self-sufficiency for colonial governments.[21]

The war itself then precipitated another major shift in attitudes towards colonial development: a new attachment to planning and a massive increase in scale. The Second World War transformed the British Government, mobilisation for the war effort pushing it into areas of public and private life it had scarcely dreamed of before. Planning, economic and social as much as military, became an ideology as well as a necessity. The forward thinkers in the Colonial Office, above all the leading economist and financial adviser, Sydney Caine, urged a more salient role for the Office itself in helping colonial governments with development planning, to bring a greater focus on economic development as well as welfare spending, and back it with a substantial increase in resources. This thinking led to the revised Colonial Development and Welfare Act of 1945 (CD&W Act) which committed £120 million in additional spending for the following 10 years. For the first time there was a willingness to offer substantial state investment from the metropolis to the colonies.[22]

This shift in thinking also owed much to the work of the Fabian Colonial Bureau (FCB). Set up in 1940 and run by the redoubtable Rita Hinden as secretary and Arthur Creech Jones as Chairman, it worked assiduously to further the case for political and economic reform in the colonies. Through its pamphlets and Parliamentary activism it helped change the climate of opinion in Britain in favour of a more forward colonial policy, and the ideas it developed during the early 1940s had a significant impact on the policies adopted by the Labour Government after 1945, not least once Creech Jones became Colonial Secretary in October 1946.[23]

For colonial officials, though, the assumption underlying this shift in thinking was that Africa would remain for the foreseeable future an agrarian society. Having made a virtue of necessity in promoting 'indirect rule' and co-opting what they chose to define as traditional 'native authorities' (or chiefs) to act as their local administration, most colonial

---

[21] Constantine, *British Colonial Development*, pp. 255–61; Morgan, *Colonial Development, Vol. I*, ch. 10.
[22] J.M. Lee and Martin Petter, *The Colonial Office, War and Development Policy* (London, Institute of Commonwealth Studies, 1982), esp. pp. 168–175; Morgan, *Colonial Development, Vol. I*, ch. 15; R.D. Pearce, *The Turning Point in Africa: British Colonial Policy, 1938–1948* (London, Cass, 1982). Interview with Sir Sydney Caine, 26 Nov 1980. On the British economic context, see W.K. Hancock and M.M. Gowing, *British War Economy* (London, HMSO, 1949).
[23] Pearce, *Turning Point*, pp. 91–112.

officials were deeply wary of the 'detribalised natives' who through education or migration to towns escaped the traditional hierarchies they had defined. In effect, they feared the destabilising consequences of what we now call 'globalisation', a direct consequence of the irreversible connection to the outside world that colonialism itself brought. Enabling Africans to remain in their rural areas and make a decent living from farming was an integral part of British imperial ideology and underpinned the work that began in the late 1930s to improve agricultural techniques and production.[24]

Colonial development in Africa

The earliest and most ambitious scheme to transform African peasant agriculture was undertaken in French West Africa where the *Office du Niger* was set up in the 1920s to bring scientific methods and greater scale to traditional farming in the Sahel. Its efforts to force local farmers to adopt intensive ploughing, irrigation and crop rotation on fixed plots of land failed dismally because the African cultivators were not persuaded of the agricultural benefits. In time, the officials came to listen to the farmers' experience of farming in the marginal lands of the Sahel and adapt their theories to the environmental and social realities that the farmers knew only too well.[25] They learnt over time that agricultural change could not be hurried. As Ormsby-Gore himself noted in 1927: 'We have to remember that in the tropics the successful introduction of new crops and the improvement in the quality and yield per acre of existing crops often depends on years of spade work at the laboratory and experimental farm, the practical application of which *cannot be hurried*.'[26]

A similar scheme was launched in the 1920s in the Anglo-Egyptian Sudan, on the Gezira plains west of the Blue Nile, which reached similar

---

[24] Sydney Caine challenged this assumption as early as 1940, presciently warning that: 'If economic development ... is to be secured, it is fairly certain that the old native society will have very largely to vanish, and if that is our aim, we must acquiesce in that social change and envisage the disintegration of native society into something more like the modern structure of this and other western countries ... Personally I think it is inevitable and must be faced because I can see no possibility of an economic development which will satisfy the nascent demand for the comforts of western civilisation on the basis of native social structures.' Caine minute, 28 Nov 1940, CO 691/179/42303/2.
[25] Monica van Beusekom, *Negotiating Development: African farmers and colonial experts at the Office du Niger, 1920–1960* (Oxford, James Currey, 2002).
[26] William Ormsby-Gore, 'British West Africa', *United Empire*, 18, Jan 1927, quoted in Hodge, *Triumph of the Expert*, p. 148 (emphasis added).

conclusions. It was designed to supply the British spinning industry with a reliable supply of long-staple cotton and was based around organised peasant production of irrigated cotton. The British Government supplied the Government of Sudan with £13 million in loans from 1919 to 1924 to build a dam and complex network of canals to provide the irrigation, but the development was undertaken by a private company, the Sudan Plantations Syndicate, financially back by the British Cotton Growing Association, which closely supervised and controlled the producers. By the 1940s, the scheme was considered a success, but only after significant trial and error.[27]

This point was not lost on colonial administrators, who increasingly saw the value of investing in agricultural and scientific research. In an important study, Joseph Hodge has argued that the 1940s witnessed a 'triumph of the expert' in British colonial policy-making, as political leaders came to rely increasingly on advice from those who had experience and expertise. But they remained acutely conscious of how little research had been done and how much there was to do. One Colonial Office official, C.Y. Carstairs, warned presciently in 1945:

> It must be recognised that in the prevailing absence of the bulk of the fundamental data required for sound planning, much of the purely developmental expenditure cannot fail to be misdirected and so wasted, together with the manpower diverted thereto. We must reconcile ourselves to a period of building upon sand, and to some extent of pouring money into the sand.[28]

In British Africa, an alternative way forward was to put the best agricultural land in the hands of white settlers who, it was invariably assumed, would bring improved agricultural experience with them. In South Africa, Rhodesia and Kenya, this was the preferred model. Some wanted to bring it to Tanganyika too. But the Depression of the 1930s put paid to this vision of a glorious and prosperous economic future for these territories, as the settlers suffered as much as anyone from the economic fall-out of the Depression and demanded greater state support to bail them out.[29]

This debate over how to develop played out in Tanganyika as it tried to put together development plans to meet the demands from the Colonial

---

[27] J. Forbes Munro, *Africa and the International Economy, 1800–1960* (London, Dent, 1976), pp. 128–9; for more detail see Tony Barnett, *The Gezira Scheme: The illusion of development* (London, Cass, 1977).

[28] Hodges, *Triumph of the Expert*, passim. C.Y. Carstairs, 'The Place of Surveys in Colonial Development Plans', 1945, CO 927/1/B, quoted in Hodge, Hödl and Kopf, *Developing Africa*, p. 25.

[29] Roberts, *Cambridge History of Africa*, pp. 576–8, 624–30 and 692–3; Bruce Berman and John Lonsdale, *Unhappy Valley: Conflict in Kenya & Africa, Vol. II* (London, James Currey, 1992).

Office. In 1940, its Central Development Committee, dominated by European non-officials (settlers and businessmen), published a report on the programmes necessary to 'make Tanganyika a country', economically autonomous from its neighbours and the metropolis. It was redolent of the assumptions of the time: that Africans needed to be encouraged to work; African agriculture was inefficient and only European farming could revolutionise production; and that government's role was to build infrastructure and support white settlement.[30] The Colonial Office vigorously disagreed, arguing that, 'African living standards could be raised by stimulating the exchange of purely native products between Africans.'[31] That report was shelved during the war, but, prodded by London, the Tanganyika Administration produced a second outline development proposal in 1944. This did indeed focus on what Africans themselves wanted – increased health and education services – but was deemed by London insufficiently 'productive'.[32] Caine had already made clear that:

> The object of any plans of Colonial development should be to increase the productivity of the Colonial Empire and so enable Colonial Dependencies to provide themselves with an increased standard of living, and not as a long term policy to provide that standard of living at the expense of this country [Britain].[33]

Sent back to try a third time, the Administration finally delivered *A Ten Year Development and Welfare Plan for Tanganyika Territory* in late 1946.[34] The total budget for the whole territory over 10 years was £18 million, with the largest proportion devoted to transport infrastructure (£7m), then health (£3m), education (£2.2m) and agriculture (£1.7m). But it was still primarily a compilation of projects, not a macro-economic plan; and while African agriculture was seen as the major source of economic growth, the aim, including of education, was to produce 'that rural middle class or yeoman type so necessary to any enduring improvement in the country.'[35] While acknowledging the effort, the Colonial Office again felt Tanganyika needed to do more,

---

[30] Tanganyika Territory, *Report of the Central Development Committee* (Dar es Salaam, Government Printer, 1940). This paragraph draws on N.J. Westcott, 'The Impact of the Second World War on Tanganyika 1939–51' (PhD thesis, Cambridge University, 1982), especially ch. 7.
[31] Minute by Clauson, 26 May 1941, CO 691/179/42303/2.
[32] Tanganyika Territory, *An Outline of Post-War Development Proposals* (Dar es Salaam, Government Printer, 1944), and minutes by Cohen and Caine of Mar–Apr 1945 in CO 691/190/42303/5.
[33] Caine minute, 20 Dec 1941, CO 852/506/19051.
[34] Published by the Government Printer, Dar es Salaam, 1946.
[35] Memorandum by Isherwood (Director of Education), 18 Nov 1944, CO 691/189/42259/5. The CO was unimpressed with the Director of Education: 'The Tanganyika Education Department is rotten bad, largely because Mr Isherwood is a rotten bad Director', noted Clauson, 11 Aug 1939, CO 691/175/42259.

particularly in terms of productive investment and education: 'If we are to keep in touch with the growing political aspirations of Africans in the Territory, and retain their confidence, we must lay the foundations of mass education', directed Cohen and Creech Jones.[36]

The Groundnut Scheme marked a new departure for colonial development in putting its faith neither in African peasants nor in European settlers, but in the colonial state; and not even the local colonial state, but the metropolitan imperial power, acting directly in territory under British control. This reflected the transformation in thinking and practice during the Second World War, and was a logical consequence of the debates that had challenged existing colonial policy during the Depression. It was not the only manifestation of this change. At the same time as the Groundnut Scheme was put in the hands of the state-run OFC, the Colonial Office created the Colonial Development Corporation (CDC) to undertake state-funded investment in colonial production. The remit of both corporations went well beyond the constraints of the CD&W Act. But whereas the successful CDC has received generous attention from historians, its ugly sister, the OFC, has been neglected. This study redresses that balance.[37]

These corporations were both a part of the 'second colonial occupation' that after 1945 was aimed at revitalising the empire both to support Britain and manage a growing demand for participation by Africans in their own political and economic development. As Anthony Low and John Lonsdale have pointed out, that effort 'to raise the level of efficiency in African production while widening the incidence of popular participation in development only too often fell into mutual opposition on the spot.'[38] But the contradiction was even more stark in the case of the Groundnut Scheme, an externally imposed project driven entirely by British domestic priorities. As the following chapters show, in this case it was a contradiction played out in debates in London as much as on the spot.

Post-colonial development: concepts and policies

The previous section set out the historical context of the discussions about development in the 1940s. Since then, the debate on what exactly

[36] Minutes by Creech Jones, 11 Jan, and Cohen, 21 Jan, and Creech Jones to Battershill, 28 Jan 1947, CO 691/197/42259/5.
[37] See ch. 6 below. On CDC, M.P. Cowen, 'The Early Years of the CDC: British state enterprise overseas during late colonialism', *African Affairs*, 83: 330 (Jan 1984), pp. 60–80.
[38] D.A.Low and J.M. Lonsdale, 'Introduction: Towards the new order' in D.A. Low and A. Smith (eds) *History of East Africa, Vol. III* (Oxford, OUP, 1976), pp. 12–15.

is 'development' and what should be the role of external aid or investment has evolved dramatically. How the Groundnut Scheme illuminates these contemporary debates is explored in more detail in the final chapter, but the main issues are worth flagging up in advance.

In relation to Africa, Cowen and Shenton have shown the continuities in development policy between the colonial and independent eras in Kenya, particularly in the perceived role of the state, and the distinction between state-driven 'development' and the 'liberal' evolution of indigenous commerce and industry. More broadly, they also pose questions over the values and assumptions underpinning our concept of 'development', and whether we mean by that simply 'Westernisation' or incorporation into a globalised world economy where inherently 'developing' or 'less developed' countries are at a structural disadvantage, or whether we should be looking at 'true' development which builds on indigenous strengths and creates a form of growth that is both more equitable and more sustainable.[39]

In 2006, William Easterly published his critique of Western aid, *The White Man's Burden,* which argued that externally organised autocratic planning, on lines initiated under colonial rule and then pushed forward by donors and multilateral development agencies, was more of a problem than a solution for reducing poverty, citing the Groundnut Scheme as a classic case of the failure of colonial development planning.[40] He followed this in 2013, in *The Tyranny of Experts,* with an analysis of how Lord Hailey's efforts to use development as a way to justify and rejuvenate the empire actually succeeded, at least for a while. But he argues it created a model of 'authoritarian development' which continues to this day, and which requires a fundamental shift towards 'free development', where people are free to define and pursue their own best interests if Africa's economic problems are to be overcome. A critical element for Easterly in this is the need for 'accountable government', which as we shall see was a key issue for the Groundnut Scheme.[41] The scheme was indeed accountable, but to a distant Parliament with different priorities. In this it reflected the imperial reality of British rule in Africa.

Other critics have condemned all forms of aid. Dambisa Moyo's 2009 book *Dead Aid* denounced the ineffectiveness of development assistance of all kinds in Africa.[42] Moyo argued in particular that 'foreign aid supports corrupt government – providing them with freely avail-

---

[39] Cowen and Shenton, *Doctrines of Development*, ch. 6 and ch. 8
[40] William Easterly, *The White Man's Burden: Why the West's efforts to aid the rest have done so much ill and so little good* (London, Penguin, 2006), pp. 281–3.
[41] William Easterly, *The Tyranny of Experts: Economists, dictators and the forgotten rights of the poor* (New York, Basic Books, 2013), pp. 81–104.
[42] Dambisa Moyo, *Dead Aid: Why aid is not working and how there is another way for Africa* (London, Allen Lane, 2009).

able cash', and that ensuring more effective accountability was a more reliable route to increased development.[43] Amartya Sen had already taken this argument further, arguing in *Development as Freedom* (1999) that the purpose of development was at heart to provide individuals with greater freedom and that the 'enhancement of human freedom is both the main object and primary means of development'.[44] These both drew on a longer tradition of critiques of state intervention and development assistance, pioneered by P.T. Bauer in the 1950s. Bauer initially challenged the benefits of the marketing boards of which the British officials were so fond in colonial Africa, arguing that they impeded the developmental operation of free markets, and moved on to criticise the underlying assumptions of foreign aid as a whole.[45]

The radical alternative critique of development, exemplified in Africa by Walter Rodney, argued that imperialism actively caused underdevelopment in 'Third World' countries, and that the economic distortions imposed by the 'free' market required a higher degree of state intervention to prevent international capital imposing its agenda.[46] The question 'what if Africa had never been colonised?' can have no definitive answer, but that imperialism created its own distortions in the economic structures that evolved in Africa is clear. Nevertheless, for many issues the challenges remain the same. On agricultural development in particular, the debate over the relative merits of state-run farms and private-sector-led enterprise continued for years, currently swinging more in favour of the latter than the former. It is an integral part of the wider debate about top-down versus bottom-up development, one of the issues taken up in the final chapter.

This study illustrates how the Groundnut Scheme exemplified the development thinking of the imperial class in the 1940s to an extreme degree. It reflected the disillusion with peasant production, an absolute faith in the ability of science to triumph over nature, and in the potential for rapid transformation – a great leap forward – in tropical agricultural

[43] Ibid., pp. 49, 147.
[44] Amartya Sen, *Development as Freedom* (New York, Anchor, 1999), p. 53
[45] P.T. Bauer, *West African Trade* (Cambridge, CUP, 1954), and *Dissent on Development: Studies and debates on development economics* (London, Weidenfeld & Nicolson, 1971).
[46] Walter Rodney, *How Europe Underdeveloped Africa* (London, Bogle l'Ouverture, 1972), especially ch. 6. Two classic studies in this mode were E.A. Brett, *Colonialism and Underdevelopment in East Africa: The politics of economic change, 1919–39* (London, Heinemann, 1973) and Colin Leys, *Underdevelopment in Kenya: The political economy of neo-colonialism* (London, Heinemann, 1975). Terminology continues to evolve, with African countries being referred to more recently as 'less developed', 'emerging economies' and even 'frontier economies' (with echoes of Hancock).

production. It also provides abundant evidence that ill-directed aid can be not only a massive misallocation of valuable resources but can do positive harm to a vulnerable economy, in this case reflecting the imperial reality of Britain in Africa.

Imperial realities

The Groundnut Scheme, like the Second World War itself, illuminates what the British Empire was *for*.

The empire had been acquired in fits and starts over the previous few centuries for a variety of reasons. Some had been taken as part of a colonising imperative; some to preserve British trading interests; some to keep it out of others' hands; and some almost by accident. Tanganyika came to Britain as a prize of war, and was welcomed as a convenient way of joining up the patches of red on the map of eastern and southern Africa. But for all the ideological justification of a civilising mission, the ultimate rationale for the colonial empire was for profit, and to support the imperial power whenever needed.[47]

The Second World War demonstrated this vividly. It saw imperialism with the gloves off.[48] Cut off from many traditional sources of supply, deprived of its most important allies in the early years, and strained to meet the physical and financial demands of total war, Britain relied increasingly heavily on the support it could draw from the Dominions, from India and from the colonies. In terms of manpower, money and materials, it had no option but to maximise the supply from colonial sources, whatever the costs and risks. Manpower was required above all for the forces, and African colonies were ordered to recruit soldiers for the West Africa Frontier Force and in East Africa for the King's African Rifles to fight in Ethiopia, North Africa and Burma. But the most critical contribution was in the form of raw materials and food,

---

[47] There is a literature too long to list. But I owe a debt in particular to: Ronald Robinson and John Gallagher with Alice Denny, *Africa and the Victorians: The official mind of imperialism* (London, Macmillan, 1961); Roger Owen and Bob Sutcliffe (eds), *Studies in the Theory of Imperialism* (London, Longman, 1971); Robert D. King and Robin W. Kilson, *The Statecraft of British Imperialism: Essays in honour of Wm Roger Louis*, special issue, *Journal of Imperial and Commonwealth History (JICH)*, 27:2, May 1999. Of more recent histories, I particularly like (and recommend) John Darwin, *Unfinished Empire: The global expansion of Britain* (London, Penguin, 2013).

[48] Nicholas Westcott, 'The impact of the Second World War on Tanganyika, 1939–49', and Michael Cowen and Nicholas Westcott, 'British imperial economic policy during the war', both in David Killingray and Richard Rathbone (eds), *Africa and the Second World War* (London, Macmillan, 1986), chapters 1 and 5.

both for consumption in Britain and for export to the United States in order to earn precious dollars to buy munitions. This meant that not just strategic raw materials but anything that could be sold to the US was of vital importance, and made Africa more important to the imperial economy than it had ever been before.[49] To secure the dollars, Britain relied on the pooling arrangements for the sterling area and the (enforced) willingness of the colonies to build up sterling balances in London – effectively an I.O.U. in sterling for dollars earned and handed over.[50]

But even then, the total resources of Britain and its empire were dwarfed by those available from the United States on which Britain came to rely increasingly heavily from the signature of the Lend-Lease agreement in March 1941 and after the United States' entry into the war following Pearl Harbour. American production far outstripped that of the Empire as a whole and Britain's wartime economic planning was dominated by the need to coordinate with the US.[51] The consequence was that with the abrupt termination of Lend-Lease in 1945, Britain was left with few alternatives other than, as Peter Clarke puts it, 'to beg, borrow or starve'.[52] In these circumstances, its dependence on imperial resources was even heavier than it had been during the war and the imperative to secure the greatest possible dollar revenue for the metropolis and the maximum supplies from sterling (i.e. imperial) sources became more powerful than ever. In particular, as Milward says: 'One result of the Second World War was to reduce the world's total available food supply', so the 'starve' option was a very real risk.[53] This is explored in more depth in Chapter 1 and was a fundamental underlying driver for the decision to launch the Groundnut Scheme.

John Gallagher has argued that the Second World War led to an intensification of imperial control in both the Middle East and especially in Africa.[54] But such an intensification carried risks, and Britain's vulnerability was evident to its own government, as was the post-war dilemma in relation to the remaining empire: of using it without losing it. The risk

---

[49] Hyam, *Britain's Declining Empire*, pp. 90–91. Darwin, *Unfinished Empire*, pp. 337–41.
[50] The fullest account of this process is in Cowen and Westcott, 'British imperial economic policy', pp. 29–40; but see also R.S. Sayers, *Financial Policy, 1939–1945* (London HMSO, 1956), and Susan Strange, *Sterling and British Policy* (Oxford, OUP, 1971), ch. 2. This is explored in detail in Chapter 1 below.
[51] Alan S. Milward, *War Economy and Society, 1939–1945* (Harmondsworth, Penguin, 1977/1987); Hancock and Gowing, *British War Economy*, ch. 9.
[52] Peter Clarke, *Hope and Glory: Britain 1900–2000* (London, Penguin, 2004), p. 227.
[53] Milward, *War Economy and Society*, p. 293.
[54] John Gallagher, *The Decline, Revival and Fall of the British Empire*, (Cambridge, CUP, 1982), pp. 141–8.

of overstretch revealing Britain's underlying weakness was emphasised by the Chief Scientific Officer, Sir Henry Tizard, who warned the Cabinet in 1946: 'We are a great nation, but if we continue to behave like a Great Power, we shall soon cease to be a great nation.'[55] The story of the Groundnut Scheme nevertheless reveals how short-term imperatives invariably trumped long-term plans. The empire was there to be used for the benefit of Britain, and used it would be, whatever the consequences. It was, after all, the *British* Empire.

But it was still a British empire *in Africa*, and Africans themselves had agency, even within the constraints of colonial rule. They were not mere peasants and workers on whom imperial instructions could be imposed. Another theme of the book is how Africans in Tanganyika responded to the unbidden incursion that the scheme made on their lives. Though sources are severely lacking, Chapters 4, 5 and 9 explore the impact of the scheme on the people of Tanganyika and their response to it, not least the fact that its very nature was the antithesis of the cautious approach to indirect rule that the British had taken up to that point.

What is true of the British Empire was also true for other European empires in Africa. Similar stories can be told of Portuguese and French efforts to develop their African colonies in the post-war period, and this study has relevance also for them.[56]

Politics and Labour

The 1945–51 Labour Government of Clement Attlee has taken on the lustre of a golden age of activist government, which transformed Britain from the depressing helplessness of the 1930s to a Keynesian model of social services, economic management and equality of opportunity – at least in the popular imagination. Historians have a more nuanced view.[57]

It is true that the party entered government with an ambitious programme of social, economic and political reform. The long-standing commitment to the socialisation of the means of production, set out explicitly in Clause 4 of the party's constitution and vigorously defended by socialist intellectuals such as Harold Laski and Stafford

---

[55] Quoted in Clarke, *Hope and Glory*, p. 233 (a lesson just as relevant today).
[56] See Hodge, Hodl and Kopf, *Developing Africa*, passim.
[57] See in general Peter Hennessy, *Never Again: Britain 1945–1951* (London, Cape 1992); John Eatwell, *The 1945–1952 Labour Governments* (London, Batsford Academic, 1979); Kenneth Harris, *Attlee* (London, Weidenfeld & Nicolson, 1982); Peter Clarke, *Hope and Glory*, ch. 7. It is notable that even John Bew's magisterial, *Citizen Clem: A biography* (London, Quercus, 2016), devotes a mere three short sentences to the Groundnut Scheme (p. 480).

Cripps, was a cause dear to their hearts and the party was committed to the nationalisation of major industries such as coal and steel, railways and power. As the Labour Party manifesto, *Let Us Face the Future*, announced: 'The Labour Party is a Socialist Party, and proud of it. Its ultimate purpose at home is the establishment of the Socialist Commonwealth of Great Britain – free, democratic, efficient, progressive, public-spirited, its material resources organised in the service of the British people.'[58] Admittedly the Fabian influence led them to propose a more pragmatic programme for the immediate future, but many of these elements remained. Essentially, it included the key elements of the 1942 Beveridge Report for the creation of a welfare state, including a National Health Service to provide free care for all citizens 'from the cradle to the grave', and a major house building programme. The scale of Labour's election victory showed that the voters wanted to give the party a clear mandate to deliver what they had promised. The people wanted change, and fast. From the moment he stepped into the Prime Minister's residence at No. 10 Downing Street, Attlee knew he would be judged on his ability to deliver.

But the economic and international realities facing the incoming government were stark. Victory had been achieved, but at a very high price. The whole country was feeling battered and bruised, exhausted rather than exhilarated. Keynes was characteristically blunt in his advice to the new government: Britain was effectively bankrupt, dependent on the United States, and pushed to the limit in terms of its resource utilisation. It was facing in effect a 'financial Dunkirk'. Drastic action was needed to avert this. If the Labour Government was to be able to implement the programmes it had promised, he argued it was essential to secure a grant or interest-free loan from the US of at least $5 billion (£1.25 billion at the then exchange rate).[59] Attlee agreed, and the Cabinet sent Keynes to Washington to negotiate it.

It is hard negotiating good terms when you have no leverage; and the US – then as now – was heavily constrained in it is charity by the democratic power of its many and various interest groups. After months of debilitating negotiations, Keynes secured a $4.4 billion loan, but at the price of 2% interest and a commitment to sterling convertibility in 18 months' time. Dollars would remain scarce for the whole of Labour's time in government, and play a big part in the story to come. This was the reality, as Britain tried to re-convert its war economy to a civilian one, restore production, create employment and recover overseas markets.

On top of the financial pressure, there was considerable hostility from private-sector business to much of Labour's programme, many

---
[58] Quoted in Eatwell, *The Labour Governments*, p. 34
[59] Robert Skidelsky, *John Maynard Keynes, Vol. III: Fighting for Britain* (London, Macmillan, 2000), ch. 12.

preferring a swift return to the pre-war order rather than a new world of centralised planning. Distrust of the private sector on the part of government was to play its part too in the evolution of the scheme, with key Labour figures determined to show that the private sector should not profit at the public's expense, and state-run enterprise could be just as, if not more, efficient than private enterprise. To deliver the new Jerusalem was therefore going to be a tough task. There was inevitably fierce competition between the different ministers for access to the scarce resources government did control. The Labour Cabinet was one of big beasts: Bevin, Morrison, Cripps, Dalton, Bevan, Shinwell and Alexander were no political novices but politicians who had been part of the wartime coalition government after spending much of the 1930s fighting the Labour Party's internal battles following the traumatic split of 1929. There were deep personal rivalries as much as party solidarity, with each committed to deliver the programmes under his responsibility, and guard his own career against the others.[60]

On top of this, the international context was immensely challenging. The war was followed by a succession of crises, inside the empire and out, and these, together with the rapid onset of the Cold War between erstwhile allies, dominated much of the Cabinet's agenda. The Colonial Office, soon under the hard-working, committed and well-intentioned Arthur Creech Jones, was therefore left largely to its own devices, except where – as with Palestine – it impinged on wider strategic and security issues. It was exceptionally hard to get any Cabinet time for colonial issues at all, let alone a development scheme in some untroubled corner of the empire. And yet, the Groundnut Scheme commanded it. This in itself was exceptional.

Finally, the post-war Labour Government was by no means the last to feel that their political project was being hindered, even actively impeded, by a civil service that was out of sympathy with its objectives and ambitions. During the war, the civil service had been transformed in scale, role and personnel. Experts had been shipped in, and a greatly expanded role fulfilled. But many individuals' attitudes remained in pre-war mode, and some assumed pre-war traditions would be resumed. There was a degree of suspicion between officials and ministers that was new to a British government, but which was also to play its part in the evolution of the scheme. While in some quarters reverence for experts and innovators had increased, in others officials were regarded as too imbued with caution and old-fashioned ideas, not in tune with the new ambitions.[61] The tension between suspicious ministers and a civil service that regarded itself as expert, impartial and defending the public interest, played out repeatedly at several points during this saga.

[60] Bew, *Attlee*, pp. 356–62
[61] Hennessy, *Never Again*, pp. 379–80.

Government enterprise and managing megaprojects

So why do governments time and again pursue large-scale projects that lead ineluctably to either predictable disaster or ever-escalating expense, or both, despite all the warnings of experts and locals? Why is optimism so pervasive and normal caution so rare? Why have so many megaprojects, both public and private, spun off-track? These are questions about the nature of government and project management that go beyond the historical specificity of a time and place or the individual circumstances of the scheme in question. But they are questions that the Groundnut Scheme illuminates with singular clarity.

In 1998, James C. Scott published *Seeing Like a State: How certain schemes to improve the human condition have failed*.[62] He argued that there has emerged, particularly in the 20th century, a form of 'authoritarian high modernism' that has a fatal tendency towards such schemes. It is based on a modernist ideology convinced of the importance of achieving 'progress', linked to an authoritarian state with an aspiration to order society, unencumbered by an active civil society or strong institutions of accountability. The result is an 'imperial or hegemonic planning mentality that excludes the necessary role of local knowledge and know-how'.[63] He examines a number of examples of this in practice, from the taming of forests to the building of ambitious new capital cities (such as Brasilia), Soviet collectivisation, and Julius Nyerere's scheme for compulsory villagisation in Tanzania (though his conclusions on both the Soviet and Tanzanian examples are contested by those who see the problem as the means of implementation rather than the objective or indeed, in some cases, the outcome). He recognises that colonial authorities were particularly susceptible to this mindset, and enforced agricultural reform was a regular target for such state engineering.

The question to be addressed, though, is not merely why they fail, but what drives a government or administration to persevere with a scheme in the face of all the evidence that it is not working as intended, will cost many times more than anticipated, or will not achieve the objectives outlined at the outset. The reasons will vary from case to case, but there are some common threads. A high level of political commitment to the project, which is seen as critical to the purpose or even the very survival of the state; a belief that the objective is so important that it justifies an ever-escalating cost; a fear of admitting failure given the reputation staked on success; and a blind faith in modernism in the face of opposition from 'ignorant', 'uneducated', 'backward' or 'reactionary'

---

[62] James C. Scott, *Seeing Like a State: How certain schemes to improve the human condition have failed* (New Haven CT, Yale University Press, 1998).
[63] Ibid., p. 6.

locals, whether peasants, pastoralists or slum-dwellers; all have played a crucial part in ensuring that obvious lessons were not learnt, or not learnt fast enough.

Scott also highlights the common ambition to 'tame nature' and impose control over its unruly reality through 'scientific' or mechanised farming and by corralling peasant or subsistence farmers who have learnt how to live with it. The neglect of local knowledge and experience is a repeated pattern in all such schemes.[64] In many ways the Groundnut Scheme is a classic example of the fundamental belief that the state (especially a 'modern' state), informed by science, can deliver results by imposing a solution that a society and economy have not come up with of their own accord before. This appears to be relatively common in efforts to achieve agrarian change.[65]

As we have seen above, the post-war Labour Government certainly had a mission, and in the colonial empire, it had the authoritarian means to take bold measures of socialist economic transformation. But it is equally clear that such failures are by no means confined to the priests of authoritarian high modernism. Any government, even in a liberal democratic state with strong and well-established institutions can be prone to pursue such disastrous schemes. In 2013, Anthony King and Ivor Crewe published *The Blunders of Our Governments*, a detailed analysis of the many failed schemes and policies undertaken by British governments between 1979 and 2010, under the Thatcher, Major and Blair administrations (all relatively successful governments, compared with those that came before and after). It concludes that a number of common factors can be identified that greatly increase the risk of failure, from cultural and operational disconnects between those taking the decisions and those implementing the project on the ground, to group-think and prejudice (especially when that becomes dogmatism), the political propensity to reach for a single dramatic solution that captures the public eye or responds to the public mood, the challenge of over-centralisation, asymmetries of expertise, and a deficit of deliberation. Altogether, as they acknowledge, the Groundnut Scheme hit almost every one of these blunder buttons, as the following pages will demonstrate.[66] But, as we will explore in the final chapter, it is by no means alone.

Not just in Britain, and not just government projects are prone to these weaknesses. Examples can be multiplied from the United States, Europe,

---

[64] Ibid., ch. 8.
[65] Sara Berry, *No Condition is Permanent: The social dynamics of agrarian change in sub-Saharan Africa* (Madison, University of Wisconsin Press, 1993), pp. 13–27; Nancy L. Johnson and Vernon W. Ruttan, 'Why Are Farms So Small?' *World Development*, 22:5, 1994, pp. 691–706.
[66] Anthony King and Ivor Crewe, *The Blunders of Our Governments* (London, Oneworld, 2013), especially p. 26.

China, India, Africa and the former Soviet Union (which specialised in such disasters), and from private sector as well as public projects. Recent research into megaprojects has illustrated the tendency to ignore rational and financial arguments, and highlighted the growing popularity of government-sponsored (though private-sector-led) projects for monocrop plantations and agricultural growth corridors.[67] The lessons of the Groundnut Scheme are more than ever relevant to these projects today.

The argument

The narrative that follows demonstrates how the Groundnut Scheme came to be, why it was backed and why it failed. It shows how some talented and imaginative men, well-intentioned but governed by certain assumptions, conceived the scheme as a solution to an urgent and vital problem; how official agricultural and financial experts raised valid and important objections to the risks the scheme would run and suggested ways to avoid those risks; but how these were overridden by politicians and businessmen – who, for their own political and commercial reasons, were in a hurry and wanted to believe that the scheme would work – and how they designed criteria to justify the risks; how men on the spot did their utmost to make the scheme work as it had been conceived, but came up against the implacable reality of the African environment and the limits of human and mechanical endeavour; how faced with impending failure, the politicians preferred to double rather than quit, deceive rather than confess, and find someone else to blame (including, in this case, the Communists) for the problems; how in the end truth could not be avoided, losses had to be admitted and the political cost had to be counted, and a scheme on which so many hopes had been hung was quietly put down.

The Groundnut Scheme was very clearly a product of its time: of the desperation to rebuild Britain after the war and improve the people's way of life, to build Labour's new Jerusalem using all the resources – domestic and imperial – at its disposal; of the conviction that things could be transformed by the power of will and the application of science; of the political hostility to civil service caution and expertise; and of the belief that African development was just waiting to be unlocked through a timely and imaginative investment. Post-war Britain needed a vision of a better future, and the Groundnut Scheme helped provide it. The vision of improvement was infectious, and irresistible.

But it is also a classic example of wider themes in politics and government: of that fatal political fear of failure that leads politicians to evade

---

[67] Seth Schindler and Simin Fadaee (eds), Megaprojects, special edition of *Environment and Society*, 10:1, 2019.

an inconvenient truth and take decisions that compound the problem while shifting the blame, driving the scheme itself ever deeper into the quagmire. It shows how organisations react as failure becomes apparent, with the rivalries, distrust and disinformation that breeds contempt and further undermines credibility. Finally, it illustrates the long-standing clash between European dreams and African realities, of bulldozers versus the bush with, on this occasion, the latter emerging victorious in the end.

Though Africa's intractable environment played its full part in killing it, the Groundnut Scheme was nevertheless fundamentally driven by British domestic politics, and died at the hands of the British Parliament. There was accountability, but not to the African inhabitants of Tanganyika; it was to the British public at home, and their interests were paramount throughout. Even so, in Africa the scheme helped shatter the myth that the white man knew best and that everything could be achieved by an effort of will alone. On the contrary, for Africans it was an outstanding example of the white man's folly, of 'mad dogs and Englishmen' pursuing an impossible dream under the tropical sun. As the final chapter reveals, however, the white man has no monopoly on folly, and the Groundnut Scheme has been re-played many times over in countries in Africa and throughout the world.

'There must be something comic about nuts', said one Tory MP during the great Parliamentary debate in 1949.[68] This story is both tragedy and farce. But if nothing else, I hope it will shine a light on why we get it so wrong, so often, and do so over and over again. Maybe, in that way, it will help us get it right in the future.

---

[68] Captain Crookshank MP, 27 Jul 1949, *House of Commons Debates* (henceforth *Hansard*), vol. 467, col. 3534.

1

Austerity

When the results of the 1945 British general election were announced on 26 July, the Labour Party was swept to its greatest electoral victory since its foundation. Though a surprise to the new Prime Minister, Clement Attlee, the victory reflected a deep-seated desire for change, a determination not to return to the pre-war world of aristocracy and depression.[1] In the aftermath of victory, people had hope for the future. It was for the Labour Government to deliver on those hopes.

They had a thumping majority to do it. With 393 MPs against 210 Tories, 12 Liberals and two Communists (their high tide in British politics, and with their own part to play in this story), Labour had an overall majority of 147. On the Labour benches were veteran leaders, including Attlee and Bevin who had served in senior roles in the wartime coalition government, and party stalwarts such as Hugh Dalton, Stafford Cripps and Sir Ben Smith. But alongside them was a new generation of MPs – 200 novices in all – including Hugh Gaitskell, Harold Wilson, John Strachey and J.P.W. 'Bill' Mallalieu.[2] Over the next six years, all of these people were to play a part, witting or unwitting, in the story of the Groundnut Scheme.

The challenges facing the incoming government were enormous. For most people at the time, after the brief euphoria of the victory celebrations and relief that the struggles of the previous six years were over, life was still pretty grim. Muriel Spark gave a graphic description of London at this time:

> The streets of the cities were lined with buildings in bad repair or no repair at all, bomb-sites piled with stony rubble, houses like giant teeth in which decay had been drilled out, leaving only the cavity. Some bomb-ripped buildings looked like the ruins of ancient castles until, at closer view, the wallpapers of various quite normal rooms

---

[1] Harris, *Attlee*, pp. 255–66; Bew, *Citizen Clem*, p. 343.
[2] Eatwell, *Labour Governments,* pp. 36–7.

would be visible, room above room exposed, as on a stage, with one wall missing.³

The contemporary Ealing comedy film, *Passport to Pimlico* (1949), set in this bombed out London landscape, revolves around a group of ingenious, down-to-earth local Londoners getting by and making do; black market spivs selling illicit supplies of rationed goods; bumbling, interfering men from the Ministry; and an unexpected find that brings momentary hope of a magical release from everyday austerity, before normal reality reimposes itself. *Austerity Britain*, the title of David Kynaston's social history of post-war Britain, conveys the atmosphere precisely.⁴

Ministering food

Food was a national obsession. War had brought not just the rationing of foodstuffs, but management of the national diet. Whether or not diet dictates or reflects the national character, the solid, stodgy, reasonably healthy but unexciting and overwhelmingly tasteless food that dominated the British diet in the 1940s reflected something of the national soul. The best had to be made of what could be got. George Orwell, no gourmet, commented in 1948 that, 'food, though not actually insufficient, is unbearably dull'. 'The food in England is worse than during the war – dry and tasteless, even at Brooks's', noted James Lees-Milne after a visit to his St James's London club. And the future doyenne of British cookery writers, Elizabeth David, stuck in a hotel in Ross-on-Wye in early 1947, recalled later: 'Conditions *were* awful, shortages *did* make catering a nightmare. And *still* there was no excuse, none, for such unspeakably dismal meals as in that dining room were put in front of me.'⁵

The weekly individual ration in May 1945 included 2 pints (1.1 litres) of milk, 4 ounces (110 grams) bacon, 2 ounces (55 g) cheese, 1 egg, and 8 ounces (220 g) each of sugar and fats (butter, margarine or lard). Bread and potatoes at least were feely available. Luxuries were not rationed but were either unavailable or unaffordable. In particular, for a country that loved its baking, the deprivation of sugar and oils and fats was particularly painful. 'Oh, for a little extra butter!' sighed Vere Hodgson in 1949.⁶

---

³ Muriel Spark, *The Girls of Slender Means* (London, 1963), p. 1.
⁴ David Kynaston, *Austerity Britain, 1945–1951* (London, Bloomsbury, 2007).
⁵ Quoted in Kynaston, *Austerity Britain*, pp. 199–200, 317. Brooks's, founded in 1762, is one of the oldest London clubs. The aristocratic James Lees-Milne was one of the founders of the (British) National Trust.
⁶ Ibid., p. 299; ration in Hennessy, *Never Again*, pp. 49–50.

Those who lived in farming areas were often slightly better off, and the national enthusiasm for growing your own vegetables in allotments or gardens continued for years. But Britain was not self-supporting in food, and availability was constrained by both money and supply at the national as much as at the individual level. It therefore mattered what was available to buy on the world market, and how much of it Britain could actually afford.

The war had profoundly disrupted and distorted the world economy. From a pre-war world where commodity and food producers were chasing each other to the bottom of the market, cutting prices below economic levels, and where agricultural land was being forced out of production, war created global shortages of food. There were widespread fears that, with population growth accelerating now the war was over, the world would run out of food. Throughout Europe, agriculture had been so disrupted by the war that few communities could feed themselves. The same was true elsewhere. In India, for example, following its disastrous famine in 1942 the export of groundnuts to the world market shrank from 500,000 tons in 1939 to zero. Pre-war exports of 1.75 million tons of edible oils from the Far East had also disappeared completely by the end of the war.[7]

The British Government responded by seeking to sign bulk-purchase agreements for food and other strategic commodities wherever they could with suppliers from within the sterling area – primarily the British Dominions and colonies but including a number of other countries willing to use sterling as their main trading currency. Sugar, wheat, cocoa, coffee, oilseeds and palm oil all became subject to such agreements, along with copper, rubber, sisal and other essentials. Where Britain had some element of control or bargaining power, for example within the empire, the contracts were secured at controlled, cost-plus prices. But the excess of demand over supply meant that in the remaining free market, which tended to be dollar-denominated, prices went through the roof.[8]

Governments did what they could. At the production end, farmers across Europe were both subsidised and protected by post-war governments to guarantee maximum production – giving rise to the tradition of agricultural protection that still bedevils world trade politics and development efforts to this day.[9] This was supplemented by whatever could be obtained overseas through bulk purchase or on the free market. Still short, governments resorted to rationing, which enabled

---

[7] For the impact of war, Milward, *War, Economy and Society*, pp. 286–93; for oils and fats, Morgan, *Colonial Development, Vol. II*, pp. 177–8.
[8] Cowen and Westcott, 'British imperial economic policy', pp. 40–49.
[9] Herman Van der Wee, *Prosperity and Upheaval: The world economy, 1945–1980* (Harmondsworth, Penguin, 1987), pp. 112–18.

them to subsidise food for the consumer, while ensuring a reasonably equitable distribution.

The Ministry of Food (MoF) had been set up in Britain at the beginning of the war to manage demand and supply. It had introduced food rationing in 1941, to public acclaim, as a way of keeping the cost of living down and spreading limited supplies fairly between rich and poor. The improvement in the diet it brought for the poorer half of the population was reflected in the overall improvement in public health in the UK during the war years. But the desperate shortages that continued after the war meant that there was no question of lifting rationing or food controls when the war ended, despite popular hopes that this would happen. Already an issue in 1945, during 1946 the level of the ration became a growing and increasingly urgent political headache for the Labour Government.[10]

Attlee had appointed a Labour stalwart, the worthy but ageing former trade unionist, Sir Ben Smith, as Minister of Food in July 1945. He struggled manfully with a deteriorating situation, but was not up to the task. In early 1946, the prospect for world food supplies was grim: European production was 25% below normal and world production 12% below. In January, Attlee set up a Ministerial Committee on World Food Supplies to oversee the Government response, chairing it himself. Every week the Cabinet reviewed some aspect of the food situation, and in April the Government published a White Paper, *The World Food Shortage* that set out starkly for the public what the difficulties were.[11]

On 5 February, Smith had to announce cuts in the bacon, poultry and egg rations. This provoked what was called at the time a 'housewives' revolt', centred on Liverpool, which gave birth to the British Housewives League. The Government's nervousness was reflected the following month when a MoF announcement that the fats ration was to be cut provoked such an uproar that it was promptly denied by No. 10. Smith found himself besieged in Parliament by an Opposition determined to demonstrate that the shortages were the result of Government incompetence as much as global dearth.[12]

Fats were particularly sensitive. A British Medical Association report in the late 1940s described the problem:

> Throughout the war the 'housewife' of the 'standard' family would have had little difficulty in obtaining the 'human needs' diet ... The picture changed somewhat in Spring 1946, for although the diet could still be obtained without much difficulty, the shortage of fats made it difficult for adults to obtain sufficient calorie intake without consid-

---

[10] Hancock and Gowing, *British War Economy*, pp. 331–2; Hennessy, *Never Again*, p. 47; Milward, *War, Economy and Society*, p. 286.
[11] *The World Food Shortage*, Cmd 6785 (London, HMSO, April 1946).
[12] Kynaston, *Austerity Britain*, p. 106.

erable strain on the digestion, this being the cause of the 'recurrent complaints' that 'people have not enough to eat'.¹³

Or as Ernest Bevin succinctly put it, eating too much of the grey (wholemeal) 'British Loaf' made him belch.¹⁴ But whether white bread or brown, the British family wanted at least margarine to put on it.

Smith flew to Washington in March to seek US support for increased supplies to Europe in general and Britain in particular, but with only limited success. In May, Attlee decided instead to send Herbert Morrison, Lord President and one of the five most senior Cabinet members, for a further go at the Americans. When Smith also fell out with Bevin, his old boss at the Transport and General Workers Union, over food supplies to Germany (a foreign policy priority for Bevin), Smith was forced finally to resign.¹⁵

To be Minister of Food in early 1946 was something of a poisoned chalice. Attlee decided it needed someone younger, more energetic and better able to present the Government's case. He picked John Strachey.

Evelyn John St Loe Strachey was an unusual Labour MP. Born in Guildford in 1901, he was the son of St Loe Strachey, one of the great editors of *The Spectator* and a cousin of the literary lion of Bloomsbury, Lytton Strachey. John's background was impeccably Establishment: conservative father, Eton and Magdalen College, Oxford, where he led an aesthetic life writing poetry and putting on plays. Passionate about cricket, he would on occasion play for Magdalen wearing a large French peasant's straw hat. But such frivolity belied an intellectual curiosity, a seriousness about ideas and an articulacy in presenting them that drew him into political life. 'A tall, aristocratic-looking man, with liquid brown eyes', as a gushing American journalist later described him, he had a wit and charm that attracted all who met him.¹⁶ His wide interest in literature and the arts as well as public affairs later made him a delightful travelling companion, including for his officials with whom he maintained an easy informality.¹⁷

But Strachey was also 'that typically English phenomenon, the Eton and Oxford Marxist'.¹⁸ He fell under the influence of the radical and passionate socialist Fenner Brockway – who liked his 'clear, persuasive

---

[13] British Medical Association report, 1949, quoted in Kynaston, *Austerity Britain*, p. 107.
[14] Hennessy, *Never Again*, p. 276.
[15] Alan Bullock, *Ernest Bevin: Foreign Secretary 1945–1951* (London, W.W. Norton, 1983), pp. 232–3; Harris, *Attlee*, p. 327.
[16] Interview in *The New Yorker*, Feb–Mar 1947 (copy in the Strachey Papers, Box 9).
[17] These paragraphs are based on Hugh Thomas, *John Strachey* (London, Eyre Methuen, 1973) and 'John Strachey', *Dictionary of National Biography, 1961–1970*. See also Eric Roll, *Crowded Hours* (London, Faber, 1985), p. 49.
[18] Wood, *Groundnut Affair*, p. 39.

Photo 1.1 John Strachey, as Minister of Food, 28 May 1946 (World Image Archive/Alamy Stock photo)

style of writing', even though 'his spelling would have disgraced a child of ten'[19] – and in 1923, he joined the Labour Party. He later claimed he became a socialist out of chagrin at being passed over for the First XI at Eton, but then began an intellectual odyssey that took him at some point into every corner of the British Left. He became friendly with Oswald Mosley, who was the best man at his first (short-lived) wedding, and moved with him to the Independent Labour Party in 1926. Through Mosley, during the General Strike of 1926, he also met Leslie Plummer, better known as Dick, who was manager of the party's newspaper, the *New Leader*. The two struck up a lifelong friendship. Elected to Parliament for Aston (near Birmingham) in 1929, Strachey became Mosley's Parliamentary Private Secretary and left Labour with him to form the New Party in 1931. But as Mosley moved to the right, Strachey was moving left. They fell out over Russia, and when Strachey lost his seat in the 1931 Election, they went their separate ways.

Thereafter Strachey became first a Marxist, then a Communist, but was more widely known to the public through his books. In 1931 Victor

[19] Fenner Brockway, quoted in ibid.

Gollancz, publisher to the British Left, published Strachey's Marxist analysis of current affairs called *The Coming Struggle for Power*.[20] Its argument that capitalism was entering its final phase and would, through wars between nations and revolution at home, lead to world socialism, attracted considerable attention. He kept company with other left-wing intellectuals and became a pillar, with Gollancz and Stafford Cripps, of the Left Book Club. With them, he began to move back towards the centre, leaving the Communist Party in the late 1930s and writing a pamphlet influenced by Keynesian economics. Many of these early friendships were to play a part in the Groundnut Scheme.

Strachey's burgeoning literary and political career was then interrupted by the war. He was conscripted into the RAF, where he became an adjutant, a role he described later as 'something like the manager of a theatrical troupe – attends to advance bookings and billets'.[21] He did it outstandingly well and, recognised for his communications skills, was promoted to be the RAF's Public Relations Officer at HQ with the rank of Squadron-Leader. He found the perfect niche in broadcasting a regular radio spot on the war in the air immediately after the *Nine o'clock News* on the BBC. Attlee enjoyed listening to it, and became a fan.[22]

As soon as the war ended, however, Strachey returned to politics and secured election as Labour MP for Dundee in the 1945 landslide. Attlee was content to regard his Mosleyite and Communist past as 'an aberration of youth', and believed that 'though he had wandered in the wilderness a bit [he] had quality',[23] later remarking that he was 'a hard worker with the intellectual humility and fearlessness to face his own ignorance'.[24] He appointed him Under-Secretary of State at the Air Ministry, a tricky job involving sensitive issues of demobilisation and service pensions. Strachey proved an efficient administrator, as well as a natural and skilful performer in the House of Commons, impressing friend and foe alike with his felicity of phrase, mental agility and debating skills. Few ministers answered so many questions, so successfully, as Strachey did in the first session of the Parliament of 1945. He was also, unusually among Labour ministers, economically literate and able to tackle the Chancellor of the Exchequer on his own terms.[25]

[20] John Strachey, *The Coming Struggle for Power* (London, Gollancz, 1931).
[21] *The New Yorker*, Feb–Mar 1947, in Strachey Papers, Box 9.
[22] Thomas, *Strachey*, p. 224.
[23] Autobiographical notes by Attlee, written in Sep 1950, Attlee Papers, Churchill College Archives (CA), Box 1/17, p. 5.
[24] Attlee article, in Frank Field (ed.) *Attlee's Great Contemporaries* (London, Continuum, 2009), p. 141.
[25] Thomas, *Strachey*, p. 227.

In early 1946, Attlee invited Strachey and his wife Celia to the Prime Minister's country house retreat, Chequers, for the weekend. He got on well with the Prime Minister, going for walks, talking politics and jumping over stiles together. Strachey admired Attlee as much as Attlee liked him. When Ben Smith resigned as Minister for Food, Strachey, though only 44 (a young age for high office in those days) was an obvious choice for promotion into this key job – which he took up on 27 May 1946, bringing with him as his Parliamentary Private Secretary his friend and fellow new MP Bill Mallalieu. His only gripe was that, though he was described as 'of Cabinet rank' and had the right to attend Cabinet for discussion of food issues, he was not a full member of the Cabinet. He wrote eloquently to Attlee putting the case for full membership, and waged a persistent campaign to attend all Cabinet discussions, but without success. Attlee, characteristically laconic, advised him to 'just get on with the job'.[26]

Strachey had a baptism of fire. The supply of wheat was becoming more precarious, and in early summer the projections for the Canadian wheat harvest were poor. The awful prospect loomed that the Government might, for the first time, have to ration bread. The Cabinet was split. First Smith, then Strachey, supported by both Attlee and Bevin, argued that bread rationing was inevitable, and in June the Cabinet bit the bullet and agreed. On the 27 June 1946, Strachey announced to Parliament that bread rationing would be introduced in July. Morrison, however, remained unpersuaded. When Attlee, Bevin, Dalton and others departed for the annual Durham Miners Gala in early July, he and Strachey decided, on the basis of some more optimistic Canadian forecasts, they could get by without it, and Morrison summoned an emergency Cabinet meeting of those ministers remaining in London to rescind the decision. Attlee and Hugh Dalton, the Chancellor of the Exchequer, were furious and rang from Durham to block the move. Rationing went ahead as planned.[27]

Dalton was not impressed and commented acerbically in his diary:

> This new Minister of Food is very disappointing. Evidently he is a weak man and there is no steel in him. A.B. [Aneurin Bevan] said at Durham that his great strength was as an expositor and as a 'perfect Man Friday'. So Oswald Mosley once found.[28]

A year later, Dalton was still hostile to Strachey: 'Once a Communist, always a crook', he shouted at a dinner party in August 1947.[29]

The debacle gave the Tories a propaganda tool they were not going to waste. As Britain faced into the worst winter of the century and fuel

---

[26] Strachey to Attlee, 5 Jul 1946, Strachey Papers, Box 9; Harris, *Attlee*, p. 328.
[27] Harris, *Attlee*, pp. 327–30; Bew, *Citizen Clem*, p. 408.
[28] Entry for 1 Aug 1946, Dalton Diaries, London School of Economics (LSE).
[29] Ben Pimlott, *Hugh Dalton* (Oxford, OUP, 1982), p. 513.

too began to run low, they coined the phrase 'Starve with Strachey and Shiver with Shinwell' (the Minister for Fuel).[30] Things were not looking good.

In October 1946, Strachey presented a paper to Cabinet describing the situation and what could be done about it. When it was discussed on the 25th, the Cabinet agreed that:

> This disclosed a serious danger of shortages for the United Kingdom and for areas of direct UK responsibility in the supplies of wheat, fats, bacon and rice ... In addition to making representations to the United States, we should increase our efforts to develop alternative sources of supply ... Pressure should also be maintained to increase exports of oil and oilseeds from Tropical Africa.[31]

Something had to be done.

Managing the money

If the food situation was grim, the financial one was grimmer. Even where food was available, Britain could not necessarily afford to buy it.

John Maynard Keynes, now Lord Keynes, was the unquestioned master of British financial policy during the war, trusted by all parties and the dominant force in Treasury policy-making. Surveying the country's post-war economic prospects in mid-1945, he acknowledged that Britain had 'spent profligately and imprudently' to ensure the Allied victory. In May 1945, he asserted that, 'it has been a prime object of policy ... that we should end the war in a financial position which did not leave us hopelessly at the mercy of the United States.'[32] But there was bound to be a reckoning.

There was, immediately, when President Truman cancelled Lend-Lease without notice on 22 August 1945. Britain was left with a distorted war economy, producing inadequate consumer and capital goods for peacetime demands, and without the wherewithal to export enough to import the goods they needed from the US which had become de facto the sole source of supply. Not only food, but imports, exports and dollars were all in short supply, as Britain emerged from the war as the world's largest debtor.[33]

---

[30] 20 Dec 1946, Dalton Diaries, LSE.
[31] Minutes of Cabinet meeting, 25 Oct 1946, CM(46)91, in CAB 128/6; Memorandum by the Minister of Food, CP(46)396 in CAB 129/14, Cabinet Office Papers, The National Archives, Kew.
[32] J.M. Keynes memorandum, "Overseas Financial Policy in Stage III', 15 May 1945, WP(45)301, reproduced in D. Moggridge (ed.), *The Collected Writings of John Maynard Keynes, Vol. XXIV* (London, Macmillan, 1979), p. 65.
[33] Skidelsky, *Keynes, Vol. III*, pp. 380–407.

This is not the place to tell the full story of Britain's post-war economic crisis and recovery, which has been well told by others.[34] But it is the essential background to understanding the subsequent discussion of and decision on the Groundnut Scheme, as well as the haste with which it was implemented. The facts set out below were weighing heavily on the minds of all those around the Cabinet table in 1946 and 1947 when that idea came floating up.

Keynes led a mission to the US in the autumn of 1945 to negotiate a dollar loan that, it was hoped, would tide the UK over the transitional period. After extremely arduous negotiations, in which the Labour Cabinet's unrealistic expectations about US generosity were exposed, Keynes finally secured in November a $4.4 billion loan (worth nearly £1.1 billion at the then fixed exchange rate of £1: $4.03 and equivalent to around £46 billion in 2019[35]), made up of $3.75 billion in new lending plus $650 million in final settlement of Lend-Lease, but with significant strings attached. Under pressure from Congress, the Truman Administration was determined to use Britain's moment of weakness to prise open British markets, including Empire markets, for US exporters. Britain had to commit to restoring sterling convertibility by mid-1947 and accepting moves towards free trade that could potentially threaten its economic reconstruction.

The consequence of this deal was that Britain was beset by recurrent economic crises over the next four years. The first struck, inevitably, when sterling convertibility was restored in July–August 1947. As sterling poured from the country and the Treasury stared disaster in the face, officials drew up a 'famine programme' to be implemented in the case of a complete meltdown. In the end it was decided to abrogate the terms of the Loan Agreement, and the US had no choice but to accede. In 1948, Marshall Aid money began to come on stream which provided some relief. But the remorseless pressure of Britain's economic decline was reflected two years later in the devaluation crisis of July–September 1949. This was in many ways the more difficult for the Labour Government, as part of Labour's political mythology was that it was the devaluation of sterling against gold in 1931 that sank the then Labour Government and led to the Conservative political domination of the 1930s. But in September 1949 they finally bit the bullet and the pound was devalued from $4.03 to $2.80 overnight.

The dollar shortage was a constant theme and threat to the Labour Government throughout the post-war years. It was impelled to ensure

---

[34] In addition to Skidelsky, for the following paragraphs see Alec Cairncross, *The Years of Recovery: British economic policy, 1945–51* (London, Methuen,1985); and Hennessy, *Never Again*, pp. 94–6, 301–5.
[35] Current equivalent value calculated using www.bankofengland.co.uk/monetary-policy/inflation/inflation-calculator (accessed 3 Mar 2020).

that Britain secured and conserved all the dollars it could, and spent those it had with the utmost care. As set out in the previous chapter, it also increased Britain's dependence on those parts of the Empire that remained under its control, especially Africa. This dependence had been concealed by Lend-Lease during the war, but afterwards the sterling area became an essential prop for the imperial metropolis.

Thanks to Keynes' negotiating skill, the US Loan Agreement at least left the sterling area intact. This comprised countries who either used sterling or had currencies tied to it, most (but not all) of them part of the British Empire. During the war this had been developed into a critical tool of Britain's economic effort, enabling the government to use empire resources to the 'greater good' of, first, winning the war, and then economic recovery at home. The key mechanisms for achieving this (as mentioned in the Introduction) were the so-called the sterling balances. Sterling balances, representing money earned from imperial exports to the UK, were held in London on behalf of empire governments, effectively under the control of the Treasury and Bank of England. They were augmented by money earned from empire exports to the US. The dollars themselves were put into the common sterling area 'dollar pool' at the Bank of England and the exporters given the sterling equivalent into their balances. This enabled the UK to control all dollars earned through raw material exports from the colonies to America.[36] In 1948, the UK's total dollar deficit was £311 million, but this could be partially reduced by the surplus of £37.5 million from colonial exports to the US.[37]

The terms of the US loan and the deteriorating balance of payments situation made it more important than ever that domestic demand was met wherever possible from sterling sources. As Dalton told Cabinet colleagues in October 1946: 'I draw my colleagues' attention ... particularly to the most urgent need of switching, as far and as fast as possible from dollar to non-dollar sources of supply'.[38] He was strongly supported by Bevin, who saw the Empire in geo-strategic as well as economic terms. He told Dalton that:

> If only we pushed on and developed Africa, we could have the U.S. dependent on us, and eating out of our hand in four or five years ... the United States is very barren of essential minerals and in Africa we have them all.[39]

Bevin believed that Britain's imperial crime wasn't exploitation, it was neglect. A strong supporter of colonial development policies, he

[36] Cowen and Westcott, 'British imperial economic policy', pp. 22–40; Cain and Hopkins, *British Imperialism, Vol. II*, ch.11.
[37] Colonial Development Corporation, *Report and Accounts for 1948* (London, HMSO, 1949), p. 7.
[38] Memorandum by Dalton, 23 Oct 1946, M.E.P.(46)10, in CAB 129/14.
[39] Dalton Diaries, 15 Oct 1948, LSE.

later told the Colonial Secretary, Arthur Creech Jones: 'If only it had been done long ago. What a different world it would have been! There would have been no dollar gap.'[40] Cripps made this very clear to Britain's African Governors when he addressed their annual conference in November 1947. The government's aim, he told them, was

> to make the sterling areas as little dependent as possible on supplies from the dollar area ... Tropical Africa is already contributing much, both in physical supplies of food and raw materials and in quite substantial earnings of dollars for the sterling pool. The further development of African resources is of the same crucial importance to the rehabilitation and strengthening of Western Europe as the restoration of European productive power is to the future progress and prosperity of Africa ... In Africa indeed is to be found a great potential for new strength and vigour in the Western European economy.[41]

In 1946–47, the Labour Government, like the British people, were looking for anything that would lighten their darkness. Into this context, from an unexpected source, came the spark of an idea.

---

[40] Bevin letter to Creech Jones, Feb 1950, quoted in Pearce, *Turning Point*, p. 95
[41] 'Speech by the Rt Hon Sir Stafford Cripps, K.C. M.P. Minister for Economic Affairs to the African Governors' Conference on 12th November 1947' (Nairobi, 1947), copy in Oxford, Bodleian Libraries, Creech Jones Papers, Box 15/III, Item 2 (formerly Rhodes House Library archives).

2

A Scheme is Born

It all began with a man called Miller.

Miller

Ralph W.R. Miller was the Director of Agriculture in Tanganyika. He was an effervescent man, as strong on ideas as he was weak in judgement. The Colonial Office considered that he was 'temperamentally ... rather volatile and needed to be kept in check.'[1] But at least he was energetic, something the territory needed badly at this time.

Tanganyika Territory was big. From Mount Kilimanjaro in the north to the Southern Highlands on the border with Northern Rhodesia (now Zambia) in the south, and from the Indian Ocean in the east to Lakes Tanganyika and Victoria in the west, it is nearly a million square kilometres (366,000 square miles), nearly twice the size of California or Spain. In 1946 its population was estimated at around 6 million people, overwhelmingly subsistence farmers, scattered across the land but concentrated mainly in the well-watered coastal and highland areas around the country's periphery. The drier interior was more lightly populated, much of it having never recovered from the devastating rinderpest epidemic that killed off most of the cattle in the 1890s and allowed the tsetse fly, which effectively prevented cattle herding, to re-infest the bush.[2]

The Second World War had transformed Tanganyika Territory from a sleepy colonial backwater, starved of funds, staff and attention during the 1930s, into a vital imperial asset, its resources mobilised to the full

---

[1] Minute by Monson, 31 Aug 1944, CO 852/609/19643/1.
[2] *African Population of Tanganyika* (East African Statistical Office, Nairobi, 1950), comprising the census data for 1948. For rinderpest, see Helge Kjekshus, *Ecology Control and Economic Development in East African History* (London, Heinemann, 1977), ch. 7.

in the cause of total war. Once the eastern empire had fallen to the Japanese in 1942, every last resource available from Africa was needed for the war effort. In Tanganyika's case, these resources were primarily agricultural, and yet, to support agricultural production, Miller had an Agricultural Department denuded of staff by the Depression and war, and a budget of just £150,000 from a total Tanganyika budget of around £5 million.[3]

Tanganyika's most vital strategic commodity was sisal, a spiky, fibrous plant used to produce naval ropes and binder twine for harvesting in the days before synthetic fibres took over. It was grown on large estates, concentrated in the eastern half of the country, and depended on thousands of migrant workers from the poorer areas to the west and south to undertake the harvesting (by hand) and processing of the fibre. Miller was close, reputedly too close, to the British, Greek and Asian sisal barons who ran the industry. They were required during the war to provide their whole crop to British markets through bulk-purchase contracts; but the settlers proved adept at driving a hard bargain and securing themselves a reasonable price for their exports.[4]

Peasant production of coffee and cotton had also begun to grow during the 1920s and '30s and brought a degree of prosperity to a small number of African peasant producers in the north and north-west of the country. But the vast majority of Africans were still subsistence farmers, producing little or no surplus.

Miller shared the common despair among colonial agricultural officials at what were seen as the primitive farming methods used by Africans. East Africa had always, until the 1930s, been land rich and people poor. So the traditional 'slash-and-burn' pattern of arable farming, and nomadic herding of pastoralists like the Maasai, made sense in a subsistence economy where any community's first priority was to feed itself. But as populations grew, land pressure also grew. Cash crop cultivation spread, and in Tanganyika – as in Kenya to the north – land alienation to white settler farmers restricted the area available to Africans in some of the most fertile areas like Kilimanjaro. In the neighbouring Pare Mountains, intensified cultivation on steep slopes meant that soil erosion also began to be perceived as a major threat to future land fertility. Here and in the Lake Province around Lake Victoria where cotton cultivation was introduced, efforts to instruct African farmers in conservation methods during the 1930s met passive resistance from

---

[3] Westcott, 'Tanganyika' in Killingray and Rathbone, *Africa and the Second World War*, pp. 144–52; Tanganyika Territory, *Estimates for 1946* (Government Printer, Dar es Salaam, 1946).

[4] N.J. Westcott, 'The East African sisal industry, 1929–49: the marketing of a colonial commodity during depression and war', in B. Ingham and C. Simmons (eds) *Development Studies and Colonial Policy* (London, Cass, 1987)

cultivators who, as elsewhere, did not see the additional effort reflected in better yields or a better return.[5]

In 1939, the Colonial Office's Development Adviser, Frank Stockdale, had warned that, 'it is necessary when considering Tanganyika not to be led away by dreams of El Dorado ... Much of the country is unpromising and ... is only "groundnut country".'[6]

The question of soil conservation was significantly more acute in neighbouring Kenya, where alienation of the best land put the greatest pressure on Africans. In mid-1946, in his Despatch No. 44, the Governor of Kenya, Sir Philip Mitchell, encapsulated the colonial administration's worries:

> I believe firmly that ... primary production by African peasants in the manner in which it has hitherto developed is already on the decline, and that in fact, far from there being any possibility of a substantial increase, populations working under that system are going to find increasing difficulty in supporting themselves at their present level ... It is now evident that, taken as a whole, East Africa is barely able to support itself in food at the present time, and would indeed be a large importer were it not for the production from European farms.[7]

Besides the need to introduce new methods of cultivation – moving beyond the hand hoe – that would enable productivity and living standards to be raised, Mitchell drew attention to the large areas of 'less readily cultivable' land, left empty due to tsetse fly, lack of water or remoteness, which needed to be brought into cultivation if the situation was to be remedied. He urged swift action by the British Government to do this.

The prospect of another area of food deficit rang alarm bells in London, and Mitchell's scepticism that peasant producers could themselves respond to price incentives to produce more food and cash crops – despite evidence to the contrary from West Africa – found a ready audience elsewhere in East Africa.

Miller was already particularly enthused about the prospects for mechanising agriculture in East Africa. He believed the northern plains of Tanganyika, around Arusha, were ideal wheat-growing country if only they could be opened up to large-scale farming. In 1942, he had promised the Allies' Middle East Supply Centre that he could provide thousands of tons of wheat to help remedy the wartime shortages in the Middle East, provided he was sent some of the scarce supplies of

---

[5] Iliffe, *Tanganyika*, pp. 347–51.
[6] Minute by Stockdale, 18 Dec 1939, CO 691/175/42303. On Stockdale, see Hodge, *Triumph of the Expert*, p. 103 et seq.
[7] Sir Philip Mitchell to the Secretary of State for the Colonies, Despatch no. 44 of 1946, quoted in *A Plan for the Mechanised Production of Groundnuts in East and Central Africa*, Cmd 7030 (Feb 1947).

machinery from the US. He was given the tractors, but his Northern Province Wheat Scheme proved ill-fated. Delay, drought and changing market conditions resulted in the scheme being closed in 1947 after four disappointing harvests, with the loss of £170,000. The machinery took longer to arrive than had been expected, and the Ardai plain in northern Tanganyika proved less amenable to mechanised agriculture and less reliable in its rainfall than had been assumed.[8] 'The Northern Province', it was noted a few years later, 'cannot be treated in the same way as the Canadian prairie.'[9]

Already in 1945, the newly arrived Governor, Sir William Battershill, had asked: 'what justification is there for keeping on this expensive and non-economic farming which incidentally is likely to do untold damage to the land because no anti-erosion measures have been undertaken?'[10] But Miller had the bit between his teeth and drove the Scheme to two more years of losses before he was forced to face reality, admit defeat, and agree to close the scheme down.

Nothing daunted by the looming failure of that scheme, when Miller received an unexpected visitor in early 1946 who asked about the potential for producing more oils and fats in Tanganyika, he expressed great enthusiasm about the potential for doing this through mechanised farming.

The United Africa Company

Miller's visitor was Frank Samuel, the Managing Director of the United Africa Company (UAC), and the second father of the Groundnut Scheme.

The UAC was formed in 1929 by the merger of Lever Brothers' Nigerian operation with its main African competitor. It was a disparate conglomerate made up of diverse businesses in over 20 British, French and Belgian colonies in Africa, ranging from commodity trading to manufacturing, from construction to palm oil plantations in the Belgian Congo. The UAC itself was a subsidiary of Unilever, the Anglo-Dutch multinational with total global assets already worth over £200 million. Though the range of its interests was vast, Unilever's core business remained focussed on the many products derived from oils and fats – from Stork and Blue Band margarine, to Wall's ice cream and Lifebuoy soap. It produced 70% of Europe's margarine and two-thirds of the soap

---

[8] 'Final Report on the Northern Province Wheat Scheme, 1942–1950', Oxford, Bodleian Libraries, N.R. Fuggles Couchman papers, MSS Afr. s. 886.
[9] J.F.R. Hill and J.P. Moffett (eds), *Tanganyika: A study of its resources and their development* (Dar es Salaam, Government Printer, 1955), p. 385.
[10] Minute by Battershill, 23 Aug 1945, TNA 30349/III. See also the correspondence in TNA 30349/I-II.

used in the British Empire, and at the end of the war the shortage of its principal raw material, vegetable oil, was an overwhelming preoccupation – a matter of life and death for some parts of the business. By 1946, 19 of its 46 oil-crushing mills in the UK stood idle for want of oilseeds to crush.[11]

Samuel had joined the UAC in the early 1930s, soon after it was created, having already made a fortune early in life by inventing the first portable gramophone and becoming chairman of the Decca Gramophone Company. When Decca was sold in 1928, he was invited by a friend to help establish the UAC where he became one of three managing directors who ran the company, along with Jasper Knight and R.H. Muir. When the latter two were recruited into government in 1940 Samuel became sole Managing Director, steering the company successfully through the war years. A genial pipe-smoker, Samuel was also a hard-headed businessman, and knew that his company faced unprecedented challenges in the post-war world.[12]

Which is why Samuel found himself, in March 1946, flying from one side of Africa to the other looking for potential new sources of vegetable oils. In northern Nigeria, African peasants already produced a large surplus of groundnuts for export, though much of it was stuck inland for want of rail transport to get it to the coast, and the colonial authorities in Nigeria deliberately blocked the UAC's proposal to expand its plantation business in the territory because they were committed to support peasant, not expatriate production.[13] So Samuel flew east, and as he flew over Tanganyika's mile after mile of empty bush (the infamous *bundu*), 'he asked himself whether this wasteland could not grow oil crops, to the benefit of the margarine ration of the British housewife and the legitimate profits of the United Africa Company'.[14]

Landing in the aptly named Dar es Salaam (Arabic for 'Haven of Peace'), the sleepy colonial capital, he was taken to see Ralph Miller by the UAC's local manager, Mr Christie, and asked him the same question. Miller later claimed: 'I was very frank with him', telling Samuel that trading companies were not nearly as much use to Tanganyika as businesses that invested in the long-term productive capacity of a

---

[11] D.K. Fieldhouse, *Merchant Capital and Economic Decolonization: the United Africa Company 1929–1987* is the definitive work on UAC; see also D.K. Fieldhouse, *Unilever Overseas: The anatomy of a multinational* (London, Croom Helm, 1978), ch. 1 and Charles Wilson, *Unilever, 1945–65* (New York, Praeger, 1968); also Forbes Munro, *Africa and the International Economy*, p. 131; R.J. Hammond, *Official History of the Second World War: Food, Vol. III* (London, HMSO, 1962), p. 490.
[12] Fieldhouse, *Merchant Capital*, pp. 12–33; see also Samuel's obituary, *The Times*, 26 Feb 1954.
[13] Fieldhouse, *Merchant Capital*, pp. 214–18.
[14] Wood, *Groundnut Affair*, p. 26–7.

country.¹⁵ He therefore responded with a short memorandum setting out 'my ideas of the scope of a scheme designed to produce 20,000 to 25,000 tons of groundnuts annually'. It would require 'at least 100,000 acres', probably in the Western Province where there was plenty of uninhabited tsetse bush, with a rotation that would keep 25% of the land under groundnuts, and the rest given over to fallow, grazing, beans and millet. Most important, however, Miller stated: 'In my opinion the economic success of any scheme would depend on its being entirely mechanised so that all operations from ploughing to lifting the groundnuts should be done entirely by machinery'.¹⁶

He had two reasons for arguing this: firstly, his conviction that mechanised farming was the way forward; and secondly his awareness that his friends in the sisal industry had difficulty enough getting the labour they needed, and used the Western Province itself as a labour reserve, where they recruited migrant workers through their own dedicated Sisal Labour Bureau (SILABU). Under no circumstances did the sisal growers want the supply of their labour force put in jeopardy by rival investors who would inevitably also bid up wages and thereby reduce profits.

And why focus on the humble groundnut? Better known elsewhere as the peanut or monkey nut, it has the great advantage of being an annual crop known to flourish in dry, sandy soils where there was a long and reliable dry season during which the nuts would mature. It has an unusually high oil content (around 40%), and the oil is particularly well suited for manufacture into margarine, with the residue making a useful cattle feed. It was already known to grow well in many parts of Tanganyika: before the war the territory had exported up to 16,000 tons a year. As an annual crop, there was little lead time for production, which could be ramped up swiftly, and yield a quick return.¹⁷

All this was music to Mr Samuel's ears. Miller had confirmed the key point on which he had been uncertain: that a mechanised scheme was feasible in Tanganyika's conditions. This became a central part of his credo, and his dictum, 'No operation will be performed by hand for which mechanical equipment is available', became one of the ground rules for the scheme.¹⁸ But his targets were somewhat more ambitious than Miller's. On the plane back to London (a two day journey including the necessary refuelling stopovers – but infinitely faster than the three-week sea voyage that most passengers still had to take), he translated what he had seen and heard into an altogether grander scheme and set it down in a memorandum for the Government.

---

¹⁵ Statement by Miller, *Tanganyika Legislative Council Proceedings*, 11 Dec 1947 (Dar es Salaam, Government Printer).
¹⁶ Miller to A.C. Christie, UAC, 15 Mar 1946, TNA 38744.
¹⁷ *Tanganyika Annual Agricultural Report,* 1935 (Dar es Salaam).
¹⁸ Scott, *Seeing Like a State*, p. 229.

Samuel multiplied the figures Miller had provided by 20 to give a total production after five years of 400,000 tons – a figure that would make a real impact on the desperate shortage of oils and fats. This, he calculated, would require an area of 2.5 million acres – nearly 4,000 square miles (1.1 million hectares). Only groundnuts as an annual crop, and only mechanised farming would enable such an increase in production in so short a time. He estimated that with an average yield of 700–800 lbs per acre, the cost of production would be £7 a ton, and the total capital cost £8 million, £3 million of it in dollars to buy the necessary equipment which could only be found in the US. It would require a labour force of only 350–400 Europeans and Asians plus 20,000 Africans. He concluded that: 'Tanganyika Territory appears to be the "Ideal Home" for this project', because of the large areas of empty land available and because the scheme would promote its economic development. But Samuel entered an important disclaimer: 'It should be made clear at the outset that the United Africa Company are not seeking to be financially interested in the project, though they would willingly give all possible advice and help in making it a success.'[19] This was a well-judged approach to the new Labour Government, given its scepticism of the private sector.

On 26 March, the Vice-Chairman of Unilever, Sir Herbert Davies, wrote to Sir Roland Wall, the second-most senior official at the Ministry of Food (MoF), attaching Samuel's memorandum and arguing that 'the world will never be able to dispense with rationing of oils and fats unless new sources of production are found'. The next day, he and Samuel called on Sir Ben Smith, still Minister of Food, at the House of Commons. Davies reinforced the case by arguing that the preferred source should be 'within the Empire' and that the Government should take the lead. Smith, in the middle of the row over the fats ration, was immediately captivated by the proposal. At the meeting, he:

> expressed his agreement with the general idea and also ... that such a scheme as this could only be carried out if it were given the highest priority as a Government venture as was done during the war with armaments etc. ... and that it would not be practicable to launch it as a private enterprise, both having regard to the finance and the necessity to obtain Government backing in order to have the necessary machinery etc. provided.[20]

There were several reasons why Unilever might encourage the Government to run the scheme rather than do it themselves, some honest, some ulterior. As the Minister said, access to the scale of finance

---

[19] 'A project for the mass production of Groundnuts in Tropical Africa', memorandum by F. Samuel, dated 26 Mar 1946, attached to letter H. Davies to R. Wall, 26 Mar 1946, Ministry of Agriculture and Fisheries (MAF) 83/1747 (former Ministry of Food papers, The National Archives, Kew)
[20] Minute by Sir R. Wall, 29 Mar 1946, MAF 83/1747.

and machinery needed would only be possible with full Government cooperation, which was more likely the more committed they were to the scheme. Samuel knew well enough he was dealing with a Labour Government that looked askance at companies like his (one official referred to 'their somewhat unsavoury reputation').[21] But he also knew this was a risky scheme. Given the uncertainties of tropical agriculture and the scale of the project, it involved a degree of risk that no sane Board of Directors of a commercial company would have endorsed. The Government would almost certainly have to turn to the UAC for expertise and help, so they could earn good money from it while running none of the financial risk. Unilever was also deeply worried about its under-utilised crushing plants in the UK which would be forced to close if additional supplies could not be found in short order. As another Unilever executive put it to the Ministry:

> The production of 400,000 tons of Groundnuts in Tanganyika (which would presumably all be shipped to this country) would not only produce about 160,000 tons of oil for margarine and cooking-fat manufacturers, and about 240,000 tons of cake for the farmers, but would also go some way towards relieving the unemployment in the crushing trade which is bound to come.[22]

So their objective in the negotiations to come was for the Government to take the risk, and Unilever to reap the profit. In the event, they achieved at least the first of those objectives.[23]

For the Ministry of Food, the proposal was also like manna from heaven. Their prayers had been answered, and Samuel – an unlikely prophet, it is true – had shown them a vision of the future which he himself put in Biblical terms, quoting Isaiah's prophecy that 'the desert shall rejoice and blossom as the rose.'[24]

In more mundane terms, though, the Ministry was easily open to persuasion. It was an unusual ministry, a fusing of government and

---

[21] Chantler minute, 8 Jan 1947, CAB 124/1090. P.C. Chantler was adviser to Morrison (as Lord President the Minister responsible for the Socialisation of Industry) and open in his view: 'You may be inclined to wonder why the United African Company itself has not undertaken the initiative in developing such a scheme if the financial prospects are as rosy as the Minister of Food suggests. Probably the answer to this is not that the U.A.C. thinks the scheme too big a risk, but that they realise they would not be allowed today (especially in view of their somewhat unsavoury reputation) to take up a concession on this scale.'
[22] Jasper Knight (on secondment from Unilever to MoF) to Sir F. Tribe (Permanent Secretary, MoF), 28 Mar 1946, MAF 83/1747.
[23] Fieldhouse, *Merchant Capital*, p. 216, notes that the UAC Board itself never discussed the Scheme: 'the initiative and drive came from Samuel himself, rather than Plantations Dept or any other part of the business ... It seems to have remained throughout the personal project of Samuel.'
[24] Isaiah, 35:1; Wood, *Groundnut Affair*, p. 41.

industry which was, in British terms, a unique feature of the war effort. At the outset of the war, the Ministry had been created by absorbing within it the relevant sections of British business best able to manage the mobilisation and control of productive forces and food supplies as efficiently as possible. So it was that the Oils and Fats Division of the Ministry was in practice run by staff seconded from ... Unilever. Foremost among them was Jasper Knight, a large, loud, and firmly opinionated director of the UAC.[25] From his seat within the Ministry he lobbied hard for the interests of his company. Though answerable through the Minister to Parliament, and clearly working to common ends during the war, conflicts of interest and divided loyalties began to become more evident with the outbreak of peace. This was to have an impact on the scrutiny the proposal was to receive within the Ministry. But even those wholly unconnected to Unilever were caught up in the enthusiasm. Herbert Broadley, later Britain's first representative to the UN Food and Agriculture Organisation, noted that it 'seems a first-class proposition. It is a pity it was not conceived earlier.'[26]

The Colonial Office

It was immediately realised that it would be vital to have the Colonial Office on board if the scheme was to get government support. They had responsibility for Tanganyika, and would in the normal run of things probably be asked to set up and oversee the scheme if indeed the Labour Government agreed to take it on. The Permanent Secretary at the Ministry of Food, Sir Frank Tribe, therefore forwarded a copy immediately to his opposite number at the Colonial Office, Sir George Gater, taking up Unilever's argument that 'the present shortage in oils and fats is likely to last for a long time', and emphasising that 'this project would provide a most valuable addition to the world's supplies of oilseeds'.[27]

In the Colonial Office, the idea received a mixed reception. Some, like Andrew Cohen, the most influential official on Africa policy, were instinctively supportive: 'this might be an immensely valuable way of developing the territory and filling the vast empty spaces along the

[25] At one meeting with Attlee and senior Ministers, Knight so irritated them with his constant interruptions that Bevin eventually leant across the table and roared at him like a lion. Knight reportedly shrank under the table. Douglas Jay, *Change and Fortune* (London, Ebury Press, 1980), pp. 141–2 (Jay worked at the Board of Trade during the war).
[26] Minute by Broadley, 1 Apr 1946, MAF 83/1747. On the Ministry of Food, 90 of whose staff were former Unilever employees, see Hammond, *Food vol.III*, pp. 435–41, and Fieldhouse, *Merchant Capital*, p. 215.
[27] Tribe to Gater, 28 Mar 1946, MAF 83/1747.

central [railway] line of Tanganyika'.[28] He was aware that Tanganyika desperately needed, and was looking for, ways to begin developing its economy beyond the existing sisal and coffee industries. But the agricultural advisers were universally sceptical. One, C.M. Roddan, picked out with uncanny prescience some of the critical problems that would afflict the scheme:

> 1. *Unreliable rainfall:* About half the stretch in question ... is in the Central Province, the most arid in the territory...
>
> 2. *Soil:* I am always suspicious when I hear of vast tracts of uninhabited fertile land. There is usually a snag, it may be soil, or lack of water, or it may be tsetse... The soil is light and easily erodable and it is certain that soil conservation measures (not estimated for) will be essential...
>
> 3. *Fertility*: Soil types vary tremendously within this area, even over quite small distances... the area is largely scrub and woodland covered and does not possess any marked degree of fertility...
>
> 4. *Rosette disease*: ...if rosette disease is to be reduced to a minimum, the optimum planting time is very limited, even a few days may make all the difference between a full crop and failure... It seems doubtful whether sowing of the vast areas can be completed in a short period without the most extravagant use of expensive machines.
>
> 5. *Distribution of labour:* The quick maturing varieties ... have growth periods of about four months. ...it is difficult to see how employment is to be provided throughout the year.
>
> 6. *Selection by aerial survey*: a preliminary selection might usefully be made in this way but it would have to be correlated with existing knowledge and a further and no doubt very considerable amount of ground work.
>
> 7. *Seed supply*: Difficulty will be found in obtaining the large amount of seed varieties which have been proved suitable under T.T. [Tanganyika Territory] conditions.
>
> From the agricultural point of view, I do not regard the project with any enthusiasm.[29]

The senior Agricultural Adviser, Sir Harold Tempany, drew attention to the 1 million acre Gezira cotton-growing scheme in Sudan which, at half the size, had taken 20 years to build up:

---

[28] Minute by Cohen, 29 Mar 1946, CO 852/603/19612/4/1 (subsequently re-numbered CO 852/603/6).

[29] Minute by Roddan, 4 Apr 1946, CO 852/603/19612/4/1. Rosette disease was a notorious plague for groundnut crops, shrivelling the leaves and reducing the size of nuts.

I frankly doubt it is possible to build up what would probably be the largest single crop plantation enterprise in the world at short notice ... I also doubt whether entire reliance can be placed on mechanical means to carry out the weeding in the early stages of growth.[30]

Another senior adviser, Gerard Clauson, also had doubts about using mechanised methods in Africa, fearing they would produce exactly the same effect as in the US dustbowl – a couple of good crops, then disastrous soil erosion.[31]

The Colonial Office also sent Samuel's memorandum immediately to the Governor of Tanganyika, with assurances that they would be willing to authorise the alienation of the necessary land and ensure the Governor was represented on the public utility board that might run it. When Miller saw it, he was surprised: 'This is a very much greater project than originally discussed with Mr Christie'.[32] Nevertheless the Governor, Sir William Battershill, who had been specifically sent out to Tanganyika to accelerate its development, responded warmly, saying he and his closest advisers 'are extremely interested and indeed enthusiastic about it; and we hope that it will come into being either on the size proposed or on a smaller scale'. But he too put in a number of caveats: firstly, Tanganyika could put up none of the capital – 'We just have not got the money'; secondly, 'Miller considers (and I agree) that it is better to leave the Central Province alone on account of its uncertain rainfall', and concentrate the project in the west, where it would usefully clear tsetse-infested bush; thirdly, yields were likely to be lower than Samuel estimated, nearer 600 lbs/acre; fourthly, transport would be difficult, and 'a great expansion of port facilities would, of course, be necessary'; and finally, both to protect Miller's friends in the sisal industry and to protect Africans themselves from the risk of conscription for any such scheme, 'we must never guarantee the Company a plentiful supply of labour'.[33]

While these exchanges were taking place, discussion of the scheme was being pushed ahead at full speed. A meeting of the Ministry of Food, Colonial Office and Treasury on 5 April 1946 noted the need to explore

---

[30] Minute by Tempany, 30 Apr 1946, ibid. (emphasis in the original). For Tempany's influence in the CO see Hodge, *Triumph of the Expert*, p. 185

[31] Letter from Clauson, 2 Apr 1946, CO 852/603/19612/4/1. These minutes are reproduced in full in Ronald Hyam (ed.), *The Labour Government and the End of Empire, 1945–1951, Part II, British Documents on the End of Empire, Series A Vol.2* (London, Institute of Commonwealth Studies, 1992 – henceforth Hyam, BDEE vol. II), doc. 2. Clauson had overall responsibility in the CO for scientific and technical cooperation: Lee and Petter, *Colonial Office, War and Development*, pp. 183–4.

[32] Miller minute, 20 Apr 1946, TNA 16583.

[33] Caine (CO) to Battershill, 5 Apr 1946 (emphasis in the original), and Battershill to Caine, 23 Apr 1946, CO 852/603/19612/4/1.

the questions raised by the agricultural advisers and agreed this should be done by an examination on the spot in Tanganyika as quickly as possible, so as to be in time for the next crop. The Treasury was surprisingly sympathetic, swayed, perhaps, by the argument that the cost to the UK of groundnuts from the scheme would be £10 15s 0d per ton as opposed to the £25 a ton it was currently paying on the world market, often in dollars. Knight rammed home the argument that without an Empire source, Britain would depend on supplies from Brazil, and 'we have no control over the Brazilian Government'.[34]

The Minister, Sir Ben Smith, desperate to show he was doing something about the situation, did not wait for detailed official advice before mentioning it to the Prime Minister, and submitting a paper on the proposal to the Cabinet Committee on World Food Supplies.[35] On 16 April, the Committee agreed to send a small expert party to investigate and report back as swiftly as possible. But it did not save Smith his job: a month later he was gone. The Colonial Secretary, George Hall, had meanwhile also been captivated by the vision and gave the Colonial Office its marching orders: 'This should be proceeded with all speed', he instructed on 6 May.[36]

Wakefield

Partly to assuage their scepticism, the Colonial Office was allowed to pick the team of expert advisers to visit Tanganyika. As head, they chose John Wakefield, with Miller and Samuel the third father of the scheme.

Wakefield had the reputation of being something of a colonial *wunderkind*, and with his domed, balding head and Attlee-style moustache he looked every inch the serious expert, in an age when experts were respected. From the age of nine years, he had wanted to be a farmer overseas. Graduating from agricultural college and Edinburgh University, he was appointed in 1922 as an Assistant Agricultural Officer in Tanganyika, and rose within 13 years to become in 1935 Director of Agriculture, at the precocious age of 35. In 1940, he was appointed Inspector General of Agriculture in the West Indies, sent specifically to tackle one of the knottiest colonial problems. He told the press he nevertheless regarded Tanganyika as his spiritual home, and was trusted by the Colonial Office to know the land and its problems and to give a

---

[34] Note of an inter-departmental meeting chaired by Sir Frank Tribe, 5 Apr 1946, CO 852/603/19612/4/1.
[35] Minute by Tribe, 8 Apr 1946, and Joint paper by CO and MOF for Cabinet Committee on Food Supplies, 10 Apr 1946, WF(46)91, in MAF 83/1747.
[36] Minute by Hall, 6 May 1946, CO 852/603/19612/4/1.

Photo 2.1 Arthur Wakefield, author of the Plan for the Mechanised Cultivation of Groundnuts in East Africa (Associated Newspapers/Shutterstock)

dispassionate view. More than that, while convalescing from a septic lung in the UK at the end of the war, he had drafted a pamphlet for the Fabian Colonial Bureau on colonial problems, which had come to the attention of Arthur Creech Jones, the Labour Party's expert on colonial affairs and now appointed by Attlee as Under-Secretary of State for the Colonies, effectively Hall's deputy. Creech Jones invited him to lunch and personally asked him to undertake the mission. With alacrity, Wakefield accepted.[37]

But there was another side to Wakefield's thinking. His papers include some random notes written early in 1946 in which he castigates the 'reactionary' thinking of the colonial administrative cadre and its insistence on exerting complete control over the activities of the technical officers and departments, thereby inhibiting their ability to work closely with ordinary Africans to drive forward progressive change. He could feel some of the contradictions of the colonial enterprise, and had clearly encountered frustrations in trying to implement his own ideas

---

[37] Interview published in the *Tanganyika Standard* (Dar es Salaam), 26 Jun 1946; Wood, *Groundnut Affair*, p. 35. For Creech Jones' attitude to colonial development, see Pearce, *Turning Point*, ch.5.

in the past. This may have weighed on the proposals he was about to make.[38]

To support him, the Colonial Office chose John Rosa. A merchant banker by profession, Rosa had spent most of his career with Helbert Wagg & Co. in the City, and combined a dapper appearance with a genial nature. During the war, he had been seconded to act as Treasury representative in Syria in 1941–42, and had then transferred to the Colonial Office as an economic and financial adviser. His familiarity with figures had made him a useful member of the small economic section, and he was added to the team as the man to make sure the finances were sound.[39]

The third member of the party was David Martin, Director of Plantations for the UAC. The Colonial Office specifically asked the UAC to nominate someone with expertise in managing tropical plantations who could assess the practical and organisational aspects of the plan. Given Samuel's role as author of the proposal, they also saw sense in having someone with inside knowledge of the company. Described as 'a man of vast girth and infinite charm, with neatly brilliantined black hair and perpetual pipe' as well as unshakeable calm, good humour and super-optimism, Martin was UAC-man incarnate.[40]

It took a while for the Colonial Office to put the team together and arrange the logistics. The UAC and the Ministry of Food both became increasingly impatient: 'I do hope you will do everything possible to make the Colonial Office get a move on in this matter', Knight urged Tribe in early May, a plea pursued by his Vice-Chairman with the Ministry two weeks later. Finally, on 20 June, the mission left by air for Africa.[41]

Over the following nine weeks, Wakefield's mission undertook a phenomenal task, surveying thousands of square miles of Africa in Kenya, Tanganyika and Northern Rhodesia (now Zambia), consulting local farmers, administrators and businessmen – all possible only because they were loaned a plane by the British Overseas Airways Corporation, and had help everywhere from UAC subsidiaries and staff. Many of the areas, especially in the Southern Province of Tanganyika, could only be surveyed from the air – at low altitude, of course.[42] But in several places they touched down for a closer look.

Their first meeting in Dar es Salaam, on 25 June with the Acting Chief Secretary (a Mr Lamb) and other senior officials, was held in the

---

[38] 'Random Notes on the Colonial system', 1946, in A.J. Wakefield Papers, Bodleian Libraries, Oxford, MSS Afr. s.352; Hodge, *Triumph of the Expert*, pp. 229–30.
[39] Rosa's CV in MAF 83/1839.
[40] Wood, *Groundnut Affair*, pp. 35–6 and 231.
[41] Knight minute to Tribe, 7 May, and Wall minute, 23 May 1946, MAF 83/1747.
[42] *Tanganyika Standard*, 16 Aug 1946.

modest but airy Secretariat building overlooking the palm-fringed harbour. Wakefield's team set out Samuel's proposals and their own plan of action. Rosa underlined that 'it was the need for greater supplies of oilseeds which gave this project the Cabinet support it had received' and that they would probably be willing to pay whatever was necessary to achieve that end. Even from the dry official minutes, it is clear there was a frisson of tension between the current Director of Agriculture, Ralph Miller, who felt ownership of the original idea, and his predecessor, Wakefield, who had been put in charge of the mission. Lamb later admitted to the Colonial Office that there was 'a conflict of personalities behind the scenes'. Miller said they had been working flat out for years to increase food production and 'would have succeeded but for the bad weather'. He urged that more attention be given to increase 'the potential of native [African] production'. The meeting nevertheless concluded that 'while there would be many difficulties to be overcome, there was no insuperable obstacle in the way of applying the project to Tanganyika.'[43]

Apart from brief side visits to Kenya and Northern Rhodesia, where the colonial administrations were equally enthusiastic and several potential areas were identified for fuller investigation later, the bulk of their time was spent in Tanganyika. On Miller's advice they concentrated initially on the Western, Lake and Southern Provinces. They were particularly impressed (from low altitude) with the well-watered Southern Province woodland around the town of Masasi, where the University Mission to Central Africa (UMCA) had run a well-established mission station for the previous 50 years. They recognised, however, that getting the groundnuts out of the area, in the absence of any passable all-weather roads, would be a problem. The province was virtually cut off from the rest of the territory throughout the six-month rainy season.[44]

Wakefield had telegraphed ahead asking to consult one or two former colleagues whose opinion he particularly valued, but arrived to find them all unaccountably on leave or on mission. Nevertheless, two consultations were particularly influential on the mission's conclusions. The first was with A.L. Gladwell, Managing Director of Gailey & Roberts, a UAC subsidiary in Tanganyika. Gladwell had unparalleled experience of clearing bush in East Africa, having done it for sisal plantations, for tsetse-clearing operations and, more recently, for the construction of airstrips in East Africa during the war. He showed the

---

[43] Minutes of meeting held on 25 Jun 1946, TNA 16583. Rosa, 'Note on meeting with J.E.S. Lamb', 16 Oct 1946, CO 852/603/19612/4/1.

[44] The itinerary of the mission is set out in its report, reprinted in the Government White Paper: *A Plan for the Mechanised Production of Groundnuts in East and Central Africa*, Cmd 7030, Feb 1947 (London, HMSO).

mission his books and the audited cost of clearing. They concluded that it could be done for £3 17s 4d per acre, a fatefully optimistic figure they included in the report and which became a basis for the whole financing of the scheme.[45]

The second consultation was more a matter of chance. In early July, an old friend of Wakefield's, a Southern Rhodesian farmer called Tom Bain who had settled near Mpwapwa in Central Province, cabled him to recommend strongly a visit to his area. The telegram survives, though lost for many years in the Tanzania National Archives (TNA): a message that may have sealed the fate of the whole scheme. It read as follows: 'Suggest you inspect half million acres Mpwapwa District ideal crop groundnuts and cerials [sic] population sparcer Fullstop If Interested wire me and I will arrange Transport accommodation etcetera.'[46] Wakefield *was* interested. Bain and the local Agricultural Officer made a preliminary survey, identifying 1,000 square miles of undulating land that looked promising, though 'the main stumbling block appears to be insufficient and inconsistent rainfall'.[47]

When the mission landed there, Bain took charge of the party, put them up at his farm and led them to well-watered parts of his patch where groundnut yields seemed to be good, equivalent to well over 1,000 lbs per acre on the plots grown by local African farmers. Wakefield was impressed. In particular, they went to a mission station north of Mpwapwa called Kongwa, near the Mlali Mountains. An apocryphal story relates how Wakefield, bending to take a soil sample from beside a bush, chanced on a spot where one of Bain's African employees had just relieved himself – and commented that the soil seemed remarkably moist. With that, they flew back to Dar es Salaam with visions of groundnuts glowing in their eyes.[48]

Nobody told them that '*kongwa*' in the dialect of the local Wagogo people meant 'to be deceived' and that the area was known to them as 'the land of perpetual drought.'[49]

As early as 15 August, Wakefield telegraphed the Colonial Secretary to say that his report would recommend a scheme similar to that outlined in London before they left. He was as good as his word. Working flat out,

[45] Wood, *Groundnut Affair*, p. 38. *Minutes of Evidence taken before the Committee of Public Accounts*, 23 Mar 1950 (House of Commons Official Reports), John Rosa evidence, question 293 (p. 46).
[46] Telegram Bain to Wakefield, 8 Jul 1946, TNA 35781 (folio 100b).
[47] 'Tour of inspection of Northern Mpwapwa District', 16–18 Jul 1946, TNA 35781 (f. 100c).
[48] Items in TNA 35781. Information from A.H. Pike, former District Officer for Dodoma (interviewed 3 Nov 1978); Wood, *Groundnut Affair*, p. 36.
[49] Judith Listowel, *The Making of Tanganyika* (London, Chatto and Windus, 1965), p. 147; Iliffe, *Tanganyika*, p. 442.

the team produced its report on 'The mass production of groundnuts in East and Central Africa' on 20 September 1946.[50]

The visionary nature of the scheme comes across clearly in the notes of the mission's first oral debrief on their return to London:

> [Wakefield] confirmed the optimistic estimates which had been cabled from East Africa and said that Tanganyika alone could provide areas of freely available land, suitable both as to soil and as to climate, which could, under modern methods of farming, provide crops far in excess of the targets contemplated in London ... In fact, East Africa would become the lowest cost producer of oil seeds in the world, able to offer them at £8–9 a ton f.o.r. [free on rail] when the project was fully in its stride.
>
> He laid great emphasis on the point that the scheme, to be successful anywhere, must completely get away from the old concepts and methods of subsistence farming, and adopt modern technique in its entirety.[51]

Like Topsy, the scheme had continued to grow. Wakefield recommended a 3.2 million acre scheme (that is 1.3 million hectares or 5,000 square miles – the size of Yorkshire) capable of producing 600,000 tons of groundnuts a year by 1951. This area would be divided into 107 units of 30,000 acres each, of which 10 units would be in Tanganyika's Western Province, 15 in Central Province and 55 in Southern Province. The remaining 27 units were in Northern Rhodesia and Kenya. The scheme would require a workforce of 500 Europeans and up to 25,000 Africans by 1950. Yields were estimated at 850 lbs per acre and, with Gladwell's figures for the cost of clearing, this gave an overall cost of production of £14 5s 6d f.o.b. [free on board]. The world market price having risen to £32 per ton, this would save the country £10 million a year once full production was reached (assuming of course that both prices remained the same). The total cost had increased to £24 million, and dollar needs were estimated at between £3–4 million, mainly for machinery. If the machinery could be obtained to start clearing in April 2007, the first crop would be harvested in May 1948.[52]

To put these costs in perspective, the total cost of the scheme would be equivalent to nearly £1 billion today (2018 prices), and was nearly five times the total annual budget of the Tanganyika Administration, which in 1946 was £5.1 million.[53]

---

[50] The original copy of the report is in MAF 83/1746. A slightly adapted version, minus some statistical annexes, was published in the White Paper, *A Plan for the Mechanised Production of Groundnuts*, Cmd 7030 (London, HMSO), hereafter cited as Cmd 7030, with the paragraph number.

[51] 'Note of Mission's preliminary oral report on their tour of investigation, 4 Sept.', in Caine (CO) to Harrison (MOF), 6 Sep 1946, MAF 83/1746.

[52] Cmd 7030, passim.

[53] Equivalent calculated using a comparator based on Retail Price Index deflator, 1946–2018 (see www.measuringworth.com/calculators/ukcompare/

The report did focus on a number of the objections that had been raised earlier. Transport was clearly a problem in the Southern Province, where a new railway and deep-water port would have to be constructed, and a branch line would be needed from the existing Central Line (which ran through Mpwapwa) to Kongwa. It was boldly asserted that

> the rainfall in all the localities selected for the project is adequate for the groundnut crop. The ill-effects of disease and of temporary cessations of rain, which have occasionally reduced crop yields under the existing primitive methods of cultivation, can be largely avoided by the methods described in the report.[54]

Scientific agriculture, in other words, had the answers to nature's uncertainty.

Great emphasis was put on the virtues of mechanisation and modern soil conservation and fertilisation methods as the *only* solution to the current world food shortage:

> No significant increase in the present output of oilseeds can be achieved, however, by the existing methods of peasant production. Nothing but the most highly mechanised agricultural methods, on a vast scale never previously envisaged, will result in any appreciable amelioration of the present disastrous world food position.[55]

While the mission had been in East Africa, the UAC had been gathering evidence on mechanised peanut farming in the US. Though less extensive than initially believed, they had found some farms in Virginia which provided some supporting evidence.[56] The team was also firmly of the view that

> [t]he nature and scope of the project rules out private enterprise as the permanent owners or operators. It would seem necessary to form a Public Corporation sponsored and financed by His Majesty's Government to operate the project.[57]

It was assumed that eventually the scheme would be turned over to local management on a cooperative basis, 'maybe a generation or two ahead', but only if the mechanised basis was retained 'to avoid reversion to primitive methods of individual effort which have proved so ineffective and ruinous to the land.'[58]

---

relativevalue.php – accessed 9 Dec 2019), which gives £984 million; other comparators produce a higher figure. For the Tanganyika budget, see Tanganyika Territory, *Estimates for 1946* (Dar es Salaam, Government Printer).
[54] Summary para. 16.
[55] Cmd 7030, Main report, para. 2.
[56] Cmd 7030, Main report, para. 62 (but see the next chapter on US experience).
[57] Cmd 7030, Summary para. 12.
[58] Cmd 7030, Summary para. 14.

As for the finances, for which Rosa was responsible, he later admitted to the Parliamentary Public Accounts Committee that the numbers were fairly speculative: 'at the time we wrote that Report no-one knew any better. We did take such advice as we could from such experts as there were [but] it was all guesswork, and our guess was as good as anybody else's.'[59]

The report as a whole was focussed on achieving the maximum output in the minimum time:

> We trust no-one will lose sight of the need for speed in getting the project started in 1947. The world's need is certainly Africa's opportunity, but the world cannot continue in hunger merely to enable a complete blueprint for Africa to be made perfect in every detail.[60]

It concluded with a rousing appeal to the spirit of wartime endeavour and overwhelming confidence that difficulties will be overcome:

> Equipment and personnel in the required numbers will be difficult to get, but the success of the project will be assured if it is undertaken with the sense of determination and urgency which the gravity of the situation demands ... The same determination is called for in the execution of this project as was needed, and found, for the conduct of the major operations of the war. Given this attitude of mind, the chances of failure are remote.[61]

The visionary quality of the report was apparent to all who read it. It seemed to provide all things to all men. To the Ministry of Food it promised swift supplies of desperately needed oils for starving British families; to the Colonial Office, development of one of its most backward territories; to Tanganyika, a major investment and source of revenue; to the Fabian Colonial Bureau, a model scheme that would put African education and labour welfare at the heart of its enterprise; to Labour politicians, a demonstration that Government enterprise could fill a gap that private enterprise could not; and to African peasants, an example of what could be done with their land if they modernised their agricultural practices.

Who could resist such a vision?

---

[59] *Evidence before the Committee of Public Accounts*, 23 Mar 1950, Rosa, question 267–8, p. 44.
[60] Cmd 7030, Main report para. 50.
[61] Cmd 7030, Summary para. 19 and Main report para. 121.

3

'The Poison of the Official Pen...'

If there was a Damascene conversion in this story, it happened on the 08.15 train from Euston to Colwyn Bay on Friday 27 September, 1946. And it happened to John Strachey.

Strachey had been Minister for four months. He had moved swiftly to transfer the Permanent Secretary, Sir Frank Tribe, to the National Audit Office, and was travelling with the man he had appointed to replace him, Sir Percival Liesching, and his Private Secretary, George Bishop. They were on their way to visit the Administrative Executive of the Ministry in north Wales. Like a good Private Secretary, Bishop leafed through the papers he had brought for the journey, including a bulky foolscap document bound in a black binding – a copy of the Wakefield Report, received in the Ministry that morning. A casual look became an engrossed read, and by the time they reached Crewe, he handed it to Strachey saying he must look at it. By the time they got back to London, Strachey was hooked.[1]

The Minister's wholesale support would prove critical. But the report nevertheless still had to run the gauntlet of inter-departmental discussion and Cabinet approval before any resources would be committed to it. Wakefield and Rosa spent the next three months pressing the case for their proposals and defending it from departmental criticisms until Strachey could put it to Cabinet. These discussions reveal much about the state of Britain's economy, its attitudes to Africa, agriculture and colonial development, and the interaction between ministers and civil servants on politically contentious issues. They are therefore worth examining in detail.

---

[1] Wood, *Groundnut Affair*, p. 40 (based on a personal account from Bishop, who sadly died before I could interview him).

Whitehall

The Ministry of Food stood four-square behind the scheme. Not just the Unilever secondees in the Oils and Fats division, but senior officials throughout the Ministry were caught up in the enthusiasm. Eric Roll, who had joined the Ministry from academia during the war and risen to a senior role, regarded it as 'a most important project which has been very thoroughly thought out and which should be given the utmost possible support ... I think our function should be to help overcome any inertia or scepticism there may be in other Departments.'[2]

For scepticism there was. The Ministry of Food noted that there was 'a cleavage of opinion in the Colonial Office'.[3] Cohen and the political side remained enthusiastic about the scheme, but the doubts of the agricultural experts were in no way allayed by Wakefield's report. The two most senior, Sir Frank Stockdale and Sir Harold Tempany, unleashed a stream of criticisms about the assumptions on yields, soil, weather and disease at an internal meeting on 1 October, warning in particular of the dangers of drought, and dismissing the idea that soil conservation techniques would be any help in limiting the damage. They believed the scheme would be lucky to achieve yields of 600 lbs/acre, and Stockdale thought it would be safer to assume that development would lag one year behind the forecasts on which the estimates were based.[4] These views were reiterated, in more muted form, at an inter-departmental meeting on 3 October, where debate focussed also on whether significant volumes could be produced before the world shortage came to a natural end. Wakefield stoutly defended the agricultural soundness of the scheme, arguing that in the Central Province 'the high yields in that area (in an extremely bad year for rain) speak for themselves', and Jasper Knight rebuffed the argument that the shortage was temporary. Knight commented afterwards to Broadley, the MoF Director in charge, that

> the attitude of the Colonial Office towards the project is really quite pathetic. I am perfectly certain that unless we force the pace, there is not the remotest chance of the necessary machinery reaching East Africa by February 1947, which will mean we shall get no production in 1948.[5]

---

[2] Minute by Roll, 2 Oct 1946, MAF 83/1746. For background see Roll, *Crowded Hours*, pp. 46–51.
[3] Note by Amos, 2 Oct 1946, ibid.
[4] 'Note of a meeting held on 1 October 1946', CO 852/603 f.94; note by C.E.I. Jones (HM Treasury), 17 Oct 1946, T 161/1371 f.57 (Treasury papers, The National Archives, Kew).
[5] Note by Amos on the inter-departmental meeting of 3 Oct, 4 Oct 1946; Note by A.J. Wakefield on 'Agricultural Soundness of the Scheme', 17 Oct 1946; and Knight to Broadley, 4 Oct 1946, all in MAF 83/1746.

But there was another obstacle to forcing the pace: Her Majesty's Treasury. They were, after all, the guardians of the public purse, and the sums of money proposed were huge. Wakefield did his best by dangling the prospect of low prices and fat profits in front of them. If the groundnuts were sold at cost price to the UK, it would save £10 million a year; if it sold them at the world market price (which he preferred), the Corporation would realise a profit of £80 million in the first 10 years – enough to pay off the capital investment and remit a sizeable profit to Her Majesty's Government (HMG). (The idea that the profit might remain in Tanganyika would never have occurred to Wakefield.)[6] But the Treasury believed both the timescale and the assumptions were over-optimistic. If world prices fell, the economics of the scheme went out the window, and the government stood to make a hefty loss. They had a good deal of sympathy with the Colonial Office's agricultural advisers and recognised that:

> the scheme does involve an element of gambling. If everything went wrong that could, e.g. labour or other troubles during the short planting period, thunderstorms, droughts, raids by rats and monkeys, serious attacks of disease etc., the estimates might prove very much out.

But they were also deeply suspicious of the Colonial Office, 'who can be relied upon to make a frightful mess of handling a big undertaking of this sort'. They felt the Colonial Office's finance department in particular was 'lamentably amateur', whereas that of the Ministry of Food, under the rigorous and redoubtable Dr E.E. Bailey, had their full respect.[7]

The Treasury was also dubious about the idea of a Government corporation, and using the UAC as a managing agent. The corporation was 'a much more speculative enterprise' than other industries which were in the process of being nationalised by the new Labour Government, a process being overseen by Herbert Morrison. Treasury officials were concerned too that the Government appeared to take all the risks while the colonial territories would cash in on the benefits – if there were any. They remained adamant that the colonies concerned should make some contribution. Rosa, who was a master of the manipulative minuting of meetings, was swiftly corrected by Winnifrith of the Treasury when he tried to slide their agreement into a note summarising the inter-departmental meetings. Treasury offi-

---

[6] Financial estimates in Wakefield to Dawson (CO), 28 Sep 1946, CO 852/603 f.11a.

[7] Notes by A.J.D. Winnifrith, 4 Oct, and W.H Fisher, 17 Oct 1946, T 161/1371. Morgan, *Colonial Development, Vol. II*, p. 235, quotes his interview many years later with Winnifrith who felt in retrospect, 'we were doomed to have a precipitate and disastrous scheme, whichever department was put in charge'.

cials prepared a note to the Chancellor recommending opposition to the scheme.[8]

Rosa fought back, reminding them that the fact this would take place in a British colony meant the Treasury would be able to retain more of the financial benefit:

> HMG, who would be undertaking this project primarily for their own benefit ... might be considered lucky to have found within the Colonial Empire land suitable for their purposes. By operating in such territories they are assured of the fullest cooperation of, and freedom from 'squeeze' by, the local Government, a happy condition which might well not result were they driven in their present extremity to turn to foreign territories for the realisation of this project.[9]

He nevertheless shared the Treasury view that

> departmental responsibility should devolve on the Ministry of Food, since the project has as its primary justification, not Colonial development, but the increase of the supply of vegetable oils ... to the UK. It is moreover important from the outset to decide whether the scheme is one having the above object as the primary aim, or whether it is one with the combined purpose of securing both the supply of fats to this country and simultaneously the betterment of the colonial territories concerned. The Colonial Office would be bound to watch the latter interest and for this reason alone it is considered that to avoid any misunderstanding and to ensure the financial interest of this country the Ministry of Food should be made responsible.[10]

On the employment of a managing agent, the Ministry of Food view was once more influenced by its Unilever secondees. Jasper Knight, unsurprisingly, told Broadley he was

> very strongly in favour of the management being entrusted to United Africa Company on an agency basis ... As a Director of United Africa Company, I am naturally a little reluctant to press this point [sic], but I am sure this is the right thing to do.

His main argument was their expertise and resources in tropical Africa which, admittedly, no-one else could match. But both the Colonial Office and Treasury remained suspicious.[11]

---

[8] 'Treasury Attitudes to the Project', note by Rosa, 28 Oct 1946, CO 852/603/19612/4/1 f.140; notes by Winnifrith, 17 Oct, and Jones, 21 Oct 1946, T 161/1371.
[9] Rosa, 'Treasury Attitudes', 28 Oct 1946, ibid.
[10] 'Departmental Views on the Report', note by Rosa, 24 Oct 1946, CO 852/603/19612/4/1 f.135.
[11] Knight to Broadley (MOF), 4 Oct 1946, MAF 83/1746.

Tanganyika

Back in East Africa, Wakefield's report also received a mixed reception. Cohen at the Colonial Office sent it to the Governor, Sir William Battershill, with strict instructions to respond swiftly and, it was hinted, positively.

Battershill himself had been sent out to Tanganyika at the end of the war to awake the territory from its torpor. Instead, it seems to have sent him to sleep. He had developed a reputation as an efficient and go-ahead official in Palestine and Cyprus before the war. Promoted to a senior job as Deputy Under-Secretary in the Colonial Office itself during the war, he was considered a modern thinker on colonial development and was sent to Dar es Salaam with high hopes. But Tanganyika didn't suit him: he was grumpy at being separated from his beloved Mediterranean, exhausted by the round of social functions that the Governor had to undertake, enervated by the humid climate, wracked by arthritis, and reputedly still shell-shocked from a near miss by a V2 rocket as he passed through Victoria Station one morning (hence his nickname 'Battered Bill'). Never one to take a decision if it could be avoided, Battershill allowed things to drift.[12]

In this he was ably assisted by his Chief Secretary and Deputy, Rex Surridge. Consummately professional, he was nevertheless a great man for letting sleeping dogs lie, and if possible, persuading them to go to sleep. Neither was hostile to the Groundnut Scheme. On the contrary, both understood well enough the importance of supporting it. But they lacked the initiative to engage with it proactively and get the Tanganyika Administration to assimilate it into its own plans for Tanganyika's future. It remained an exotic alien plant amongst the native species of their neglected garden.[13]

Miller was still sceptical on the agricultural side, particularly about the poor soils and lack of reliable rainfall in the Mpwapwa area which he regarded as 'an extremely doubtful proposition'. But even he was convinced that courage and vision could overcome the problems and that '£3,000,000 of artificial manures will make a silk purse out of a sow's ear'. He was also impressed that production on the scale proposed would double the territory's exports and revolutionise its economy. This alone made the risk worth taking.[14]

---

[12] Battershill's correspondence with his mother, Battershill Papers, Box 5, Mss Brit. Emp. s. 467, BLCAS, Oxford. Interviews with M.J. Davies, former Private Secretary to Battershill in the Tanganyika Colonial Service, 8 Jun 1978 and 1 Jun 1979.
[13] Sir Rex Surridge, interview recorded in Mss Afr. s. 1813, Bodleian Libraries, Oxford; Surridge to Colonial Secretary, 2 Mar 1949, CO 691/204/4.
[14] Notes by Miller, 18 Sep 1946, TNA 16758, and 8 Oct 1946, TNA 35781; Miller to Engledow (CO Agricultural Adviser), 27 Mar 1947, CO 852/912/1 f.94a.

Two other things preoccupied them: labour and transport. The sisal growers were as nervous as ever that the scheme would steal their labour, or – just as bad – force wages up. But Tanganyika's Labour Commissioner had scant sympathy for them given the poor wages and conditions they currently provided, despite the huge profits they were making: 'the sisal industry will only have themselves to blame if they suffer from this scheme', he noted. But he did advise against starting the scheme in the Western Province because the government were themselves recruiting labour to build a railway extension to the Mpanda lead mines in that region that were just beginning to the opened up (though in the end that project too came to a disappointing end).[15]

On transport questions, the normally dour General Manager of Railways, Farquharson, proved wildly optimistic that the existing Central Line network could manage the requirements of the scheme. He was confident they could export the volumes of groundnuts expected, but seems to have failed completely to assess the volume of *inward* traffic. It was as if all the necessary tractors, equipment, people and material would appear in the bush by magic. More realistic was the assessment of the proposed Southern Province railway by the Nairobi-based manager of the Kenya and Uganda Railways and Harbours, R.E. Robins. He warned of the enormous cost of an isolated railway line unconnected to existing networks, because of the need to duplicate the rolling stock and maintenance facilities, a prediction that proved all too accurate.[16]

Battershill replied to the Colonial Office, reflecting some of the concerns about labour and resources, but re-emphasising their willingness to have the scheme in Tanganyika. He could take a hint, and despite the sound advice of men on the spot, no fundamental objections were raised.[17]

Cabinet

With the official-level discussions threatening to get bogged down, Strachey decided to add impetus by raising it to a political level. He was keen to put the proposal to Cabinet as swiftly as possible, bearing in mind the urgent wish to secure a crop in 1948, but wanted to be assured of a favourable reception. That meant at the very least getting Creech Jones, who had replaced Hall as Colonial Secretary when the latter retired for health reasons, and Hugh Dalton, the Chancellor, on board.

---

[15] Minute by Molohan (Acting Labour Commissioner), 9 Oct 1946, TNA 35781.
[16] Note by Farquharson, 30 Oct 1946, and Robins to Cavendish Bentinck, 5 Oct 1946, TNA 35781.
[17] Battershill to Caine, 23 Sep, and Battershill to Colonial Secretary, 4 Nov 1946, CO 852/603/19612/4/1 f.102, 151.

Strachey was an effective political operator and understood the need to do this through personal contact, so in late October 1946 he engaged himself fully in the task.

In the event, Creech Jones proved the easier to persuade. He had already devoted years of his life to defending African interests in Parliament and through the Fabian Colonial Bureau, and was very much engaged with the need to modernise African agriculture. He had written to Strachey in mid-October saying that the Colonial Office wanted to be closely involved, but conceding at the outset that if the scheme went ahead the Ministry of Food should have lead responsibility for it. This was not least because Colonial Office resources for such schemes were constrained by Treasury rules and the terms of the 1945 Colonial Development and Welfare Act, whereas the Ministry could fund it without having to go back to Parliament for more money. But he still had doubts about using the UAC as managing agents and his experts were still troubled about the scheme's viability. Strachey and his officials prepared a reply suggesting that the Ministry set up a Special Section, including a Colonial Office representative, to complete a thorough examination of the Wakefield report. The draft argued that the use of the UAC was essential if an early start was to be made, though it should be handed over as soon as possible to a Government-run corporation and eventually to the colonial territories themselves; and therefore accepted that in those circumstances, the Ministry of Food would take responsibility. Before the reply was sent, however, Strachey spoke to Samuel, Samuel spoke to Creech Jones, and Creech Jones then spoke directly to Strachey on 25 October. The result was that the two ministers agreed to put a joint paper to Cabinet the following week recommending an immediate start using the UAC while the Special Section completed its work.[18]

Dalton was now the critical factor. His sceptical officials had been assuaged by the thought that no decision would be taken until the Ministry of Food finance section had given the proposals a thorough going over. Only R.W.B. Clarke (known as 'Otto' Clarke), a senior official on the international side of the Treasury, showed much enthusiasm for the scheme. He thought the £7 million of US equipment well worth spending and was in favour of pressing ahead fast. On 29 October, Strachey went to see the Chancellor. Aware of Dalton's personal antipathy to him, he went with Creech Jones, but his silver tongue did the trick. Clarke reported:

> The Minister of Food has spoken to the Chancellor about this, and it all fits so closely with the Chancellor's plans for developing food production in the sterling area and Europe that I think we should apply ginger

---

[18] Creech Jones to Strachey, 15 Oct, Strachey's draft reply to Creech Jones, 24 Oct, and Feavearyear's minute to Bailey, 24 Oct 1946, all in MAF 83/1746; minute by Caine, 26 Oct 1946, CO 852/603/19612/4/1.

rather than morphia. But if we don't look out, the C.O. will get away with murder.[19]

The last point was widely felt in the Treasury. Its note to the Chancellor ahead of the meeting had put their scepticism of the Colonial Office's fitness to run the project bluntly:

> The Treasury have no doubt that it is essential for the Ministry of Food and not the Colonial Office to run it. If the Colonial Office run it, the scheme is bound to be a financial failure, since the Colonial Office will, all along, tend to look at it not as a commercial venture in which H.M. Government have invested money which they expect to see returned, but as a scheme for the betterment of the Colonies concerned. The Colonial Office would be quite happy to see the scheme used as a means of extracting further financial benefit for these Colonies from this country.[20]

Dalton agreed not to oppose the proposal to commit £3 million now to allow an immediate start on the scheme, with a further consideration of the full scheme once the Special Section reported back.[21]

The joint Strachey-Creech Jones paper for Cabinet was circulated on 30 October for the Cabinet meeting the following day. It summarised Wakefield's proposals, with the one change that estimated yields were reduced from 850 to 750 lbs/acre, and said that the Special Section in the Ministry of Food would complete a thorough examination of the scheme by the end of November. In the meantime, committing £3 million now would enable some crop to be produced in 1948, without prejudice to the full £25 million scheme. It put off the decision whether any eventual scheme should be run by a public corporation, and was deliberately vague on the use of agents ('e.g. the United Africa Company and similar organisations'). But the overriding argument was that the scheme held out the prospect of 'an early and substantial contribution to the present shortage of oils and fats'.[22]

Other Cabinet ministers were taken by surprise. 'Is it really necessary to buy this £3,000,000 pig-in-a-poke?' asked one of the advisers to Herbert Morrison who, as Lord President, had an overall responsibility for economic policy.[23] Attlee's Private Secretary, Gorell Barnes, admitted that there had not been time to form a balanced judgement, and was concerned that the demand for excavators for this project

[19] Minute by Clarke (HMT), 29 Oct 1946, T 161/1371.
[20] Note on 'Groundnuts in East and Central Africa', J.I.C. Crombie (HMT), 28 Oct 1946, T 161/1371 f.83 (reproduced in Hyam, *BDEE*, vol. II, doc. 114, p. 241).
[21] E.E. Bailey (MOF Finance) to Liesching, 30 Oct 1946, MAF 128/11.
[22] 'Project for Growing Groundnuts in East and Central Africa', 29 Oct 1946, CP(46)402, CAB 129/14.
[23] Minute by Chantler, 30 Oct 1946, CAB 124/1090.

might divert them from opencast coal mining, which was even more urgent. But only six days before, the Cabinet had had a notably gloomy discussion of the food situation, and any steps to alleviate it were likely to be welcomed.[24]

At Cabinet the next day, Strachey emphasised the importance of developing Empire sources of oils and fats, which at present covered only 60% of British needs. Creech Jones spoke in favour, but noted that the money could not come from Colonial Development and Welfare funds. As promised, Dalton supported on two conditions: that the project was run by the Ministry of Food, and that the whole crop would be made available solely to the UK, not to some international pool. Cabinet added a third condition, that no machinery should be diverted from other priorities, such as coal mining. Strachey tried to assuage such fears by gaily suggesting (without a shred of evidence) 'that a good deal of the equipment required could be improvised from material available in Africa'. With that, Attlee concluded that the £3 million start-up funding was approved.[25]

Strachey immediately wanted to cement the deal by making a statement to Parliament. This, however, meant coming off the fence about the Government's intentions for managing the scheme – through a corporation, a managing agent, or a bit of both. Treasury officials were still sceptical. If the scheme was such an attractive proposition, why would the UAC not do it with their own money? And if it was too risky, why should the public's money be put at risk? The tug of war went through November, with the Treasury trying to excise all reference to a public corporation. Eventually, Strachey went straight back to the Chancellor. Following their conversation on 23 November, Dalton curtly told his officials: 'I took, and take, the view that, if it goes on, it must be a public show.'[26]

As Rosa commented:

> The position is not so much that the Treasury have agreed, as that the Chancellor has kept ahead of his officials and has proved much more amenable than they, with the result that the Government is already virtually committed to setting up a Corporation.[27]

Strachey also secured Dalton's agreement that the UAC should undertake the work, at least in the start-up phase. As one Ministry of Food official put it, 'the Minister is convinced of the necessity of employing United Africa from the beginning and is not disposed to yield on this.'

---

[24] Gorell Barnes to Prime Minister, 30 Oct 1946, Gorell Barnes Papers, BARN 2/1 (Churchill College Archives, Cambridge).
[25] Cabinet minutes, 31 Oct 1946, CM(46)93rd Conclusions, CAB 128/6.
[26] Minutes by Sir Herbert Brittain, Dalton and Shaw (HMT), 23 Nov 1946, T 161/1371.
[27] Minute by Rosa, 24 Dec 1946 CO 852/603.

In any case, he had already told Samuel in October that he wanted the UAC to start work on it.[28]

So, on 25 November 1946, eight months after the scheme was first conceived, Strachey announced to Parliament the initiation of the Groundnut Scheme. He reported the Cabinet's agreement to launch the first year's operations, emphasising the urgency of the work and the implications for the margarine ration. Further study, he assured MPs, was under way on the full scheme, on which:

> It is the Government's intention that the full undertaking, should it be initiated, shall be owned and financed entirely by His Majesty's Government, probably through a Government-owned corporation. But in order to get the work going in Africa without delay I have invited the United Africa Company to act as managing agents for the present limited scheme pending a decision on the long term project.[29]

The Opposition asked about the funding, the UAC's experience, the diversion of machines from British agriculture, whether any Africans would be dispossessed of their land, and whether the scheme would need a subsidy. Strachey was reassuring on all points. He promised a supplementary estimate, that 'the natives would be very greatly benefited', no forced labour would be used, and, while admitting that nobody had direct experience of this kind of operation before, 'groundnuts produced in these areas by this method will be one of the cheapest sources of raw material in the world'. For now, the scheme appeared to have the whole-hearted backing of Parliament.[30]

The Special Section

The papers of the Special Section set up by Strachey within the Ministry of Food occupy many shelves in the Ministry's archive. A small team was set up, led by Frank Hollins of the Ministry, reporting direct to the formidable Under-Secretary for Finance, Dr E.E. Bailey, and including William Faure, a UAC Board member, and John Rosa from the Colonial Office (Samuel had wanted F.J. Pedler, a Colonial Office (CO) official who later went on to have a distinguished career in the UAC, but the CO said that Rosa was 'the best, and only, man available'). It worked at a frenetic pace, checking the Wakefield proposals, instructed to report back as swiftly as possible.[31]

---

[28] Minute Bailey to Hollins, 1 Nov 1946, MAF 128/11.
[29] *Hansard*, vol. 430, cols 1262–6, 25 Nov 1946.
[30] Ibid.
[31] The Special Section's files are in MAF 83/1746–2005. There is a detailed account of the Section's work and report in Morgan, *Colonial Development, Vol. II*, pp. 238–50.

The review and subsequent debates bear out the claim by Joseph Morgan Hodge that this period could be deemed the 'Triumph of the Expert' in colonial development policy.[32] Of course, the Wakefield team themselves were intended to be experts, though under interrogation by the Public Accounts Committee four years later, John Rosa confessed: 'I think it is hardly fair to call me an expert in any context, but certainly not in the matter of soil, rainfall and agriculture'.[33] The agricultural aspects were examined by the head of chemistry at Rothamsted Experimental Station and the Principal of Wye Agricultural College, though neither of them knew East Africa well; the labour requirements were given a thorough review by Major G. St J. Orde-Browne, the CO's long-standing Labour Adviser, who *did* know East Africa well (but was himself not well, and died shortly after); and the commercial prospects were looked at by J.A. Dyson, the director of costings at the Ministry, a long-standing civil servant.[34]

David Martin of the UAC was sent to the US to look in more detail at the mechanisation of peanut farming there. Given the US antipathy to socialist enterprise, it was agreed to 'soft-pedal' the governmental angle in his discussions with the US authorities lest they prove reluctant to sell the necessary machinery to the British Government. But so firm were assumptions about American technical prowess by the end of the war, that hopes were high of finding the answers to the challenges of mechanised farming already sorted by US farmers. To his own surprise, Martin telegraphed back in early December:

> After visiting South Georgia growing areas and finding how little mechanisation of worthwhile nature has been accomplished, we decided similar investigations Virginia Carolina not justified. Mules still more favoured than tractors ... And both farmers and research works confirm that to neglect weeding seriously jeopardizes crop prospects.

It was also apparent that mechanical harvesting brought with it a considerable amount of straw and stones in with the nuts, which meant 'we will have to face much heavier expenditure on decortication machinery than allowed in our report.'[35]

Other gaps were found. The Special Section noted that Wakefield's report did not cover potential expenditure on school buildings, equipment and teachers; wells and water supply for African settlements; the cost of clearing land for African farms; 'inducement goods' for African

---

[32] Hodge, *Triumph of the Expert*, ch.7.
[33] *Evidence before the Committee of Public Accounts*, 23 Mar 1950, Rosa, qn 290, p. 45.
[34] Morgan, *Colonial Development, Vol. II*, p. 240; note by Orde Browne, 12 Nov 1946, CO 852/603.
[35] Martin to Special Section, 4 and 6 Dec 1946, MAF 83/1760.

labour (traditionally cloth and cooking utensils); roads, light railways and rolling stock; or clearing airstrips. Serious risks were identified over the supply of equipment and labour, over the phasing and the financing of the scheme. Nevertheless, the estimated costs of production per ton were increased only by a further £2 to £16 8s 0d.[36]

But whatever the caveats, qualifications or questions in the detailed studies, it is clear that Hollins had political instructions from Strachey to endorse the proposals. The conclusions of the Special Section's report, submitted on 5 December, were written by Mr Hollins alone and not endorsed by the rest of the Section. They stated baldly that the scheme was 'a practicable plan', 'involves no unjustifiable finance risks', would be of as much benefit to Africans as it would to the UK, and was essential given the world prospects for oils and fats.[37]

It is striking that the full report was never signed, published, or even circulated widely outside the Ministry of Food. But even within the Ministry, the whole process left two very unhappy people, both holding financial responsibility for the scheme: Dr Bailey, the Under-Secretary for Finance, and Sir Percival Liesching, the Permanent Secretary.

Dr Bailey took the unusual step of submitting a formal memorandum of dissent to Liesching: 'I have read their Report with care but regret that I cannot associate myself with its Conclusions ... in my judgement the evidence now so laboriously and skilfully assembled leads to different conclusions.' He listed significant risks in relation to providing equipment and labour and to the overall costs of the scheme. 'I find it no part of my duty to recommend the hazarding of public money however high the cause or the stakes [marked with large question and exclamation marks in the margin, in Strachey's hand]. If it is to be decided that the risks should be run, that decision should, in my view be taken at Ministerial or Cabinet Level'. 'Of course', annotated Strachey.[38]

Liesching submitted Bailey's memo to Strachey with a covering note, in his capacity as Accounting Officer for the Ministry, which gave him responsibility not only to the Minister, but directly to the House of Commons through the Public Accounts Committee. He pointed out, firstly, that in his view the scheme was primarily one of colonial development and was not covered by the formal remit given to the Ministry of Food when it was decided to make it permanent in November 1945.

---

[36] Hollins note, 13 Nov 1946, MAF 83/1746. Other material in MAF 83/1753, 83/1755, 83/1764.
[37] 'Report of the Special Section', 5 Dec 1946, MAF 83/1758. Its conclusions are quoted in Morgan, *Colonial Development, Vol. II*, pp. 238–40. See also, the important retrospective note by Bailey (MoF Finance), 6 Oct 1949, MAF 85/589.
[38] Bailey to Liesching, 20 Dec 1946, attaching his memorandum (on which are Strachey's annotations), MAF 85/589.

Secondly, the success of the scheme depended fundamentally on the adequate provision of African labour, over which he had no control and therefore no means of ensuring the success of the scheme.[39] In the genteel world of the British civil service, this was strong stuff: the two most senior officials responsible for the financing of the scheme rejecting the conclusions of their own department's assessment and refusing to take responsibility for delivering it on budget, making clear they would only proceed under explicit Ministerial instruction, a 'direction' as it is known.

Strachey decided to hang on to the papers until after the Cabinet discussion.

Back to the Cabinet

With the report of the Special Section completed, Strachey could now go back to Cabinet for endorsement of the full scheme. On 4 January 1947, he circulated a paper to Cabinet colleagues with the conclusions (only) of the Special Section assessment, and financial calculations which showed that the debt to the Treasury would be repaid by 1964 and a net profit of £17 million achieved by 1971. He said nothing of his senior officials' reservations, but instead added a second, personal memo of his own. This is a masterpiece of political rhetoric and the political foundation stone of the whole Scheme. It deserves quoting at length. Strachey admitted that the yields had been revised down and the costs per ton revised up (to £17 18s 0d), and acknowledged frankly that this was a big and risky undertaking:

> But what I would ask my colleagues to consider is the risks of not undertaking this project. If we do not make a determined effort such as this to open up a new supply of oils and fats, we shall risk two things. First in 1950 [the date of the next election] we may have the same or a lower margarine ration than today. Or second: in 1950 we may have to spend so many dollars on buying fats from dollar sources, that we shall have too few left to buy other indispensable dollar imports.
>
> Again, a large enterprise of this type is the only way in which our Central African possessions can be rapidly developed, so that they may become an economic and strategic asset instead of a liability, as to a large extent they now are.
>
> It may be objected that public money should not be used in an enterprise of this kind. But shall we not have failed as a Government unless we can on suitable occasions, substitute public, socialist enterprise for private enterprise? The alternative would be to turn the whole thing over to Unilevers with a blank cheque to do what they liked. There

---

[39] Minute by Liesching to Minister, 20 Dec 1946, MAF 85/589.

are a dozen reasons why the Colonial Secretary, and indeed all my colleagues, would not allow us to do that.[40]

As identified in the Introduction, the Attlee Government were on a mission: to remedy the failures of the Conservative governments during the Depression; to demonstrate that socialism worked; and to salvage the country from its post-war mess. Strachey pressed all the right political buttons, and craftily insulated himself from criticism down the road that if things did not go according to plan, the scheme was invalid. Even if it was losing money, he had ensured that it would still be justified on the grounds of future savings of dollars and helping win the next election.

Anticipating further Treasury obstruction, Strachey once more met Dalton in advance, on 8 January, to secure his support in Cabinet. The Chancellor agreed, on three conditions: there should be annual reports to ministers on the progress of the scheme; the groundnuts must come to the UK; and the colonial government should make a contribution to the capital cost of the scheme. It would, as Dalton succinctly put it, 'Develop the Empire and grow more fat.'[41]

Nevertheless, Strachey's rhetoric failed to convince one sceptic. Max Nicholson, Secretary to Herbert Morrison in the Lord President's Office, had seen all this before during his wartime stint in the Middle East Supply Centre, where no doubt he had received all of Ralph Miller's extravagant promises of supply from the Northern Province Wheat Scheme. He was blunt in his advice to Morrison:

> I have grave misgivings about sinking £25 million or anything like it on an untried crop in East Africa. Whether owing to climatic conditions, bad luck or local inefficiency, the various ambitious projects on these lines which were put up from East Africa at intervals during the war all proved fruitless – some after considerable resources had been sunk in them ... I doubt whether any commercial firm would seriously consider sinking a really large sum like this on an untried plantation crop in a part of the world where there is no adequate previous experience of success in growing it and where there is a long history of expensive failures.
>
> I think Ministers should be quite clear before agreeing:
>
> (a) that there is a real risk of having to report to Parliament that a considerable part of the capital has been lost;

---

[40] 'East African Groundnuts Scheme', memoranda by the Minister of Food, 4 Jan 1946, CP(47)4 and CP(47)10, CAB 129/16. The latter is printed in Hyam, *BDEE*, vol. II, document 116, p. 243.
[41] Minutes by Miss Shaw, 8 and 10 Jan 1947, with annotation by Dalton on the latter, T 161/1371.

(b) there is an even greater risk that the supply will not come forward on schedule and that it may be of much less value by the time any does come through; and

(c) that the very heavy draft on our resources already budgeted cannot on past experience be regarded as a safe upper limit: heavy supplementary demands are always liable to arise and cannot be resisted without sacrificing what has already been invested.

He was prepared to bet you could get more groundnuts through a long-term contract with French West African producers 'with immensely less risk of being landed with an embarrassing white elephant'.[42]

It would have been hard to put a clearer, more succinct or more accurate prediction of precisely what would come to pass before the second-most powerful minister in the Government.

But when Cabinet met on 13 January, Morrison kept his head down, asking only for more frequent progress reports. Dalton duly supported, setting out his conditions. Creech Jones did too, though refusing to commit himself to what contribution the colonies would make. Strachey emphasised the dollar savings, and had a ready answer to every question: Where would the fertiliser come from? New deposits of phosphates had just been found in Uganda. Were there enough soil chemists? The Colonial Service had plenty already there. Wasn't machinery short? It could all be found in Canada. Whether any of these answers were true or not did not seem to bother anyone, then or later. Attlee summed up that the proposals – to spend £23 million of government money and establish a public corporation to run the scheme – were approved, and asked Strachey to publish a White Paper and prepare the necessary legislation. The deed was done. The full scheme was launched.[43]

In the end, for all the doubts and dodgy facts, the Cabinet supported because they wanted to believe in it. It seemed an answer to their prayers. Experts had said it could be done and, as during the war, they believed a big enough effort would ensure it succeeded. Three other things stand out: firstly, major risks were glossed over and inadequate answers too easily accepted; secondly, the decision to go ahead was not based on cost effectiveness or technical feasibility but on the need to save dollars, so, as costs escalated and problems arose, it did not seem to

[42] Nicholson to Lord President, 11 Jan 1947, CAB 124/1090. This was not the only occasion on which Max Nicholson was ahead of his time: see Chapter 9 below. He might almost have been heeding Adam Smith's advice in *The Wealth of Nations* (ch. 11) where he warned: 'Comparisons, however, between the profit and expense of new projects are commonly very fallacious, and in nothing more so than in agriculture'.
[43] Cabinet minutes of 13 Jan 1947, CM(47)5th Conclusions, CAB 128/9 (printed in Hyam, *BDEE*, vol. II, doc. 117).

undermine the rationale for the scheme; and thirdly, the whole process was conducted in great haste to a political timetable, which allowed serious challenges, doubts and justified queries by experienced officials to be brushed aside rather than closely examined. The political bulldozer flattened any objection, however well-founded, because they were politically inconvenient, and perhaps because, at this particular time after the end of the war, there was a feeling that risks *needed* to be taken, not mitigated, if challenges were to be overcome. Many, or all, of these ingredients can be found over and again in one failed government project after another in the years that followed, as explored in the final chapter.

On Christmas Eve 1946, before the deed was finally done, John Rosa anticipated (and celebrated) the approaching victory:

> It has in fact been a general feature of the passage of this project through its various stages, that Ministers have travelled faster and much less cautiously than their officials, and that in most cases the Ministerial mind has already been made up before the poison of the official pen had had time to reach Ministers, let alone influence them.[44]

Not for the last time...

Three years later, in 1949, Dr Bailey drew in retrospect three rather different lessons from the events of these months:

> In the first place, extreme Ministerial pressure on officials who are charged with forming objective judgements is a bad thing and may lead to disastrous results. In the second place, the Private Office channel of communication should be used with great discretion, and should never be allowed to cut across the Civil Service channel ... Finally, the objective judgement of officials is difficult, if not impossible, in the face of conflicting Ministerial decision in the same field.[45]

Immediately after Cabinet, Strachey minuted back to Liesching about his earlier concerns:

> I have spoken in detail to the Chancellor on this point and he is fully assured, as I am, that your position will be fully covered at the PAC by the decision which the Cabinet took today. Now what we have to do in order to discharge our duties is to see that the most efficient possible public Corporation is set up to operate the G'nuts decision.'[46]

It was full steam ahead.

---

[44] Minute by Rosa, 24 Dec 1946, CO 852/603.
[45] Note by Bailey, 6 Oct 1949, MAF 85/589.
[46] Strachey to Liesching, 13 Jan 1947, MAF 85/589.

The practice of imperialism

Three loose ends left by the Cabinet reveal a great deal about the realities of British imperialism in the 1940s: the strategic decision on which railway to build; the scale of the colonial contribution to the scheme; and the relations between the Government and the private sector, specifically the UAC. The first two in particular went to the heart of what the Empire was for, as identified in the Introduction. The third relates to the wider issue, with us to this day, of the relationship between governments and the private sector, and on what financial terms these relations should be based. The argument over the managing agent contract echoes the arguments continuing in recent years over the public-private partnerships and outsourcing of government work. Once again, there are lessons that should have been learnt by now.

Railways had since the end of the 19th century been one of the arteries of empire. Where they were built revealed much about imperial strategy. The war had shown Britain that their African colonies were significantly more vital than they had sometimes thought during the 1930s. One element of the 'second colonial occupation' of the continent was how it would be secured for the future, garrisoned and supplied. There had long been a dream of a Cape to Cairo railway that linked all British possessions on the eastern and southern side of Africa. But in the cash-strapped inter-war years this idea had been shelved. The idea was now taken down and dusted off. Late in 1947, Britain's grandest soldier, Field Marshall Lord Montgomery of Alamein, the Chief of Staff, was sent on a tour of Africa to look at strategic defence issues.[47]

The question was asked: if a connecting line was built between Tanganyika and Northern Rhodesia, joining the southern African network with the East African one, could this be used to evacuate the groundnuts from the largest proposed area in southern Tanganyika? But the decision-making on the Groundnut Scheme was very fast, and that on railways very slow. The challenge of joining or unifying systems of different gauges and the doubtful economics of the Central African connection meant that, though the military regarded the railway as 'strategically desirable', it was not essential and they were not willing to put any money towards it. Nor were any of the proposed groundnut ports in southern Tanganyika of any strategic value to the military, being too far from the Middle East. So, with no funding from the military and no strategic imperative to direct otherwise, the Groundnut Scheme was left to build its own, self-standing branch line from the coast, where a new deep-water port was to be built at Mtwara,

---

[47] Hyam, *Britain's Declining Empire*, p. 142.

to its proposed inland units, miles from anywhere in the Southern Province.[48]

The strategic opportunity to build an integrated transport network between southern and eastern Africa passed. It was not until the 1970s that the challenge was taken up by independent Africa's new friends, the Chinese, to build the link between eastern and southern African systems through the Tazara railway linking Dar es Salaam in Tanzania to Kapiri-Mposhi in Zambia – albeit in a different gauge from either of the existing rail networks, so everything had to be transhipped. One can speculate that, but for the Groundnut Scheme, eastern and southern Africa might have been linked by an integrated rail network 20 years earlier, to the benefit of all the economies along the route.[49]

The Chancellor's insistence that the colonies should pay their fair share of the costs of the scheme, on the grounds that they would benefit, caused trouble in Tanganyika. The Governor and his staff were distinctly unhappy at the prospect of having to pay anything for this scheme wished upon them by London. But issues of land, tax and infrastructure needed to be settled, and all had a bearing on the economic and political relations between Britain and her colonies.

Land rights in African colonies were complex. But broadly, all land not explicitly owned by someone possessing an established legal title was deemed to belong to the state, and colonial governments claimed rent for any land alienated to foreign enterprises or farmers. The Tanganyika Administration was willing to forego rent for the scheme, as there was little alternative economic value in the land. But they were not willing to give up royalties on the timber that would be cut to clear the land, particularly in the south where the timber was of good quality and logging companies were already established. The UAC, as managing agents, and the Ministry of Food wanted simply to slash and burn the timber as the quickest (and cheapest) way to clear the land. The wood did, however, have a real economic value, and the Colonial Office and local Administration feared they would be accused of 'mining' the land and setting a bad precedent if they collected no royalty. After a long argument, they settled for a small revenue and agreement that the scheme would build a sawmill to use the timber productively.[50]

---

[48] Key papers in CO 537/3633 and CO 537/5148; draft report of Chiefs of Staff on transport in Africa, Feb 1947, in Hyam, *BDEE*, vol. II, doc.118. A full assessment of this issue is in Michelle Bourbonniere, 'Ripple Effects: The groundnut scheme failure and railway planning for colonial development in Tanganyika, 1947–1952', *Canadian Journal of African Studies*, 47:3, 2013, pp. 365–83. See also Hyam, *Britain's Declining Empire*, p. 134.

[49] Bourbonniere, 'Ripple Effects', p. 378. On the Tazara railway, see Jamie Monson, *Africa's Freedom Railway* (Indiana University Press, 2011).

[50] See TNA 35114 for the forestry discussion.

Tax was the most contentious point. To pay tax on the profits of the scheme struck some in the Ministry of Food and the Treasury as robbing Peter (the British taxpayer) to pay Paul (the Tanganyika Administration and ultimately Africans), even though the scheme was bringing development to their country. From the Treasury's point of view it was unacceptable that not only did the colony refuse to pay for the scheme, it expected to profit from it. To Andrew Cohen in the Colonial Office, however, to exempt the scheme from tax 'would savour of nothing less than old-fashioned colonial exploitation'. Wise heads suggested waiting until the scheme actually turned in a profit. But the Chancellor, Dalton, was having none of it: *'These Colonial Governments must be made to pay a reasonable share of the costs'*, he insisted.[51] So an ingenious formula was eventually found which satisfied all – tax receipts would be paid into a non-interest bearing fund that would be used to buy a share in the scheme by helping repay the Treasury loan.

The one area where the Tanganyika Administration acknowledged some financial role was in the provision of infrastructure. Given the British Government's refusal to fund a railway connection to the southern area on strategic grounds, the full cost of building a new deep-water harbour and a 100-mile railway in the Southern Province had to be found elsewhere. The Administration reluctantly agreed to improve the port of Dar es Salaam and to build a 20-mile branch line to Kongwa in the Central Province at its own expense. But it insisted that the scheme cover the capital cost of the southern railway. This added another £2 million to the bill just agreed by the Cabinet.[52] Later, other arguments arose over who would pay for the schools, police and other services for staff working on the scheme when they came. It became increasingly clear that the great model scheme presumed a level of infrastructure that simply did not exist and the colonial government simply could not afford.

It is worth noting that at no point during the scheme's short life was there ever any suggestion whatsoever that the groundnuts produced might be crushed and processed in Tanganyika itself. Leaving aside that part of the very purpose of the scheme was to provide an increased supply of raw material for Unilever's crushing plants in the UK and thereby help preserve employment there, at this stage of colonial development thinking the very concept of industrialising the colonies to increase the value of their exports and thereby the benefit of the colony itself was positively antithetical to the underlying purpose of empire as it was understood in the 1940s. Even for the export of raw materials themselves, it was only those producers with *political* power, like the

---

[51] Dalton minute, 18 Mar 1947 (emphasis in the original) and other papers in T 161/1371; Cohen minute, 9 May 1947, and papers in CO 852/912/1.
[52] The Central Line railway extension is discussed in TNA 35110, and Morgan, *Colonial Development*, Vol. II, pp. 262–6.

sisal barons in Tanganyika, who were able to secure anything like the world market price for their produce at this time.[53] Ironically, the price at which the UK would buy the Groundnut Scheme's produce never became an issue, if only because there was never any produce to buy. But that part of the story is still to come.

Finally, the terms of the Managing Agency to be undertaken by the UAC had to be settled. From October 1946, the UAC was confident that it would be engaged by Strachey, and knew well enough that if the Government wanted to make a quick start they had no option. So through November and December they bargained hard for the maximum financial freedom from Government control, leaving them free to spend as they saw fit 'within certain global figures'. They also insisted on the freedom to give out sub-contracts to whichever contractor they preferred, i.e. not strictly to the lowest bidder, enabling them to push most of the work to their own local subsidiaries such as Gailey & Roberts. Neither made much sense for a temporary managing agency which would soon hand over to a Corporation: it was a predictable recipe for disaster. But the UAC had the Government over a barrel if they had any hopes of getting a harvest for 1948, and more or less got whatever they wanted. They did, however, magnanimously agree to waive any explicit fee for their services, which they valued at £250,000. But any contract on a cost-plus basis in untried circumstances, without competitive tender or any effective comparator, was bound to leave the assessment of 'cost' entirely in the hands of the contractor. Nothing daunted, Strachey blithely assured the Chancellor that the eventual agreement signed was

> a very good bargain from the Government's point of view, and is satisfactory to the Company because they realise the prospect of their being able to get more groundnuts into the UK, and so to re-open some of the closed-down Unilever crushing mills depends upon the success of their own efforts to grow groundnuts quickly.[54]

A win-win formula, for the company.[55]

Relations between business and government in British colonial Africa remain under-researched. The relationship was more complex than often assumed, with a colonial administration that presumed its

[53] Westcott, 'Sisal industry', pp. 210–28; see also Cain and Hopkins, *British Imperialism, Vol. II*, ch.9.
[54] Strachey to Dalton, 30 Apr 1947, MAF 83/1839 and T 161/1371.
[55] The full unedifying story of these negotiations is contained in MAF 83/1763 and summarised in Morgan, *Colonial Development, Vol. II*, pp. 266–8. The Heads of Agreement between UAC and MoF is reproduced in *Evidence to the Public Accounts Committee*, Appendix 4, p. 116. See also Fieldhouse, *Merchant Capital*, p. 217.

role was to stay out of economic production, but provide a conducive environment for private enterprise, whether British, African or foreign. In Tanganyika a large part of the sisal industry – the country's biggest – was owned by Asian or Greek, not British, farmers. There were significant economic and regulatory barriers to Africans entering large-scale production or commerce, and an assumption that these were services that could, and should, be provided by expatriate business. Compared to West Africa, the UAC presence in Tanganyika was comparatively small and their relations with the colonial administration relatively undeveloped. But in the context of the scheme, it was the relations in the UK that were dominant, and the UAC played on their relationship with the British Government in London to maximum effect.[56]

The scene was set. In February 1947, as Britain faced up to the longest, coldest winter it had suffered in 50 years, with a blast of publicity, the Government published a White Paper entitled *A Plan for the Mechanised Cultivation of Groundnuts in East and Central Africa* (Cmd 7030), price 1/- (one shilling). Admittedly in Tanganyika the paper shortage meant that it was more a brown paper than a white one. But news of the scheme spread around the world. Experts and politicians from the US, France, Brazil, India all came to visit the scheme, including it seems an Indian prince who wished to modernise agriculture in his domains. Even the Russians asked to visit, but were turned down on security grounds.[57]

The public and press response was almost universally enthusiastic. *The Times*, the *Manchester Guardian*, *Nature* and the *British Medical Journal* all gave it a warm welcome.[58] Even *The Economist*, that bastion of free-market thinking, described it as 'the sort of economic planning that is needed to change the face of the colonial empire', and praised not only its vision but 'the hard-headed practical thinking and costing which have gone into the immediate plan for producing groundnuts.'[59] The well-known Anglo-American economist, Edith Penrose, wrote a glowing assessment of the scheme in *The Scientific Monthly*, arguing that such large-scale schemes were essential to feed the world and

---

[56] For business in British colonial Africa see Fieldhouse, *Merchant Capital*; Dimier and Stockwell, *Business of Development*; Cain and Hopkins, *British Imperialism, Vol. II*, ch. 9.
[57] Reports in *Tanganyika Standard* and *The Times* (London) in Feb 1947. The brown paper version is in TNA 35147. The Russian visit is discussed in CO 936/31/4. The Indian Prince was referred to by Strachey, Cabinet memorandum, Jun 1947, CP(47)176, CAB 129/19. The great freeze is described in Kynaston, *Austerity Britain*, pp. 189–200.
[58] *The Times* and *Manchester Guardian* for Feb 1947, *Nature* and *British Medical Journal* for Aug 1947, quoted in Esselborn, 'Environment, Memory and the Groundnut Scheme', pp. 70–71.
[59] *The Economist* (London), 15 Mar 1947.

show Africans how to modernise their agriculture.[60] Rita Hinden, who ran the Fabian Colonial Bureau, the best informed and most critical of the lobby groups, also wrote in its journal *African World* in May 1947:

> This scheme has the makings of a revolutionary change in the whole standard of life of the peoples of Africa ... For Africa, this might mean the introduction of a technique which will at last cut through the vicious circle of low productivity [and] through the conservatism and the futility of the past ... It may be that in this groundnut scheme we have discovered the weapon which will bring about Africa's economic revolution.[61]

The whole world seemed sold on what a great and innovative initiative this was.

It has been important to examine these debates, before even a furrow had been ploughed, in some detail because they reveal fundamentally why the scheme was doomed to fail, and why so many megaprojects suffer the same fate. A political objective, fixed because it seems to meet public or political need, becomes self-justifying and enables all rational debate about feasibility and cost to be stifled rather than addressed. The debates also reveal that even within the imperial project, despite the firm assumption in the official mind that imperial objectives were to the benefit of all people, British and colonial subjects alike, there were tensions and conflicts between the interests of the colonies and those of the metropolis, even if it was very clear which hand held the whip.

But even before the White Paper was published, while the Whitehall warriors waged their paper battles over policies and pounds, an advance party was pegging out what was to become the scheme's headquarters deep in the Tanganyikan bush.

---

[60] Edith T. Penrose, 'A Great African Project', *The Scientific Monthly*, LVI (1948), p. 325.
[61] Article by Rita Hinden in *African World*, May 1947, FCB papers, Box 52 file 6, Oxford, Bodleian Libraries.

4

The Groundnut Army

Soon after dawn on 10 February 1947 a small band of pioneers came over the range of mountains that lies between the Central Line station at Gulwe and the small mission station of Kongwa. They had their first sight of the vast, dry, bush-covered plain that had been selected as the first location for the new scheme. One of them, Hugh Bunting, later recalled: 'We had been bitten almost to pieces by mosquitoes the night before at the railway rest-house; we were tired; we were pretty hungry, but the inspiration of that first moment I think has been unforgettable for all of us.'[1] They faced the same challenges as many pioneers, bringing a scheme seen at the time as at the cutting edge of modernisation into a place that was, to say the least, off the beaten track. This chapter looks at how they approached the questions of land, labour, transport and material in the effort to make the scheme work as conceived.

Kongwa

The advance party, ominously numbering 13 in all, had left a bleak, frozen, snow-covered London airport on 30 January. Their flight to Tanganyika was delayed two days when the wartime Lancastrian (a civilian version of the Lancaster bomber) they were flying in developed engine trouble in Khartoum. But their arrival in Dar es Salaam on 4 February caused a sensation: the town had never seen a plane as big as a Lancastrian before, and even the Chief Magistrate had to suspend hearings as everyone in the courthouse rushed out to watch it fly over. The team were put up in an old RAF transit camp and taken round to see the relevant government officials before boarding the train for the 24-hour journey to Gulwe.[2]

From there they set off overland. They set up camp at a place called Sagara, 14 miles from Kongwa, in a pleasant glade up against the

---

[1] Quoted in Wood, *Groundnut Affair*, p. 57.
[2] Ibid., p. 55–7.

hills, with a spring of good but rather hard water. They were greeted by George Nestlé, a larger than life white hunter with a slouch hat and huge moustache, taken on by the UAC to look after the party as they settled in. He served them up a larger than life breakfast – 40 eggs and a heap of ham, all piled on one plate, with a single knife, fork and spoon to eat them with, washed down with Harvey's Bristol Cream sherry. On their first sortie from camp, up the hill behind to view the terrain, two of the party met and were chased off by a large band of baboons.[3]

Who were they, these first pioneers of the Groundnut Army? Besides Wakefield and David Martin, who was to be the UAC's manager on the spot, there were three men from Pauling and Co., the company that had been selected to do the land clearing. It was run by Sir John Gibson, the man whose drive and imagination had made possible the Mulberry Harbours used during the D-Day landings in Normandy. He chose Major Peter Rush, a veteran engineer who had spent the war running a company that repaired airfields, built roads, railways and bridges, all under the most extreme wartime conditions. Rush brought with him two other veterans who had served with him, Messrs McBride and Hoare, and many more former comrades in arms were to join them later. Tom Whalley, a cheerful, moustachioed native of Cheshire, came from the UAC to help assess the clearing work. The UAC also sent Mac McGaw and David Bostock, veteran convoy drivers from the Abyssinian campaign against the Italians, with a couple of lorries to help set up the camp.

Three others had crucial roles to play in the early days. Colonel Marchant was Chief Labour Officer, having spent part of the war organising underground resistance to the Japanese in the Solomon Islands. Major-General Tom Woods had been seconded from the Army Medical Corps in response to Strachey's appeal to the Minister of War, and asked to set up the scheme's medical services 'more or less on army lines', as he had done for the Indian Armoured Division during the war.[4]

Then there was Dr Hugh Bunting, the Chief Scientific Officer, who was to play a decisive role in the future of the scheme. Handpicked by Wakefield from the British Agricultural Research Station at Rothamsted, Bunting was a young agronomist from South Africa. Descended from Dr Jabez Bunting, a firebrand Methodist preacher who led the Wesleyan Missionary Society in the early 19th century, Hugh's own father, the solicitor Sidney Bunting, was one of the founders of the South African Communist Party and devoted his life to the advancement of African peoples. Hugh was brought up with a similar determination to

---

[3] Maj.-Gen.T.F.M. Woods. 'Organising a Health Service: An account of the first two years with the East Africa Groundnut Scheme', Woods Papers, folder 4, Liddell Hart Archives, King's College, London.
[4] Woods Papers, King's College, London, folder 4, p. 1.

help the Africans, but his nature led him to do it through the pursuit of science. After studying botany and ecology at Witwatersrand, in 1938 he became a Rhodes scholar at Oriel College, Oxford. When he completed his doctorate in 1941, he was immediately appointed to Rothamsted to undertake essential war work on increasing agricultural production. It was there Wakefield met him in 1946 and recruited him on the spot.[5]

Bunting's first task was to find out whether the soil in the areas chosen was suitable for groundnuts. Bunting described many years later in an interview how 'none of us, including me, knew enough to judge which area was best'. He had asked Wakefield, but the latter admitted that there was no basic information yet available: 'It's your job to find it', he told Bunting.[6]

So why did the scheme start in Kongwa, at first sight the most risky of the three areas in Tanganyika? Speed and convenience, mainly. Though Wakefield recommended the Southern Province as the best groundnut country, communications were almost completely lacking and there was no chance of beginning serious operations until the roads had been improved and a port and railway built. The bush was also much more dense there, large parts of it thickly forested. The two areas along the Central Railway line already had reasonable communications, and were more lightly wooded. Of the two, the Tanganyika Government requested that the scheme leave the Western Province alone until the rail extension to the Mpanda lead mines had been completed, so as not to compete for labour there. The UAC, supported by the MoF, therefore took the decision to send the advance party to Kongwa. The question remained: would groundnuts grow well there?[7]

By the end of March, Bunting had completed his first survey and concluded:

> On grounds of accessibility, rainfall and temperature, topography and soil fertility, the Mpwapwa [Kongwa] area stands out as being by far the best of those so far surveyed. It is evident from the vegetation and the soils that the rainfall is higher than has been supposed. It is therefore recommended that production be developed to the fullest possible extent there.[8]

---

[5] A.H. Bunting, 'A Personal Note', Bunting Papers (privately held). Allison Drew, *Between Empire and Revolution: The life of Sidney Bunting* (London, Pickering and Chatto, 2007).
[6] Interview with Prof. Hugh Bunting, conducted by David Betts, 9 Apr 2002 (only one month before he died), disc and transcript held by Reading University Archives.
[7] 'Choice of Locality for Initial Operations', note by Hollins, 19 Nov 1946, MAF 83/1775; OFC, *First Annual Report and Statement of Accounts* (London, HMSO No. 252, 27 Sep 1949), p. 7.
[8] Report of Chief Scientific Officer, attached to Managing Agent's Second Progress Report, 23 Feb–31 Mar 1947, MAF 83/1778.

Even so, it was known to be risky because of the erratic nature of the rains. Albert Walter, director of the East African Meteorological Service, warned them it was 'definitely unfavourable' with a high risk of periodic drought, and Rosa justified it at the time only because the choice was to take the risk and hope for some harvest in 1948, or accept there would be no crop until 1949 – which was politically unacceptable.[9]

Throughout the first year, there was an overwhelming sense that speed was of the essence. As the White Paper noted, the Government were determined that 'clearing should be started as soon and on as large a scale as possible in order to ensure the planting of the maximum possible acreage of groundnuts in 1948'. In a phrase in their handover report to the Overseas Food Corporation (OFC) the following year, which came back to haunt the scheme, the Managing Agents referred to 'the decision to proceed immediately in a headlong manner on an improvised basis.'[10]

It was not just headlong – it was more like hell-for-leather. To deliver some kind of crop in 1948, the UAC, as Managing Agent, had to find three things: men, material for them to use, and transport to get everything to Kongwa. Using the freedom in their contract with the MoF, the UAC sub-contracted clearing in the three areas to Pauling & Co. (Kongwa), Mowlems (Southern Province) and their own subsidiary Gailey & Roberts, re-named Earthmoving and Construction Ltd (Western Province), all on a cost-plus basis. It was 'do what you need and damn the cost'.[11]

Men

Recruitment proved the easiest task. In Britain, over 100,000 applicants responded to the advertisements for the 1,200 jobs – from demobbed soldiers at a loose end or looking to find the challenge and camaraderie they had enjoyed in the forces; from people who had stuck it out at home and were desperate to escape the drudgery, austerity and cold of post-war life in Britain; and from people inspired by Strachey's vision of transforming Africa into a modern, prosperous continent.[12]

'Operation Groundnuts' as Strachey called it, was influenced by his own experience, recorded at the time, watching the Allied landings in North Africa in 1942:

---

[9] A. Walter to Wakefield, 28 Jun 1947, Walter Papers, Oxford, Bodleian Libraries; Rosa to Dawson, 13 Mar 1947, MAF 83/1775; Morgan, *Colonial Development, Vol. II*, pp. 295–6.
[10] OFC, *First Annual Report*, p. 10; see also the original *Plan*, Cmd 7030, p. 5.
[11] OFC, *First Annual Report*, p. 91; the contracts are in MAF 83/1817.
[12] A.T.P. Seabrook, 'The Groundnut Scheme in Retrospect', *Tanganyika Notes and Records*, 46 (Jan 1957), p. 88.

> A score or so of ships, in close company ... must impress the onlooker with a sense of weight and purpose. It is visibly an expedition. Thus far it has been possible to produce these collective efforts for the purposes of war alone. What could not be done if an expedition of this scope could be fitted out, not in order, as this one is, to decide who should have the right to develop Africa, but in order *actually* to develop Africa?[13]

He felt he had now been offered the opportunity to fulfil that vision.

Comparing it explicitly to the launch of a military operation, he told the new recruits that they were in the front line of the struggle for more food and faster development:

> On your success depends more than on any other single factor whether the harassed housewives of Great Britain get more margarine, cooking fats and soap in the reasonably near future. [Equally], the world will not tolerate any failure to develop the vast latent resources of these areas. But if we British show the way that the wealth of these areas can be developed to the immense good, not only of Britain but also of the native inhabitants of the areas ... then I am convinced that our Commonwealth will enter the most glorious period of its existence.[14]

A newsreel of the time, sonorously narrated by Lawrence Olivier, passionately orchestrated by Benjamin Britten, was even more purple: 'A new spirit is abroad ... In the dark jungle, battalions of bulldozers are clearing land for the Ground Nut Scheme ... It means a great deal to Europe and a New Deal for Africa.'[15]

People responded. They wanted adventure, and they wanted to do good. The pioneer spirit and commitment to the project of the first recruits was remarkable. They came from all walks of life, and they came not just from the UK. The Scientific Department soon boasted three Dutchmen – Harkenseeker, Bosswinkle and Bos van Coolen – and a number of Italians were recruited to the scheme (see below). But the diversity itself caused some alarm to the public school-educated officer class in the Tanganyika Administration. While recognising that many of the recruits were first class, they decried 'a large swarm who were definitely fifth class', many of whom had never set foot in Africa before. Barclay Leechman, the Administration's Labour Officer, remembered seeing one plane load of 25 being flown out of Kongwa:

---

[13] Strachey's speech on the ORD Bill, *Hansard*, vol. 443, 6 Nov 1947, col. 2034 (emphasis added).

[14] Strachey to Faure (UAC), 29 Sep 1947, MAF 83/1752.

[15] Replayed in the BBC Radio 4 documentary, 'The Great Groundnut Scandal', 28 Jul 1982. Sheila Unwin, based in Kongwa, commented in a letter home: 'We did get a laugh from that broadcast – "The tractor roars – the jungle parts". We only wish it was as easy as that.' Letter of 29 Dec 1948, Unwin Papers (see note 17 below).

They were, I think, in general appearance and the manner in which they were behaving, even at the airport, the lowest types of Europeans I have ever seen in my life. David Martin told me these people had been recruited in Liverpool ... and had been quite useless; they had refused to work and behaved like a set of hooligans. He had been compelled to get a charter plane to fly them out to get rid of them.[16]

For those that stuck it, life was pretty rough. The only accommodation was in tents, water was scarce, and there were occasional encounters with the local wildlife – hyenas, snakes, scorpions, buffalo, the odd rhinoceros, and the solitary leopard that lived on the hill. Above all in the dry season there was dust. Sheila Unwin, accompanying her new husband Tom Unwin, was one of the first women recruited to the scheme as a secretary in August 1947. Like many, both she and Tom had served in the forces during the war, in her case the Women's Royal Naval Service (known as the Wrens), and had had her fair share of adventure and hardship. Arriving in Kongwa in early August, however, she was struck by the tough conditions: 'What roads! Sandy and incredibly bumpy and dust, dust, dust. It is now the dry season here and the wind blows ... and loads of thick red dust envelope[s] everything, and it's impossible to keep clean at all!'[17] Sleeping in dusty, leaky tents, it was no surprise that those on the scheme referred to themselves, only half in jest, as the 'groundnutters'.[18] But at least they ate well, Chief Medical Officer Woods reporting that the Europeans received more and better food in Kongwa than in England.[19]

The military atmosphere was overwhelming. At the outset the pioneers tended to refer to each other by rank rather than name: among the first four secretaries recruited there were 'two ex-Wrens and a Waaf' (Women's Auxiliary Air Force).[20] Military terms and practices dominated. Most found this helpful and strangely comforting. Even

[16] Listowel, *Making of Tanganyika*, p. 147. Other information from Peter Le Mare, interviewed Oct 2007.
[17] Letter from Sheila Unwin to her mother, 8 Aug 1947, Unwin Papers (by kind permission of her daughter, Vicky Unwin). Sheila (née Mills) married Tom Unwin in December 1946, having been a naval cypher officer during the war in the Middle East, ending in 1945 as Head of Department at the Harwich Cypher Office. She took a close interest in everything the scheme was doing and, with Tom, an agricultural officer, was one of the few people to stay with the scheme from 1947 to 1951. Her letters to her mother are an invaluable source for how the European staff saw the scheme. For the background see the published collection of her wartime letters in Vicky Unwin, *Love and War in the WRNS* (Stroud, The History Press, 2015).
[18] Letter of 6 Dec 1947, Unwin Papers.
[19] 'Second Progress Report', Feb–Mar 1947, MAF 83/1778; Wood, *Groundnut Affair*, p. 69.
[20] Undated letter of Aug 1947, Unwin Papers.

the layout had a military air. Another of the secretaries recruited by the scheme, Vivienne Bell, arriving by plane described Kongwa as 'resembling an army encampment dumped in the middle of a huge plain with trails leading off in all directions disappearing into the hazy distance.'[21]

Material

The monumental task of procuring everything the scheme might need began at once. But what did a Groundnut Scheme need, asked the puzzled young Unilever procurement officer, Clive van den Berg: 'Have you ever seen one? Do they need boots? Could they use water carts? What do they sit on?' (He decided it was three-piece suites, and ordered 40.) Major-Gen. Woods, who shared his office before flying out, watched him in fascination 'apparently buying everything in the world by phone'.[22]

The post-war world was awash with army surplus equipment being sold off in job lots, and the Managing Agent's rule of thumb seems to have been that, since this was going to be the largest agricultural development scheme the world had ever seen, and because they needed the kit quick, they should buy almost anything going. So they did. Over three-quarters of the scheme's supplies were army surplus. There was, indeed, no other source of supply available and, as Strachey (never one to miss the silver lining in every cloud) argued, this simply put the money straight back into the Exchequer. But with the supplies they *did* want often came much that they did not; and it tended to arrive in no particular order, and no particular shape.[23]

The sleepy port of Dar es Salaam had never seen anything like it. Tumbling onto the quayside came a cornucopia of second-hand goods:

> 300 brushes, paint, 4oz, bristle mixture
> 2,780 buckets, 3 gallon
> 5,000 buckets, 2 gallon
> 240 watering cans, with roses
> 2,500 each, knives, spoons, forks
> 5,000 pots, cooking

---

[21] Vivienne Bell, *Blown by the Wind of Change* (Lewes, The Book Guild, 1986), p. 28. See also the recollections in David Read, *Beating About the Bush* (London, David Read, 2000), p. 187.
[22] Woods Papers, King's College, London, file 4 pp. 7–8; Progress Report No. 6, Jul 1947, MAF 83/1778.
[23] Seabrook, 'The Groundnut Scheme in Retrospect', p. 89.

Plus, unsorted:

Bedding, mosquito nets, rakes, bricklaying equipment, lamps, fridges, fire extinguishers, weighing machines, kettles, flit sprays, filing cabinets, mirrors, light bulbs, typewriters, telephones, fire engine trailers, hosepipes, tablecloths, vacuum flasks, wheelbarrows, tin openers, alarm clocks, etc.[24]

The lists go on and on. As Strachey himself commented later, things were simply delivered by the ton: 'no-one who has not witnessed it can fully imagine the chaotic state in which many of the cargoes of war surplus stores arrive in Dar es Salaam'.[25]

But some of the most crucial items were the hardest to get. In February 1947, of 84,650 hoes ordered, only 8,438 had arrived. Getting basic trucks for transport was especially challenging: a diligent buyer for Unilever inspected 900 trucks put up for sale in Belgium and identified only 150 sound enough to purchase. Aware that there was a risk the good would be substituted with bad ones when they were shipped, the buyer secretly marked the driver's door on each of the selected trucks, and had them sent to East Africa. On arrival in Kongwa, the doors were checked and the secret marks found. But as soon as they tried to drive them around the camp, they found the trucks to be useless. The dealer, it seems, had taken the marked doors off the good trucks and put them on some that were complete write-offs before they were shipped. Even where sound supplies of essential goods were found to be available relatively nearby in Egypt, getting them to Tanganyika proved a challenge: the supplies had finally been loaded on board ship in Alexandria when an outbreak of the plague put all shipping in the port in quarantine for a month. Getting cement anywhere proved 'extremely difficult', and the indispensable tractors were the slowest of all to arrive.[26]

Even when things did reach Tanganyika, there were no proper accounts of what was received nor any systematic storekeeping. It was hard, as Faure of the UAC explained later, when 'shiploads of unidentified and unidentifiable goods, mixed in cases, badly packed' were dumped on the quayside in Dar es Salaam.[27] Coopers Bros, the accountants, were finally brought in to report on the situation in August 1948.

---

[24] Lists of purchases in MAF 83/1801; former Lend-Lease equipment purchases in MAF 83/1805; see also Progress Report No. 1, Jan 1947, MAF 83/1778.
[25] Strachey memo to Cabinet, 6 Jul 1948, CP(48)175, CAB 129/28; also his speech in *Hansard*, vol. 453, col. 873, 12 Jul 1948.
[26] Van den Bergh to 'Dear Mac', 21 Feb 1947, MAF 83/1801; see also the multiple stories about the efforts to procure supplies given to the Parliamentary Accounts Committee by W.A. Faure and David Martin in *PAC Evidence*, 9 May 1950, questions 1946–2100 (Belgian truck story at qn.1970, p. 87).
[27] Faure, *PAC Evidence*, 9 May 1950, qn 1952, p. 84.

Photo 4.1 Unloading a bulldozer onto a lighter, Dar es Salaam port, 1948 (Trinity Mirror/Mirrorpix/Alamy Stock photo)

They delivered a devastating report, and both the Chief Supply Officer and his Deputy swiftly departed the scheme.[28] But what the rush and muddle did store up was trouble for the future.

Transport

Dar es Salaam port had never before had to cope with the quantities of goods that now began to arrive. It was a lighterage port without a deep-water berth, requiring all goods to be transhipped from the cargo vessels to lighters with a shallower draft, from which they were then

---

[28] 'Memorandum presented by Messrs Cooper Brothers & Co. to the Board of the OFC', 3 Aug 1948, *PAC Evidence*, Appendix 1, p. 112.

unloaded onto the dock. It was a cumbersome and labour-intensive process and, without strict control of paper-work and process, the arrival and storage of goods would soon fall into a state of chaos, as Strachey himself had seen and informed Cabinet. By August 1947, the Managing Agents reported that

> congestion at the port of Dar es Salaam has brought work to a complete standstill owing to the rapid arrival of large cargoes. A breakdown in electrical power ... and complete overtaxing of European supervision led to an unparalleled state of affairs.'[29]

Sheila Unwin's luggage 'got stuck in a lighter in Dar harbour for weeks owing to there being no wharf space. The whole place is completely bunged up, and so little haulage and transport to remove it.'[30]

This degenerated further the following month when the long hours for dock workers, together with stagnant wages and rising prices, provoked a general strike (see below). This merely compounded the problem of getting the equipment to Kongwa fast. The storage depots were soon full as the railways lacked the rolling stock to shift the material up country. They were particularly short of flat-bed trucks to shift the bulldozers and tractors needed to start bush-clearing. In Whitehall, the scheme was given ever-increasing priority in the allocation of shipping, for example to bring the tractors from Canada. Supplies arrived in Dar es Salaam from every corner of the world: from the US, UK, Canada, Egypt, India, Ceylon, the Philippines, West Africa ... In that sense the scheme was a truly global one.

The journey of the first 10 reconditioned heavy tractors typified the challenge. Bought in January 1947, they were held up first in the UK by the fuel crisis, then held at port for over two weeks by fogs and storms. Finally shipped at the end of February, they reached Tanganyika at the end of March. They were further delayed by the breaching of a railway embankment due to flood and so they finally reached Kongwa only at the end of April, four months later.[31]

One of the recognised constraints was that all rail traffic had to unload at Msagali junction, 20 miles from Kongwa, and be transported from there by truck along rough tracks. It was therefore agreed in December 1946 that a branch line should be built to Kongwa. In the event, with material shortages and occasional wash-aways due to floods, it took until the end of September 1947 to complete the extension. As the Governor said, 'Very slow work. 9 months for 22 miles!'[32] In the end, the railways situation only really improved when, as part of a

---

[29] Progress Report No. 7, Aug 1947, MAF 83/1788.
[30] Letter of 8 Nov 1947, Unwin Papers.
[31] *East African Groundnut Scheme: Review of progress to November 1947*, Cmd 7314 (London, HMSO, Jan 1948).
[32] Battershill minute, 6 Sep 1947, and other papers in TNA 35110.

larger scheme, Tanganyika's railways were amalgamated into the new East African Railways and Harbours organisation in 1948.

To help overcome the congestion in the port of Dar es Salaam, the UAC set up a series of convoys to bring supplies down by truck from Nairobi. This was scarcely an easy option, requiring a crossing of the crocodile-infested Ruvu river on an ancient ferry that finally sank under the strain, and a long drive through miles of uninhabited bush.[33] A small team led by Clive van den Berg, Unilever's procurement expert, was set up by the UAC in Acacia Avenue, Dar es Salaam to try and bring some order to the chaos of supplies. They faced other distractions:

> The windows overlooked one of the hotels in Dar, and all day beautiful women seemed to find it necessary for one reason or another to parade on the hotel balconies in little, if any, clothing. After a day or two of this, it was amicably agreed that as many as possible of the occupants of our offices should work with their backs to the windows. Work then went on according to plan.[34]

Through their heroic efforts, the bulk of the supplies landed were eventually shifted up country.

The impact on Tanganyika: land and labour

Aside from the balcony beauties, both the British and African inhabitants of Tanganyika watched this invasion with a certain bemusement. One of the first British journalists to visit the scheme was James Cameron, then of the *Daily Express*. He noted that the arrival of the groundnutters was met by the existing white residents with a gaze of highly watchful reserve: 'If you ever saw a party of Commandoes entering the lounge of a residential hotel in Cheltenham you will know what I mean'.[35]

The hotel management, of course, were fully supportive: they were paid to be. Governor Battershill welcomed the new arrivals, helped provide accommodation for them in Dar es Salaam, and was inclined to let them get on with it. So too was Miller, who appears to have had as little to do with the scheme as possible (at least, there is no record of him ever having visited it). The Provincial and District administrators

---

[33] I have taken the road by bus, and even in the 1980s it was terrible, arriving in Dodoma shattered and bruised.

[34] Van den Bergh article in *Our World*, the Groundnut Scheme's in-house magazine, quoted by Wood, *Groundnut Affair*, p. 61. There is a good deal of additional colourful detail in Alan Wood's account, chs 5–8.

[35] Wood, *Groundnut Affair*, p. 62. Cameron himself did not impress the groundnutters, who regarded him as 'a rather peculiar sort of pansy boy', letter of 15 Mar 1948, Unwin Papers.

had their hands full with the government's own post-war development plans, and, with barely 200 British officials for the whole territory, were focussed on just keeping their heads above water. One official who was there at the time likened their arrival to the Army undertaking land manoeuvres on the deck of an otherwise deserted battleship at sea. Occasional ratings crossing the deck would point out where the sea was and advise that they avoid it. The local veterinary officer helped pull one of the Nairobi convoys out of the black cotton soil they had got themselves stuck in, and shot some impala for their dinner while he was about it. A minority, including the editor of the *Tanganyika Standard*, who were passionately committed to the territory's development applauded the scheme loudly.[36]

But for the long-term expatriate residents, 'a Groundnutter was something not quite nice to know.'[37] As Seabrook recalled, the locals considered that they overcrowded the hotels, railway trains and aeroplanes. Sheila Unwin told her mother: 'Most people here dislike the G-nuts people on principle because of the benefits we're getting and they haven't got!'[38] Very soon there were more Europeans living in Kongwa than in the capital, Dar es Salaam. They had a fanatical faith in their scheme; and demanded top priority for all their imports and building requirements. Everything had to be done instantly. Worst of all, they drove up the price of gin. For people who had been starved of imports and luxuries since the outbreak of war, it was galling to see their own needs by-passed.

One man at least was happy – Tom Bain. Having taken the initiative to get the scheme to Kongwa, he was well-placed as the only commercial farmer for hundreds of miles around, to take on the job of supplying food to the men camped there. He became a regular at the local cattle markets, buying up meat for the groundnutters' rations, to the disgruntlement of the local Somali cattle traders who had bid for the same contract and lost. At least someone was doing nicely out of the whole project.[39]

For most Africans in the Territory, except those living in Dar es Salaam or around Kongwa, the scheme passed largely unnoticed. Those most directly affected by the invasion were the Wagogo people who inhabited the area around Mpwapwa, Originally pastoralists, they had taken to growing crops and settled in scattered homesteads throughout the area, the better to use the thin grazing and scarce water.

---

[36] Read, *Beating About the Bush*, p. 175; Hill and Moffett, *Tanganyika*, p. 135.
[37] Seabrook, 'Retrospect', *TNR* 46, p. 88.
[38] Letter of Aug 1947, Unwin Papers.
[39] Progress Report No. 2, Mar 1947, MAF 83/1778; Listowell, *Making of Tanganyika*, p. 144; for Bain's unorthodox business methods, see Read, *Beating About the Bush*, pp. 185–7.

Their small fields – *shambas* – of groundnuts and millet had impressed Wakefield. But this was because they practised a form of agriculture that was appropriate to an environment with poor soils and erratic rainfall. Like other Africans in similar circumstances, they used the extensive, shifting cultivation, sometimes called 'slash and burn', that was anathema to the scientific agriculturalists from Rothamsted, but of proven effectiveness over generations of cultivation. Land would be cleared from virgin bush with the debris burnt on the spot to provide both nitrogenous fertiliser from the ash and so that the heat would kill the weeds still in the soil. They would cultivate a number of different crops on a deliberately scattered number of plots, in order to take advantages of different types of soil and spread the risk of crop failure from disease or drought, rainfall being notoriously patchy where it depended on thunderous cloudbursts.[40]

The Wagogo knew all this – but nobody asked them. Like most subsistence farmers, they were cautious people, and watched the scheme with puzzlement and wariness. With reason, as nearly 300 families had to be moved from the area where the scheme would operate to other land.

Land alienation was an especially sensitive issue in Britain's African colonial territories. Tanganyika was at the fulcrum of the debate between proponents of settler production and peasant production as a means to develop the African colonies. Under German rule, the settlers had secured the upper hand so that, like South Africa or Kenya, they saw the African inhabitants primarily as a source of labour for farms and businesses to be run by and for Europeans. When, however, it passed to Britain under a League of Nations Mandate, which set explicit protections on the rights of the native people, this policy was reversed and the Colonial Office decreed that it should follow the path defined by its West African territories and be 'primarily a Black man's country'.[41] But the European settlers who established themselves on the old German farms in the fertile northern highlands nevertheless aspired to unite with Kenya's settlers in an East African federation that would take South Africa as its ideal.[42] The Colonial Office, however, was conscious not only of the risk of unrest from displaced African farmers, but was under sustained pressure from the 'native rights' lobby in Parliament, who were closely linked to both church interests and the Fabian Colonial Bureau, both powerful and influential in the Labour Party. The radical

---

[40] Esselborn, 'Environment, Memory and the Groundnut Scheme', pp. 87–9. A good account of this form of cultivation, from Northern Rhodesia (now Zambia) where conditions were very similar, is in Sara Berry, *No Condition is Permanent*, pp. 88–100. See also Wood, *Groundnut Affair*, ch. 7.
[41] Sir Charles Strachey, 'Land policy in Tanganyika', 29 Apr 1922, CO/691/60/148, quoted in Iliffe, *Tanganyika*, p. 262, and see pp. 373–4.
[42] Nicholas Westcott, 'Closer Union and the Future of East Africa, 1939–1948', *JICH*, 10:1, Oct 1981.

Labour left-wing MP Fenner Brockway, well known to both Strachey and Creech Jones, was a formidable champion of African rights and neither minister would risk crossing him in this matter.[43]

In the aftermath of war, the old League of Nations Mandates were transferred to the oversight of the new United Nations, who established a Trusteeship Council in New York to call to account those imperial powers entrusted with administration of Germany's former territories. The Foreign Office as well as the Colonial Office now had a concern to ensure that Britain's international reputation for fair play and respect for the rule of law was preserved in this very public forum. Both the Government and the Tanganyika Administration therefore handled this operation with kid gloves. In early 1947, David Martin for the Managing Agents, 'stressed that every hour was now of importance since they were already behind schedule and ... they could not allow small individual rights to impede progress'. But in Kongwa the Administration made sure the local Wagogo native authorities were scrupulously consulted and the families (relatively) generously compensated for the forced move. They also publicly pledged that the alienation of the land would be strictly temporary. In these circumstances the moves passed off peacefully, no challenge was made and no complaints from the Wagogo communities are recorded.[44]

In the Southern Province, the number to be moved was larger, and the resistance firmer. The Provincial Commissioner reported at the end of 1947 that in Liwale District the evacuation of 3,660 families 'was only carried through by the tremendous efforts of the District Commissioner and his officers who had to contend with considerable passive resistance to the evacuation.' A further 3,000 families were left on the land in the hope that they could be integrated into the scheme.[45]

Labour was another sensitive issue for colonial authorities, not just because the scheme would compete with the sisal growers, but because the White Paper had promised that the scheme would be a model employer and no scandal could be risked. Still, the scheme's need was urgent and it set about recruiting at once. Among the first and most enthusiastic recruits were Africa's own demobbed soldiers, many of whom had fought in the King's African Rifles during the war. A few had learnt or retained skills that the scheme now needed – tractor drivers, mechanics, clerks – but most were unskilled, though they were at least in tune with the military ethos of the project. With training, African workers demonstrated a real aptitude for driving

---

[43] See P.S. Gupta, *Imperialism and the British Labour Movement* (London, Palgrave Macmillan, 1975).
[44] 'Notes of a meeting on the Groundnut Scheme and Native Land Rights', 25 Apr 1947, Cohen to Surridge, 15 May 1947, and other papers in TNA 35147.
[45] Southern Province Annual Report, 1947 (T.O. Pike), TNA.

tractors, and those taken on as drivers became known as 'Paulingis' after the clearing company, Pauling & Co.[46] But this took time, and to meet the immediate needs for skilled labour the scheme had to look elsewhere.

One of the scheme's first British recruits was N.R.F. Fuggles-Couchman, who had served as an agricultural officer on the Northern Province Wheat Scheme. There he had employed as tractor drivers a number of Italian detainees and prisoners of war, held in Tanganyika after being captured in the Ethiopian campaign earlier in the war. He was promptly despatched to Italy to hunt them down and recruit 275 of them for the Groundnut Scheme. They began to arrive in the late summer of 1947, but things did not go smoothly. By December there were disagreements with British staff, protests about racism following a members' vote to exclude them from the Kongwa Club (which had to be overturned by the scheme's management, who took over the Club) and internal squabbles among the Italians themselves; most of them were sooner or later packed off back home.[47]

Another source of skilled clerical staff lay on the other side of the continent, in the Gold Coast, now Ghana. With a higher level of secondary education than in Tanganyika, the West African colony had a surplus of literate school leavers willing to take up jobs elsewhere. The first batch of clerks arrived in August 1947, including one Mr Danquah who was responsible for managing the Kongwa airstrip. His iron grip, resolute efficiency and eloquent English quickly made him a legendary figure around the Scheme.[48] Mauritians too were imported for their carpentry skills, though the caste distinctions between them became almost impossible to manage. Altogether, Africans from other British territories found themselves in a slightly uncomfortable position between the local Tanganyikan Africans who undertook the bulk of the manual work, and the *wazungu* (the Swahili term for Europeans, literally 'those who make your head spin'), who supervised and sat in the offices.

Though planned as a fully mechanised operation, the scheme still required a substantial supply of unskilled manual labour, which the Plan had put at around 20,000. But the recruitment of African labour was particularly tricky.

Hitherto, the dominant sisal industry had had more or less a free hand to recruit wherever they wanted at whatever wage they wanted. Predictably, they did not welcome the competition for labour that the

---

[46] Peter Le Mare, interview 12 Oct 2007.
[47] Progress Reports Nos 5 (Jun), 10 (Nov) and 11 (Dec) 1947, MAF 83/1778. There is a colourful account of the whole affair in Sheila Mills letter of 22 Feb 1948, Unwin Papers.
[48] Peter Le Mare interview; Wood, *Groundnut Affair*, p. 171; Drew to Dashwood, 6 Sep 1947, TNA 35147.

Groundnut Scheme brought. As one correspondent put it to the *Tanganyika Standard* newspaper, 'I can't see the sisal-owners kissing the Secretary of State when they see the Western tribesmen marching off to the Empire's oil-nut farms instead of to the coast under Silabu's [the Sisal Labour Bureau's] quasi-military escort.'[49] The settlers in the Northern Province, around Kilimanjaro, complained: 'By bringing the Ground-nut Scheme in there was now an even shorter supply of labour for the Territory than before.'[50] Meetings were arranged with the Tanganyika Sisal Growers' Association at which its irascible Chairman, Sir Eldred Hitchcock, tried to force the Administration to help maintain their labour supply, which was estimated at around 140,000 workers in 1949. But Battershill was adamant: 'the Government is not a recruiting agency'. So the rival employers were left to fight it out through competitive wages. According to local missionaries, this led to a long overdue increase in wages for sisal workers who, until then, had been roundly exploited. In Tanganyika, unlike in Kenya, the settlers were too few and too politically weak to force the colonial administration to distort the local labour market in their favour.[51]

In practice, Africans living close to the scheme, including the Wagogo, were the least likely to seek employment with it, preferring instead to follow in the footsteps of Mr Bain. As was later observed in the southern areas, there were many African farmers,

> who do not wish to be employed for the simple reason that they can make quite a good living by selling their own produce i.e. chicken, eggs, fruit etc., the prices of which have risen considerably with the influx of the very well-paid groundnut European employers who are willing and able to pay ridiculous high prices.[52]

That it was possible for Africans too to seize the opportunity that the scheme provided is illustrated by the life history of one African entre-

---

[49] Letter from 'Agronom', *Tanganyika Standard*, 28 Jun 1946
[50] Message from Moshi-Arusha Production Committee (chaired by Anderson), 29 Jun 1947, TNA 36033.
[51] Correspondence between Hitchcock and Mellor (UAC), Battershill minute 24 Oct 1947, and other papers in TNA 16758; Capper (missionary in Lindi) to Broomfield (UMCA), 7 Apr 1948, UMCA Papers, SF 134, Bodleian Libraries, Oxford; Westcott, 'Sisal industry', pp. 220–24; sisal employee numbers in minute by Molohan, Labour Commissioner, 3 May 1950, TNA 19417/II; wages rose from under Shs 20/- per kipande (roughly a month) in the war to Shs 26/- plus rations in 1948 and Shs 39/- in 1951, see Westcott, 'Impact of War', p. 222. Compare, Frederick Cooper, *Decolonization and African Society: The labour question in French and British Africa* (Cambridge, CUP, 1996), chs 5–6.
[52] Labour Officer, Southern Province Annual Report, 1948, quoted in Matteo Rizzo, 'What was left of the Groundnut Scheme? Development disaster and labour market in southern Tanganyika, 1946–1952', *Journal of Agrarian Change*, 6:2, Apr 2006, pp. 227–9.

preneur in the south, Julius Mtenda. Having accumulated enough savings as a soldier during the war, Mtenda bought a small shop in his village, Mnyambe in Southern Province, when he returned in 1946. Hearing about the scheme, in 1948 he visited its headquarters at Nachingwea and swiftly moved his business there to profit from the almost unlimited demand: as Matteo Rizzo says, 'from 1949 until 1951 he accumulated wealth at an astonishing speed', selling goods such as milk, tea, cigarettes, sesame oil, soap, dates, coffee, lamp oil, bicycle oil, matches, earrings, hoes, envelopes and pencils. His wife also set up and managed a restaurant and bar. It was the making of him, becoming in the 1950s one of the richest African traders in the south.[53]

Hundreds, and in due course thousands, of Africans did come to work for the scheme on an extended basis, many from distant parts of the country: 'All kinds of tribes arrived here', said Mtenda, including the Chagga from the north and Arabs from the coast.[54] As paid employment went, it offered relatively attractive wages – Shs 70/- per month for a 'house boy', compared to around Shs 25–30/- per month for a sisal worker.[55] They lived in a large, shambling settlement over to one side of the site, initially in tents but increasingly in locally built huts of wood and mud and – when available – corrugated iron for the roof. Unfortunately sources are scarce to provide an African voice or perspective on the experience of working for the scheme, and there is considerable scope for more research on this aspect to complement the work done by Rizzo in the Southern Province. The colonial perspective, reflecting established assumptions, focussed on the problems of securing stable labour. Some grumbled that even those who were happy to take up paid employment tended to disappear as soon as the rains arrived in order to plant their own *shambas* and maintain their own food supply, to the deep frustration of the contractors. There was equal frustration that others would work for a short time, then disappear with some piece of company property, neither of them to be seen again. The Administration accused the scheme of attracting 'thieves and other miscreants from all parts of the Territory', causing a crime wave that put a serious strain on local police resources.[56] But Sheila Unwin noted the contradiction: an African was sentenced to 12 months for taking some wood to make themselves a bed, whereas Europeans helped themselves to the same with impunity.[57]

In order to get African workers to stay, the scheme had to offer them not only money but accommodation and – even more importantly –

[53] Matteo Rizzo, 'Becoming Wealthy: The life history of a rural entrepreneur in Tanzania, 1922–1980s', *Journal of Eastern African Studies*, 3:2, 2009, pp. 221–39.
[54] Ibid., p. 227.
[55] Letter of 27 Jul 1949, Unwin Papers; Tanganyika Territory, *Labour Report*, 1948.
[56] Surridge (Acting Governor) to Colonial Secretary, 2 Mar 1949, CO 691/204/4.
[57] Letter of 3 Jul 1949, Unwin Papers.

access to food and consumer goods. As Kongwa was so distant from other major settlements, the nearest being Mpwapwa, 20 kms away and Dodoma, capital of Central Province, over 80 kms distant, the scheme had to create its own supply chain of traders, both African and Asian, to supply the African workers' need for food, housing and material goods. The problem here, as throughout the territory, was the lack of imports. This included items as critical as agricultural hoes – the basic hand tool of African agriculture. The normally phlegmatic Dodoma District Commissioner, W.A. Forbes, in whose district Kongwa fell, lamented:

> It is somewhat incongruous that vast quantities of expensive imported machinery can be obtained for the groundnut project, yet year after year the local Mgogo living in an endemic famine area is unable to obtain the primitive and easily produced hoes so necessary for the cultivation of his plot.[58]

In 1947, two years after the war, he noted that there was still 'a great shortage of clothes, hoes and most of the articles required by natives. As a result prices are high in spite of controls'.[59] At least in that year the rains were good; two droughts in the previous four years (1943 and 1946) had brought serious famine to many Wagogo areas, and the rains of 1947 were celebrated with much beer-making and dancing. Nevertheless, one study of the Wagogo concluded that by diverting labour from subsistence farming, the scheme actually exacerbated famine in the region during the next drought in 1949.[60]

But the choice of bulldozers over hoes was an imperial one, deliberately made for the benefit of the metropolitan power, despite the significant consequences for Tanganyika and its people.

Given the intensity of public scrutiny that the scheme received, and the high principles on which it was established, every effort was made to ensure that the local labourers had a reasonable standard of living. Gradually the mud huts were replaced with more solid accommodation in labour lines, and the food supplies for African workers were improved. So generous were these efforts that in mid-1949 Herbert Morrison wrote to the Colonial Secretary begging him to reduce the meat ration on the scheme, so that more could be exported to 'our own meat starved citizens' in the UK.[61] At first, African workers' families were excluded from the labour camp, until this attracted too many of the 'wrong sort' of female migrants. So families were permitted for African as for European workers, and with their arrival schools and

---

[58] Dodoma District Annual Report (DAR), 1948 (W.A. Forbes), TNA.
[59] Ibid., 1947.
[60] Studies by G.H. Maddox, quoted in Esselborn, 'Environment, Memory and the Groundnut Scheme', p. 83.
[61] Morrison to Creech Jones, 17 Aug 1949, CAB 124/1092.

additional medical facilities were needed for the African children too – yet another expenditure not included in the original estimates.[62]

With the influx of African workers, families and assorted hangers-on from all over the country, maintaining law and order made increasing demands on the local administration and taxed the Tanganyika police force beyond its modest means. The scheme began to recruit its own police, but this provoked a swift response from the Colonial Office which wanted no freelance, private-sector arrangements on its Territory. Law and order in the colonial context was to be the exclusive prerogative of the colonial state. There was no question over who would control the monopoly of force in British East Africa. Extra police were found.[63]

The scheme and its work force accentuated the contradiction between Britain's 'civilising mission', and its attachment to traditional African societies as a means of political and social control under colonial rule. It raised new fears that 'detribalised natives' working on the scheme, from all over the country, would sit outside the purview of the native authorities which were the bastion of Britain's indirect rule in Tanganyika. In practice the local Wagogo chiefs had no role or authority at Kongwa, and the full burden of administration fell on the British.[64] The colonial administration therefore established a new District Office, or *Boma*, at Kongwa itself in 1949. The new District Commissioner, Robin Johnston, and District Officer, Ian Norton, recruited Sheila Unwin as an assistant. She noted that their work, which was relentless,

> consists mainly of taking court (they are magistrates and try dozens of cases a week) and dealing with all kinds of queer things that turn up during the day, from seeing that the local shopkeepers don't charge too much for eggs, to settling the trouble of an old illiterate African who comes in to say that his wife has run off with another man. And of course all the incidentals such as attending to the removal of a thousand head of people, plus their cattle, from the land which is wanted by the O.F.C. and arranging compensation therefor. We are surrounded by books of law, and some frightfully efficient African clerks, whom I've never seen bettered.[65]

In practice, the Groundnut Scheme was only one of a number of factors that were accelerating change for the African inhabitants

---

[62] Dodoma DAR, 1949, TNA. For the role of prostitution in Tanganyika in the 1940s as one of the few avenues for female capital accumulation, see Westcott, 'The Impact of the Second World War' (PhD), pp. 290–4. But a proper study is awaited.

[63] Creech Jones to Cohen, 3 Aug 1949, CO 691/205/2. See also Provincial Commissioner's Annual Reports, Central Province, 1947 and 1948, TNA.

[64] Cooper, *Decolonization and African Society*, p. 12; Iliffe, *Tanganyika*, ch.12; papers in TNA 16758 and TNA 4/1088 (initiating sociological studies of the impact of the scheme; there is sadly no sign of the finished studies).

[65] Letter of 20 May 1949, Unwin Papers.

of Tanganyika and eliciting new responses. The surge in imports for the scheme put such pressure on the port that it undoubtedly contributed to the dockworkers strike that broke out in September 1947.

This was one of the seminal moments in Tanganyika's history, the first time African workers of all kinds and in all parts of the territory united in protest against the authorities. It was the first serious, modern challenge to colonial rule in the Territory.[66] Even the Governor broke off his usual litany of complaints about arthritis and boredom to tell his mother about it in his letters.[67] Beginning with the Dar es Salaam dockworkers, as had previous strikes in 1939 and 1943, this time the strike spread along the railway line, reaching Kongwa on 15 September, where the whole African workforce downed tools for three days. They initially made no specific demand other than for 'more pay', better food and better accommodation than mere tents, and the Labour Officer reported that: 'the men were all in good humour and although picketing and some intimidation occurred there was no untoward incident.'[68] While they waited for a detachment of African police to arrive from Dodoma, many of the European staff were sworn in as Special Constables, and tried to prevent their personal cooks and servants from joining the strike, but with little effect. As Sheila Unwin reported home: 'our houseboy had been told by the strikers that if he didn't strike too he would be beaten up. So off he went, with all the other personal boys and of course cooks and mess boys ... so we all set to in the cookhouse preparing meals, setting tables and washing up. For two whole days.'[69] In the end, no pay rise was given to the scheme's workers, but they returned when news came that the strike in Dar es Salaam was over. Labour relations were watched carefully thereafter.

That a group of African workers which had only been assembled in the previous few months should show such immediate and complete solidarity with their fellow workers in Dar es Salaam demonstrated the speed with which the transformation of African attitudes was taking place, whether the British liked it or not. The celebrated author Evelyn Waugh, visiting Tanganyika later, attributed the strike to the Labour Government's determination to spread socialist-style trade unionism throughout the colonial empire as well as at home. This was not wholly untrue: the Colonial Office had just sent a British trade unionist, Norman Pearson, to support the nascent unions in the Territory. But the

---

[66] Iliffe, 'Dockworkers', *TNR* 71, pp. 131–3, and Iliffe, *Tanganyika*, pp. 402–4.
[67] Battershill Papers, Box 5, BLCAS.
[68] Progress report No. 8, Sep 1947, MAF 83/1778. Wood, *Groundnut Affair*, pp. 79–82.
[69] Letter of 20 Sep 1947, Unwin Papers.

change came from within African society, and the Groundnut Scheme accelerated it.[70]

The strike came and went. The scheme itself had bigger problems to worry about – getting the land cleared, planted and harvested in time for the 1948 season. So it was with military spirit and determination that the groundnutters set to work, singing (to the tune of *Lili Marlene*):

> We remember clearly
> Not so long ago
> When we came to Kongwa
> To make the Groundnuts grow,
> The Honourable Strachey told us then:
> 'You are the men, we've got the gen
> You are the Groundnut Army
> You're Mr Strachey's Own.'[71]

---

[70] Evelyn Waugh, *A Tourist in Africa* (London, Chapman and Hall, 1960); see Norman Pearson, 'Trade Unionist on Safari', unpublished manuscript book, Bodleian Libraries, Oxford.
[71] Quoted in Wood, *Groundnut Affair*, p. 202. Originally a German song, *Lili Marlene* became the signature tune of both the Axis and Allied armies in North Africa during the war.

5

Beating about the Bush

Even as the men and material assembled, the process of actually clearing the bush and starting production was already under way. This chapter looks at the progress made and the difficulties encountered, as well as the kind of life the 'groundnutters' lived.

Bush-bashing

The African bush around Kongwa might have inspired the old Africa hands' acronym, 'MMBA – miles and miles of bloody Africa'. There were small patches of grassland, called *mbugas*, where there had once been lake beds. But the rest was a uniform low scrub of densely packed thorn bushes with the occasional giant baobab rising like an island from the tangled sea. No lush jungle this, but an impenetrable wilderness, almost never before farmed.

The first and greatest challenge was simply to clear the bush. Wakefield's plan proposed the clearing of 150,000 acres in the first year, and to do this with tractors – man mastering nature in an almost elemental way. By 1950, it was estimated the scheme would need 1,000 tractors in all. In the medium term, new tractors were ordered from Massey-Harris in Canada. But in the short term all that was available were 125 reconditioned caterpillar tractors from the UK, up to 300 army surplus bulldozers bought up second hand from the beaches of the Philippines and 50 old Lend-Lease tractors in the Middle East. As we have seen, simply getting them to Kongwa was difficult, but even when they arrived, many were found to be in a terrible state. 'Reconditioning' was a relative term, amounting in some cases to little more than a lick of paint; and many of those from the Philippines turned out to be too rusty to use. Before the railway extension was completed, they had to be driven the 20 miles from Msagali to Kongwa. Some did not make it, and stood like derelict sentinels along the road for years to come.

Photo 5.1 Bulldozer clearing bush at Kongwa (Overseas Food Corporation/Crown Copyright)

Others made it, but never moved again, cannibalised for parts for their healthier brethren.[1]

But some worked, and as soon as the first tractors arrived in Kongwa at the end of April 1947, 'bush-bashing' began. It was gruelling work. The pioneer team was led by the tanned and grizzled Frank Richards, a veteran army bulldozer driver who would set off into the bush at dawn to cut a 'trace' – a road that ran in a straight line for mile after mile, along which the units could be sub-divided. He and his colleagues would sometimes disappear into the bush for days and return with stories of being attacked by wild bees, or being forced to hide under the tractor for hours by an angry elephant.

Once the traces were cut, the serious clearing began. The tractor drivers quickly discovered two things: firstly, bulldozers bounce off baobabs – the vast trees that dominate parts of the African landscape and appear all trunk and no leaves. They could not be flattened, so were simply circumvented, which was probably just as well given that several of the largest baobabs were sacred to the local people. One

---

[1] This and other information in this chapter is drawn mainly from the Managing Agents' Progress Reports for 1947, in MAF 83/1778, and Wood, *Groundnut Affair*, pp. 64–8, 85–8. Wood's book is an invaluable contemporary source. Before writing it, Alan Wood had been the head of the OFC Information Division from 1948–50 and therefore both a frequent visitor to Kongwa and a reliable witness. An Australian with a gifted academic background, he had been President of the Oxford Union and served during the war as a gunner, an intelligence officer, and as a war correspondent with the British Airborne Divisions at Arnhem and the Rhine crossings, in the course of which he lost a leg, before becoming a journalist. He died tragically young in 1957.

driver, endeavouring to knock a baobab down, found himself showered with a skull and bones that had been dislodged from a hole in the trunk.[2]

Secondly, simply flattening the bush might be fine for airstrips, but not for cultivation. The roots had to come out too; and these were not to be moved. To survive in this arid environment, the thorn bushes put down a mass of deep, intertwined roots. The Managing Agents had foreseen the need for rooting, and had brought out 40 Le Tourneau Rooters – large harrows with long tines that were dragged through the ground, designed to rip out the roots to a depth of about a foot. At least, that was the theory. In practice, the African bush made short work of them. Within a day or two, most of them were too bent or broken to be of further use. In the spirit of 'make-do-and mend', the mechanics tried welding on lateral plates, which made them more effective. But the work of rooting still took many times longer than expected.

It was tough work for both the tractors and their drivers. Covered in dust and detritus, both suffered from heat exhaustion, the first through boiling radiators, the latter from dehydration and thirst, as well as bee stings. As the *Tanganyika Standard* reported at the time, the African bush put up a stiff fight against the new invaders.[3] As they cleared each patch of bush, the drivers never knew what wildlife would spring out at them. The occasional lion, and even rhinoceros were disturbed, though no casualties were reported among either man or beast. The most frequent casualties were the tractors themselves. Of the 70 tractors on site by the end of June, only 27 were operational. By the end of August, 200 had been delivered but two-thirds of them had broken down. The poor condition of the second-hand purchases, the resistance put up by the bush, and the initial lack of experience of many of the African drivers combined to cause a high rate of attrition. Tractors continued to arrive until, by the end of 1948, the General Manager reported that 'we have more tractors in Kongwa alone than Montgomery had tanks in the desert.'[4] But the capacity to repair them did not increase commensurately. The workshops – the need for which had scarcely been mentioned in the Wakefield Report – did their best, but crucial spares were lacking, one bulk order for spares from the US having mysteriously gone astray en route. Throughout 1947, the scheme rarely had more than 60 tractors operating at any one time.

As the old groundnutter joke ran: 'Give us the job and we'll finish the tools'.[5]

---

[2] The General Manager of the Scheme, Maj.-Gen. Harrison, regarded baobabs as 'probably one of the most useless trees on the face of the earth', D. Harrison, 'Civil Engineering Problems of the East African Groundnuts Scheme', *The Engineer*, 30 Jul 1948, p. 121, quoted in Esselborn, 'Environment, Memory and the Groundnut Scheme', p. 73.
[3] *Tanganyika Standard*, 21 Jul 1947.
[4] Maj.-Gen. Harrison, *Our World*, Dec 1948, p. 3; OFC, *First Annual Report*, p. 9.
[5] Wood, *Groundnut Affair*, p. 77.

The logistics of supplying the fleet of tractors as well as keeping them repaired also taxed the local infrastructure and suppliers. The tractors consumed 40,000 gallons of diesel *a week*, but the transport system could only deliver a supply of 22,000 gallons a week because of constraints on the railway line and road tankers. So for months the tractors could only operate for two and a half days a week. All this massively increased the costs, way beyond the initial estimates in Wakefield's plan. In the end, it was found to be substantially cheaper and more effective to do a lot of clearing at Kongwa by manual labour. But this was significantly slower and required a far larger workforce than had been anticipated.[6]

Clearing was further slowed by the need to take anti-soil erosion measures. The dustbowl disaster in the American West, only 20 years before, was a recent experience and left a legacy of caution among the agricultural staff on the scheme: great care was taken to avoid a recurrence. The uprooted vegetation was bulldozed into windrows along the contours, and then burnt to provide both nitrogen for the soil and a ridge to prevent rainwater carrying the soil away. One of the scheme's scientific staff, Peter Le Mare, vividly remembered the striking sight of the windrows burning at night, long lines of fire stretching far into the distance towards a hidden horizon.[7]

By late September, the UAC's General Manager at Kongwa, David Martin, wrote to Unilever admitting that they would be lucky to clear 15,000 acres in time for the planting season in December – one tenth of the target. The delays had a dramatic impact on the cost. Wakefield's original estimate for the cost of clearing had been under £4 an acre. When an estimate was finally made of the actual cost, it was said to be 10 times that amount, and informal estimates put the initial cost at over £60 an acre.[8] On the basis of cost-plus contracts, the British taxpayer was going to have to pay significantly more than had been promised. This fundamental flaw in the initial estimates, however, took a long time to sink in.

One of the abiding characteristics of the scheme, also inherited from the war, was its ability to improvise. To meet the lack of available tractors, Wakefield hit on a modern version of beating swords into ploughshares – turning tanks into tractors. After an ill-fated experiment with an old Valentine tank, the arms company Vickers-Armstrong succeeded in converting Sherman tanks into caterpillar tractors by removing the turrets and armour plating and reconstructing them with a bulldozer front. The result was known as a 'Shervick', and eventually some 580

[6] Hogendorn and Scott, 'Lessons of the East African Groundnut Scheme', pp. 176, 182.
[7] Le Mare interview, 12 Oct 2007.
[8] *Picture Post* (London), 19 Nov 1949, p. 21; OFC, *First Annual Report*, p. 17.

Shermans were bought from War Disposals for conversion, and transported out to the scheme.[9]

The scheme attracted other innovations too. As senior scientific officer, Hugh Bunting ('a very clever and brilliant man, as well as an outstanding personality', according to Sheila Unwin[10]) started up an experimental farm which devoted itself to testing every available variety of groundnut to see which flourished best at Kongwa, every type of tilling and weeding that would yield the best result, every combination of fertiliser, and an array of supplementary crops, including sunflower, sorghum and soya, that could complement the groundnuts themselves. Path-breaking work was done by the small but dedicated team, the results recorded at length in the scientific reports.[11]

The scheme had a particular problem with cars. Almost all transport at the outset was by Bedford truck. A delivery was taken of new Vauxhalls, but they all fell apart within weeks on the un-metalled roads. Perhaps the most lasting innovation was a new kind of vehicle that was first tried out at Kongwa. The final monthly report from the Managing Agents, in March 1948, records that a prototype Land Rover was inspected and tested. The results were positive, and a British alternative to the Jeep was at last available. Fifty were ordered.[12] Seventy years on, the Land Rover Defender is a recognisable descendant of that prototype, and perhaps the most lasting legacy of the Groundnut Scheme as a whole.

Half London

Gradually, the camp at Kongwa evolved, as numbers grew and building began. Until June 1947, everyone was still living in tents. Even in mid-1949 new arrivals still had to share a tent for the first few weeks, as Vivienne Bell found to her disgust.[13] At least by then electricity was more widely available: in 1947, when Sheila Unwin arrived, only the main buildings were supplied, and those by a giant diesel generator that had a tendency to explode, plunging the whole camp into pitch darkness.[14] But the ambitions of the scheme, its time horizons, and the

---

[9] Wood, *Groundnut Affair*, p. 87. The story of the Shermans is continued in Chapter 9 below.
[10] ... whose judgements were usually sound; letter of 6 Feb 1951, Unwin Papers.
[11] Attached to the Progress Reports in MAF 83/1778; also A.H. Bunting, 'Agricultural Research in the Groundnut Scheme, 1947–51', *Nature*, 168, 10 Nov 1951, pp. 804–9; Bunting interview, 2002.
[12] Progress Report No. 14, Mar 1948, MAF 83/1778; Le Mare interview, 2007.
[13] Bell, *Wind of Change*, p. 28
[14] Letter of 8 Aug 1947, Unwin papers.

basic needs of the European and African staff who began to flood in, all required something more permanent.

Building began as soon as cement could be found. By the end of 1948 there were 166 houses, and more being built. Posh three-roomed houses were provided up the hill for the executives, along 'Millionaires Row' as it was known. But lower down, for the workers, there were row upon row of 'Landcrete' houses which 'bore an uncanny resemblance to rows of prefabricated houses on a London bomb-site'. It helped people to feel at home, no doubt. But Kongwa was not a pretty sight, as Alan Wood admitted: 'The only time Kongwa did not look ugly was after dark'.[15]

It was not only the buildings that were familiar. So were many of the faces. Newly arrived groundnutters would remark that 'half London seemed to be here', and the name stuck, at least among the locals, who were flattered. Road names followed suit, with its Piccadilly Circus, Strand and Park Lane; and so too, from the outset, did the social life. Almost all of those who arrived in the early months worked extraordinarily long hours, determined to do all they could to make the scheme a success. Tom Unwin regularly left for work supervising the clearing on one of the Units at 6.30 in the morning and would not return until after 8.00 pm in the evening.[16] Many worked through the weekends, which seemed easy when there were not too many distractions. But some recreation was needed, and by all accounts the groundnutters certainly knew how to party.

The tone was set by the advance party who, when moving from their initial camp at Sagara to the permanent site at Kongwa, discovered, abandoned in the mess store, four bottles of champagne and two of gin. None of the bottles made it as far as Kongwa, and the four discoverers, led by Hugh Bunting, only just did, thanks to some ferocious – if erratic – driving across soggy marshland by Jeep. As everywhere across the Empire, the British took their virtues and their vices with them: cricket teams were formed, a golf course created (with browns instead of greens), tennis courts laid out (*very* hard courts indeed), and a makeshift cinema arranged from May 1947 – the only problem being that the cinematographer arrived in Kongwa with a stock of only pre-war films (somehow strangely appropriate for Tanganyika). Sing-alongs and parties were regular. A bawdy pantomime was laid on for Christmas ('a very local version of Cinderella, with take-offs of all the high-ups, racketeers, glamorous, lazy secretaries, copy-typists etc … slick and

---

[15] Wood, *Groundnut Affair*, p. 118. The following paragraphs draw on Wood, *Our World*, and interviews with Le Mare, Pike and Surridge, as well as Sheila Unwin's vivid letters. There is now a wealth of photographs available online recording the lives of British groundnutters, e.g. the Lithgow collection (www.flickr.com/photos/83874554@N00/sets/72157629437682125 – accessed 18 Jan 2020).

[16] Letter of 29 Dec 1948, Unwin Papers.

most amusing' reported Sheila Unwin[17]), and the traditional festivals of the British abroad – St George's, Burns Night and all – were marked in their traditional fashion at the Kongwa Club, housed in an army surplus Nissen hut. Mess arrangements were strictly hierarchical: No. 1 Mess for the bigwigs, No. 2 Mess for the scientists, professionals and married couples, No. 3 Mess, the male-only preserve of the working bachelors. Most Africans ate at home in the evening.

Life for the expatriates became a bit more civilised once married quarters were provided and more wives allowed to come out (from January 1948, at the specific rate of 15 per month).[18] But life was tough for them too. Many of the normal educational and medical facilities of life overseas were absent or had to be improvised from scratch. Present instead were a plentiful supply of rats, scorpions, snakes and cockroaches. But as the town grew, so did activities and amenities. 'In a few minutes I am off to a Young Wives Meeting (!!) whereat the local padre is going to talk on "the problem of suffering"', Unwin informed her mother.[19] A 400-bed hospital, the largest and best equipped in the whole of Tanganyika, was opened in late 1948 – the remains of which I saw 34 years later. It had a staff of 7 doctors and 13 European nurses, nearly as many as in the rest of the country put together. The OFC annual reports indicate that the most common complaint for Europeans was a new, prophylaxis-resistant strain of malaria; for the Africans it was respiratory illnesses. A school was set up for the European children that began to multiply, taught by some of the mothers. Lessons in Swahili were started and some of the more civilised arts cultivated. Dancing lessons began and a camera club was launched.

If there was not enough to do at Kongwa, one could always travel. Peter Le Mare recalled a group of (expat) Paulingis putting their arm chairs in the back of a Bedford truck and driving from Kongwa to Mombasa for the weekend (a distance of more than 380 miles) – returning no doubt both shaken and stirred by the expedition.[20] Others preferred nearer outings or domestic pleasures.

The small number of single women who came to Kongwa as secretaries or nurses found themselves much in demand. Romance flourished, even if the groundnuts didn't. The delay in building married quarters that prevented the arrival of wives and families provided plenty of opportunity. 'Immorality was rife' recalled Vivienne Bell – though not for her, despite being invited one night to a traditional Wagogo Mating Dance.[21] The more respectable activities were reported

[17] Letter of 4 Jan 1949, Unwin Papers.
[18] Drew to Dashwood, 12 Nov 1947, TNA 36826.
[19] Letter of 5 Sep 1949, Unwin Papers.
[20] Le Mare interview, 12 Oct 2007.
[21] Bell, *Wind of Change*, p. 31. Her book is worth reading for the account of the

in the scheme's own newspaper, *Our World*, which appeared monthly, and included useful information on, for example, recipes that could be made with local ingredients – such as groundnut stew.[22]

Food was never short, but it was expensive. A shop was set up for the European workers, but had a hard time making ends meet – scarcely surprising when they brought in a European sales assistant on a salary of £1,000 a year (a new District Officer earned around £500 a year).[23] Prices were so high that many preferred to shop in the local African market. A *Picture Post* photograph from 1949 shows two European women, elegantly dressed in the New Look and wearing sunglasses, picking fruit from a stall manned by an African trader wearing a trilby, both the height of fashion in their own way.[24]

Though the African workers were housed in the neighbouring settlement, and were all day working in close proximity on the scheme itself, there was little or no social interaction between the races. The scheme was still a world unto itself, and for most Africans another mystery visited on them by their colonial masters. By November 1947, there were 400 Europeans and 5,500 Africans at Kongwa. By 1949, it was the second largest town in Tanganyika.[25]

The local Wagogo tribesmen found the groundnutters not just puzzling but hugely amusing. Always musical, they were often asked to perform dances, *ngoma*, for European visitors, and would accompany the dance with satirical songs in their own language – *kigogo* – observing the white man's incomprehensible impatience, anger, peculiar habits and inappropriate ways of living in the bush, all for the benefit of the beaming, oblivious European spectators from Kongwa.[26]

The southern front

Though Kongwa was the initial focus of activity, the Managing Agents also began opening up the vast areas in southern Tanganyika that had been earmarked for the scheme.

Mating Dance alone. Sheila Unwin comments more discretely on the mating rituals of both Europeans and Africans in her letters.
[22] Copies of *Our World* are hard to find. One is in the Fabian Colonial Bureau papers, Box 55, Bodleian Libraries, Oxford, and some extracts in TNA files. I am grateful to Peter Le Mare for sharing his personal copies.
[23] Letter from Mills, 25 Jan 1949, Unwin Papers.
[24] *Picture Post*, 19 Nov 1949.
[25] Strachey to Cripps (Chancellor of the Exchequer), 10 Oct 1949, CO 691/204/4; *East African Groundnut Scheme: Review of Progress to the end of November 1947*, Cmd 7314, p. 6.
[26] Article by Sister Bullard of the Church Missionary Society, *Our World*, Dec 1948; Wood, *Groundnut Affair*, p. 73.

This was inevitably a slower task because of the poor transport and communications to the region. If Tanganyika had been the Cinderella of the colonial empire, the Southern Province was Cinderella's Cinderella. Much of it remained scarcely touched by the outside world, agriculture was predominantly subsistence and, apart from a few whiskery missionaries and the odd naturalist, precious few white men had ventured into the interior since Dr Livingstone. Wild animals still roamed the bush and, near the mission station at Mahenge in 1949, a tribe of baboons forced one village to abandon their *shambas* and move out, while one rogue lion alone was reported to have killed 17 people during the year. While the rainfall was more reliable than in the Central Province, the geology of the area meant that there was almost no surface water, and therefore a very sparse local population – the very reason it was free for the scheme. With no opportunity to pursue commercial farming, those who lived there tended to be regarded as a labour supply for the sisal estates further north, though some Makonde had already migrated south to work on the Rand's gold mines in South Africa. The Groundnut Scheme had to begin more or less everything from scratch.[27]

The first questions were where to site the port, and where to build the railway. Samuel insisted that they plan for the long term and not jeopardise the future for temporary expediency. The biggest existing port in the province was Lindi. But this had a shallow harbour that would not allow a deep-water berth, requiring a complete dependence on lighterage. As a result, the Ministry of Food sent out a Mr Millbourn in February 1947 to look at the options. Reading his report, they were 'forced to conclude that Lindi is an unsatisfactory site', even though developing an alternative would delay production in the south by six months. The Treasury was concerned that such a delay would mean missing the scheme's production targets.[28] But 25 miles further south, at a place called Mtwara near the village of Mikindani, was a perfect natural harbour that seemed ideally suited, as Livingstone himself had identified when he landed there in 1866. Thus the decision was made to build a brand new 'Port Peanut'.[29]

Balfour Beatty won the contract to build the new dock, a single, long deep-water berth, for £600,000. Work was due to start in late 1947 and the new port to be operational by the end of 1950. By the end of 1947, a crane had arrived, but nothing for it to lift. By mid-1948, there was still little sign of progress. No work could really begin until proper commu-

[27] Southern Province Annual Reports, 1946–49, TNA. Rooke-Johnson (Provincial Commissioner) to Chief Secretary, 13 Feb 1947, TNA 35147/90; Rizzo, 'Groundnut Scheme', passim; Strachey comments in *Hansard*, 14 Mar 1949, col. 1789.
[28] Huntley (MoF) to Fisher (HMT), 19 Mar 1947, MAF 83/1748; Fisher minute 21 Mar 1947, T 161/1371.
[29] Wood, *Groundnut Affair*, ch. 11.

Photo 5.2 Mtwara deep-water quay under construction, 1950 (East African Railways and Harbours)

nications had been built to the site. By March 1950, the European living quarters and African labour lines had been completed, and things were almost ready for construction itself to begin. By 1955, the magnificent new dock was completed.[30] But by then, things had changed. So the scheme continued to use the port at Lindi, with the help of some LCTs (landing craft tanks) from War Disposals in the Middle East, which enabled them to get the tractors ashore.

In practice, the railway came first. Despite the failure to link the scheme's needs to those of imperial strategy, David Martin for one was optimistic that railway construction would not be difficult. He himself had helped pull up the old German tramway which ran up country from Lindi to the inland mission station of Masasi, and was confident the whole thing, including port, could be built for £1.25 million.[31] But getting the equipment there to build it proved a nightmare. Everything had to come from Dar es Salaam, and could not wait for the three-monthly ships. The only road from Dar es Salaam down the coast was virtu-

---

[30] OFC, *First Annual Report*, p. 24; OFC *[Second] Annual Report and Statement of Accounts to 31 March 1950*, 28 Jul 1950 (London, HMSO, No. 147); J.P. Moffett, *A Handbook of Tanganyika* (Dar es Salaam, Government Printer, 1958), p. 226.
[31] 'Note of discussion on evacuation of groundnuts from Masasi area of Southern Province', 15 Aug 1946, TNA 16583/161.

ally impassable for half the year during the rains, and involved a perilous crossing of the (also crocodile-infested) Rufiji River on a trestle balanced on four canoes paddled by the local tribesmen. The 18-year-old son of one groundnutter fell into the river during one crossing and was indeed eaten by crocodiles – the only such casualty recorded. Even in good conditions the journey took three full days. Peter Le Mare, based in the south in early 1948 to start up the experimental farm there, was completely stuck when their lone tractor broke down. The only spare part was in Kongwa, 500 miles away. By truck, plane and train, he did the round trip in three days, which was reckoned an extraordinary feat. The cost of that repair fell on the broad back of the British taxpayer.[32]

Much of the construction work on the railway was therefore done by hand. It had been decided that the scheme's headquarters in the south should be 107 miles inland from Lindi, at a village called Nachingwea, judged to be the centre of the best groundnut country. Dr Leader Stirling, a pioneering missionary doctor in the Masasi district since 1935, recorded a surreal encounter in early 1949. Driving miles from Nachingwea, along the roughest of tracks, his ambulance stuck, as so often, in the thick mud. 'Luckily a gang of 50 men were building a railway nearby for the great groundnut fiasco ... and for a reasonably small consideration they all pulled on our tow rope and soon got us out.'[33] At least they were useful to someone. The railway finally opened on 25 October 1949.

The pressure to open up the area was immense, especially given that its rainfall was so much more reliable than that of Kongwa. Bunting advised against trying any agricultural operations there for two years until the infrastructure was in place, but was overruled. At great expense of effort and money, tractors were brought in and clearing begun. In addition to the railway, an oil pipeline was built to bring fuel to Nachingwea. Part of the bargain with Tanganyika had also been to ensure that the rich timber resources of the south were not just cut and burnt, but put to good use. A whole, brand new sawmill, 'the most modern in Africa' capable of turning 100 trees a day into five furnished prefabricated houses at the cost of £1,500 each, was therefore imported and assembled at a place called Noli, before they discovered that the quality of timber in that particular area was not good enough, and better logs had to be shipped in from further afield to try to make the sawmill pay its way. It never did.[34]

[32] Le Mare interview, 13 Oct 2007; *Our World*, Dec 1948, p. 9.
[33] Leader Stirling, *Come Over and Help Us: A doctor in Africa* (Dar es Salaam, AMREF, 1995). Dr Stirling became Tanzania's Minister of Health after independence.
[34] Col. Stanley, *Hansard*, vol. 470, col. 68, 21 Nov 1949; Surridge to Sir T.K. Lloyd (CO), 6 May 1949, CO 691/205/1; OFC, *Second Annual Report*, p. 23; Alan Jenkins, *On Site, 1921–71: First 50 years of Taylor Woodrow* (London, Heinemann, 1971), p. 52; Wood, *Groundnut Affair*, p. 134.

While Balfour Beatty worked on the port and Paulings on the railway, Mowlems were contracted to start clearing the land. Having three separate contractors with no effective coordinating mechanism proved disastrous, each competing against the other for the scarce supplies, and no-one taking overall responsibility. Two pioneers were sent down by the Managing Agents to start opening up the area and establish a headquarters, but they did not have authority to manage anyone else. Arwen Llewellyn Jones and Christopher Perrin Brown became legendary figures, camped amidst the tall trees of the plateau, driving traces through herds of elephants and tracking down water supplies where none had been thought to exist. But all their heroism could not bring order from the chaos. Supplies were lost or stolen or destroyed by accident, camps were built in the wrong place, and work was physically constrained by the fierce and proprietorial elephant population who regularly made work impossible between 3.00 and 6.00 pm when they were on the move. More than one groundnutter fled the field pursued by an elephant. On top of the physical constraints, personal relations were also reported to be particularly combustible. The Unwins were transferred there in 1950 and found the scheme staff 'very cliquey', to the extent that Sheila told her mother 'I should hate to think I had to live in Nachingwea for the rest of my days'.[35]

The Universities Mission to Central Africa (UMCA) had been active in the area since the 19th century, and sent the Rev. E.H. Capper to Lindi as a missionary to the scheme, because it represented 'one of the biggest opportunities and responsibilities ever to come the church's way in East Africa'. Lord Hailey, author of the magisterial *African Survey* and Chairman of the UMCA, also wrote to *The Times* to insist that religious instruction be included in plans for the scheme.[36] Capper found those missionaries already in the region to be rather less positive, denouncing 'this accursed groundnut scheme which will ruin the spiritual lives of thousands of Africans.'[37] In February 1948, his superior on the spot, Archdeacon Kidner, was still fulminating that:

> the whole plan has brought tremendous economic and social problems. An influx of undesirable women from other parts of the country and the virtual sale of local girls by their elders to be temporary or secondary wives of employees of the scheme is one of the horrible results of bringing thousands of men from their own families and tribal life to be concentrated in this scheme ... As always, one of the curses of bringing a large number of men together out of their normal life is that drinking becomes the favourite form of 'recreation'.[38]

[35] Wood, *Groundnut Affair*, ch. 11. Letters of 1 and 27 Oct 1950, Unwin Papers.
[36] Rev. Canon G.W. Bloomfield (Secretary General of the UMCA) to Rev. E.H. Capper, 3 Jul 1947, UMCA Papers, SF 134, Bodleian Libraries, Oxford.
[37] Letter from Capper to Bloomfield, 17 Dec 1947, ibid.
[38] Letter from Kidner to Bloomfield, 15 Feb 1948, ibid. Also Maj.-Gen. Harrison quoted in the BBC's R4 programme 'The Great Groundnut Scandal'.

The Administration shared the missionaries' concern. The District Officer in Masasi worried about 'the lessening of the general morality of the inhabitants', and the Chief Secretary wrote to the Colonial Office complaining that 'mushroom villages of an insanitary type, which are the haunts of prostitutes and other undesirables, have sprung up in the vicinity of the groundnut camps.'[39] This played into one of the strongest preoccupations of the older colonial officials, that 'detribalised natives' would upset the delicate equilibrium they tried to achieve by maintaining what they believed to be traditional tribal structures as a vehicle for enforcing colonial authority. Again, it all came back to the delicate colonial business of keeping political control over a society which the scheme itself was helping bulldoze into a new phase of development. This contradiction of post-war colonial policy, as well as the well-meaning but rather paternalist assumptions of the colonial enterprise, were starkly illuminated by the scheme.[40]

The missionaries (like the administration) were equally worried about the 'unsuitable' European employees brought in by the contractors for fear they might undermine the carefully constructed image of the white man as an educated, superior and principled figure. Of the 200 Europeans imported by Mowlems, Rev. Capper reported:

> The leaders and managers are very nice people, some of them churchgoers etc. But numbers of drivers etc. ... are certainly the toughest type of European that Southern Tanganyika has ever seen and we wonder what effect *they* will have on the African.[41]

One was prosecuted for breaking into an African's hut in pursuit of the man's wife, and several were dismissed and sent home for 'a disgraceful episode with a heavy lorry while drunk'.[42]

The problem was that there was little other recreation to be had. Vivienne Bell, arriving fresh from freezing post-war London into the basic facilities of the camp at Nachingwea to work as a secretary, was horrified to find herself living in a mud hut, shared with sundry lizards and beetles, and swiftly sniffed out by the local leopard. The only facilities were a long-drop, 20 yards away across snake-infested grassland. This was not the Africa of her imagination, all verandas, lawns and sundowners, and she swiftly demanded a transfer to the relative civilisation of Kongwa.[43]

For most Africans, however, the arrival of the Groundnut Scheme was warmly welcomed and remembered as 'these days of great prosper-

---

[39] Surridge to Creech Jones, 2 Mar 1949, CO 691/204/4; Rizzo, 'Groundnut Scheme', p. 232.
[40] Cooper, *Decolonization and African Society*, pp. 261–9
[41] Capper to Broomfield, 23 Apr 1948 UMCA Papers, SF 134.
[42] Ibid.
[43] Bell, *Wind of Change*, pp. 20–27.

ity'.[44] Suddenly money was pouring in. The railway construction alone employed 4,600 men. Africans could at last demand a decent wage, and did so. More money could be made from selling food to the scheme, so most labour tended to be seasonal here too. Labour was adequate during the dry season, but as soon as the rains arrived, the African staff left. In only one year, 1950, did the local managers not complain about the shortage of labour. Bicycles – long a luxury – began to proliferate: 'everybody bought one', recalled Dr Stirling.[45] In short, the Groundnut Scheme brought something the Southern Province had never had before: prosperity. It quickly became 'the dominating factor' in the local economy because of its seemingly unlimited demand for food supplies, trade goods and labour. The Newala District Officer reported: 'Money as easy as never before, and a man could sell his crops, his goats and his labour at prices that would have seemed fantastic a few years ago.'[46] That pioneer African entrepreneur, Julius Mtenda, was one of several who made the most of the Southern Province's moment in the economic sun.[47]

Globalisation, warts and all, was reaching even the Cinderella province, thanks to the Groundnut Scheme.

Urambo

In March 1947, Hugh Bunting made his first trip to assess the fertility of the soils in the western-most areas identified by Wakefield. Beyond the small town of Tabora, he found suitable conditions for groundnut growing at Urambo, though the soil was so deficient in phosphates he reckoned large quantities of fertiliser would be essential to provide a good yield. The vegetation here was *miombo* woodland (predominantly *Brachystegia* trees), much more open than the dense thorn bush scrub at Kongwa, and with lighter tree cover than the forested slopes of southern Tanganyika. The rainfall was more reliable too.[48]

In August 1947, the Managing Agents sent a UAC team to set up the operation there. Partly because it had good communications, lying directly on the railway line, and partly because it was competently managed, Urambo was the most civilised and effective of the groundnut areas. Once the tsetse flies had been cleared from the camp,

---

[44] Mr Makwinja, letter in *Habari za Nachingwea katika Kiswahili* (Nachingwea News in Swahili), TNA 16/32/35, quoted in Rizzo, 'Groundnut Scheme', p. 212.
[45] Stirling, *Doctor*, p. 132; Rizzo, 'Groundnut Scheme', passim.
[46] Newala DAR, 1948, TNA 16/11/260, quoted in Rizzo, 'Groundnut Scheme', p. 218.
[47] Rizzo, 'Becoming Wealthy', pp. 225–6, see Chapter 5 above.
[48] A.H. Bunting, 'Field survey of Western Tabora District', 4 Mar 1947, TNA 35113.

pleasant accommodation was set up, with decent housing for the African workers, and good amenities. Urambo swiftly developed the best cricket team in western Tanganyika.

Clearing was entrusted to A.L. Gladwell, the expert who had advised Wakefield and who now ran the Earth Moving and Construction Co. He proceeded more slowly, but more steadily with the project and Urambo developed a good reputation for clearing, though even here the casualty rate among tractors was as high as ever, limiting the acreage cleared. Some 2,800 acres were cleared in 1948. The only trouble was that experiments showed that groundnuts did not grow well here, being particularly prone to rosette disease. As a result, 2,000 of those acres were planted with sunflower. Here too a saw mill was set up to use the cut trees for timber. Though more of a Heath Robinson contraption than the mill in Noli, it produced enough to provide furniture for everyone.[49] But the effort was too much for Gladwell. In November 1948, at the age of 58, he died, to universal regret – the first senior casualty of the scheme.[50]

In the first 18 months of the scheme, under Managing Agent control, tremendous effort had been expended, miracles of improvisation and endeavour had been achieved, parts of Tanganyika barely touched by British rule had been abruptly brought into contact with the modern world; and yet it felt as though the scheme was merely scratching the surface, barely making a start on the great project that had been foreseen. It was hoped the transition in management to the Government-run OFC would accelerate things.

[49] OFC, *First Annual Report*, pp. 21–2; Wood, *Groundnut Affair*, pp. 122–5.
[50] *Our World*, Dec 1948.

6

The Overseas Food Corporation

As work in Africa under the Managing Agents fell further and further behind, in London John Strachey determined to speed up the transfer of the scheme's management to the public corporation which Cabinet had agreed should be established to run it. This was no mean task, requiring the passage of the necessary implementing legislation through Parliament, and the selection of a suitably qualified management team. Both reveal much about how the post-war Labour Government, and John Strachey personally, worked.

Above all, it forced the Labour Government to come face to face with the question of what exactly they were trying to do in developing Britain's colonial territories, and where the balance lay between benefit to the imperial power and benefit to the African people. Naturally, as we have seen, the Government asserted that it would benefit both. But to assert that something is true does not necessarily make it so. Then, as now, putting something into legislation tends to pinpoint the ambiguities that politicians so often prefer to slide over.[1]

The Overseas Resources Development Act: development or exploitation?

Strachey's objective was to get legislation establishing a public corporation to run the Groundnut Scheme through Parliament as swiftly as possible, but it immediately raised both wider questions of principle that needed to be resolved first, and became entangled with the Colonial Office's ambition to create their own corporation to pursue more commercial forms of colonial development than were permitted under the Colonial Development and Welfare (CD&W) Act of 1940.

---

[1] Something the 2019 legislation to implement Brexit illustrated vividly in our own day.

For some time the Colonial Office had been dissatisfied with the limitations imposed on their efforts to develop the African territories by the CD&W Act. They wanted something that would be more flexible, less bound by Treasury rules, and able to mobilise larger sums of money. The CD&W funds were being spent predominantly on the provision of basic social services, and public works and utilities, not on what would be considered 'productive' projects to increase the supply of foodstuffs, raw materials and other commodities, nor to initiate genuine industrial development. In 1943, the Colonial Office's main economic thinker, Sidney Caine, had floated the idea of a body 'to conceive and carry out major projects' in the context of overall development planning, in the form of 'a company clothed in commercial form ... working as an agent of Government ... not intended to be operated in a commercial spirit' but acting 'with the comparative freedom of a commercial concern', freed from the 'portentously heavy machinery' of government.[2] In March 1947, the month after the publication of the Groundnuts White Paper and following the Cabinet decision to use a public corporation to run it, he firmed up this idea in a memo to the Colonial Economic Development Council (CEDC), proposing the establishment of a 'Colonial Development Corporation' (CDC). The Chairman of the CEDC, Lord Portal, forwarded the idea to Attlee on 10 April with the suggestion that it should have an initial borrowing limit of £100 million.[3] Attlee asked Creech Jones to take the idea forward with the Chancellor. Creech Jones accordingly wrote to Dalton on 28 April outlining the idea of a corporation backed by government funds that would invest in new companies and big ad hoc development schemes undertaking commercially viable activities – i.e. designed to at least break even – but which were unlikely to attract private capital. This also reflected the Colonial Office view that 'on grounds of general policy big industrial developments in the Colonies ought not to be exploited by private enterprise'.[4] His officials immediately started drafting legislation to put such a public corporation into place

Dalton was enthusiastic: 'This is a Big Idea and we must back it', he declared, urging the fastest possible implementation of the proposal.[5] He liked the idea for exactly the same reason he had agreed to back the Groundnut Scheme: it would help increase production from the sterling area and reduce Britain's dependence on dollar imports. But the idea was less well received in the Ministry of Food. They feared that a

---

[2] Caine memo of Aug 1943, quoted in C. Brain and M. Cable, *CDC: Pioneering development* (London, CDC, 2008), p. 10.

[3] Ibid.; Portal to Attlee, 10 Apr 1947, PREM 8/457 (Prime Minister's Office papers, The National Archives, Kew), quoted in M. Cowen, 'Early Years of the CDC', p. 66.

[4] Creech Jones to Dalton, 28 Apr 1947, Helsby (HMT) minute of 9 May, and other papers in T 220/31. PM minute of 26 Mar 1947 and other papers in CO 537/2002.

[5] Fisher to Helsby, 19 Jun, and Dalton minute 21 June 1947, T 220/31.

corporation on these lines would not serve their purpose, as it would be too focussed on the developmental benefits for the colonies rather than the food requirements of the UK. It could not therefore be used to establish a corporation to run the Groundnut Scheme, and risked slowing up Parliamentary consideration of their own proposal because it would be more controversial in proposing the industrial development of the colonies. They therefore drafted their own bill, focussed purely on growing food, but not necessarily exclusively within the colonial empire.[6]

The Colonial Office in turn objected that to prioritise a limited proposal establishing a corporation for a single project would delay the acceptance of their own, wider scheme by up to two years. They feared it would be attacked as 'a measure exploiting colonies for the benefit of the consumer in this country.'[7] The two departments were at loggerheads, each believing the other wanted to seize control of colonial development projects for their own ends. Strachey met Creech Jones in May, but failed to resolve the impasse. The matter was about to be passed to Herbert Morrison who, as Lord President, had overall responsibility for the socialisation of industry and the establishment of government corporations, when Strachey, having spoken to Morrison, called first Creech Jones and then the Chancellor and talked both into a compromise.[8]

As a consequence, in early June Strachey and Creech Jones jointly presented the Cabinet with a proposal for a single piece of legislation establishing two separate corporations, with two distinct purposes:

> the Colonial Development Corporation would have wider powers to develop mineral resources, improve communications, develop water power etc. as well as produce food and other agricultural products such as rubber, cotton, fibres and so forth; in so far as it produces food in the Colonies it would normally do so as part of its plans for the general development of the Colonial Empire, whereas the Overseas Food Corporation would be concerned primarily with the production of food for export to the UK as part of the Ministry of Food's overseas procurement programme.[9]

'This all seems a bit messy', commented Attlee's Private Secretary.[10] But at their meeting on 10 June the Cabinet went along with the proposal, provided the Chancellor agreed capital limits with the ministers, and

---

[6] Morgan, *Colonial Development*, Vol.II, pp. 271–2.
[7] Minutes by Monson, Eastwood and Caine, May 1947, CO 537/2002.
[8] Note of Creech Jones meeting with Strachey, 15 May 1947, CO 537/2002; Note of CO meeting with MoF, 30 May 1947, MAF 83/1748. Bishop (MoF) to Nicholson, and minute by Nicholson to Morrison, both 9 Jun 1947, CAB 124/1090.
[9] Memo by Minister of Food, 8 Jun 1947, CP(47)176, CAB 129/19 (reprinted in *BDEE*, II, no. 120).
[10] Gorell Barnes to PM, 9 Jun 1947, Gorell Barnes Papers BARN 2/9, Churchill College Archives.

(at Bevin's behest) the CDC recruited professional managers for its schemes.[11]

The money was soon fixed. Dalton was willing to put some impressive headline figures in the bill, and agreed total lending limits of £100 million for the CDC and £50 million for the OFC – £25m of it for the Groundnut Scheme and the same again for other schemes it might identify, plus a further £5 million for experimental work.[12] But wrangling over the precise terms of the Overseas Resources Development (ORD) Bill continued. At issue was the overlap in their functions in relation to the production of food within the colonies, and how this would be seen by others. The Colonial Office wanted to limit the OFC's remit effectively to just the Groundnut Scheme within the colonies. Strachey was determined to keep open the possibility of other schemes. With ministers unable to agree, the matter was referred to Attlee, who sought advice from the dependable Foreign Secretary. Bevin was clear:

> We must be careful that our plans for the development of our colonial Dependencies cannot in any way be represented as springing solely from our own selfish interests. It is, above all, important that in their presentation there is no possible suggestion of exploitation of the Colonial populations. In either case, we may find ourselves exposed to bitter criticism in the United Nations, and be obliged to defend ourselves against quite baseless charges. We know from experience that the possibilities of misrepresentation in this field are almost endless.[13]

For now, ministers reached a compromise whereby the Ministry of Food would seek the agreement of the Colonial Secretary before launching any further projects in colonial territories.

The debate nevertheless continued both inside government and in public as the Parliamentary process proceeded. In January 1948, the Cabinet Secretary, Sir Norman Brook, put the presentational risks of the ORD Bill to Attlee bluntly:

> It could, I suppose, be said to fall within the ordinary definition of 'Imperialism'. And at the level of a political broadcast, it might be represented as a policy of exploiting native peoples in order to support the standards of living of the workers in this country.
>
> This policy is doubtless inevitable – there are compelling reasons, both economic and international for adopting it. But if it is disclosed incautiously or incidentally, without proper justification and explanation, may it not be something of a shock to Government supporters – and, indeed, to enlightened public opinion generally? It would certainly

[11] Cabinet minutes, 10 Jun 1947, CM(47)53rd, CAB 128/10.
[12] Minutes in T 220/31.
[13] Bevin to PM, 4 Oct 1947, PM/47/139, PREM 8/456 (also quoted in Morgan, *Colonial Development, Vol. II*, p. 275).

expose a Labour Government to very damaging misrepresentation. It can, of course, be argued that the more rapid development of Africa's resources will bring social and economic advantages to the native peoples in addition to buttressing the political and economic influence of the United Kingdom. I should have thought, however, that some care and preparation would be needed in order to put this argument across successfully, both here and in Africa.[14]

So was the Groundnut Scheme development or exploitation? The Cabinet itself recognised the economic imperative for Britain of securing more supplies from guaranteed sterling sources within the colonial empire to enable speedy post-war economic recovery. But it had at least to look as though there would be equal benefit for the colonies themselves. In John Strachey's mind there was never any doubt that the two objectives could be reconciled, that the scheme would develop Africa for the benefit of Africans while also helping the British consumer – just as the Gezira cotton scheme in Sudan was deemed to help Lancashire as well as the Sudanese peasant. But others were more conscious of the moral, presentational and economic dilemmas. These were real, as seen in the debate over Tanganyika's contribution to the scheme through taxation policy (in Chapter 3). Had the scheme been successful, these dilemmas could have become a political bone of contention for nationalist politicians. But they were to be spared that problem.

When it came to presentation, no-one could be more eloquent than John Strachey in leading the Government side in the Commons Second Reading debate on 6 November 1947. In a *tour de force*, Strachey set out the vision, the logic and the details behind the twin corporations. Starting from the premise that '[w]e are the greatest of Colonial powers, and we cannot afford a deserted Empire', he described what he liked to call 'Operation Groundnuts' as a righteous campaign against

> the tsetse fly, the climate, the stubborn African bush, the ignorance of the cultivator, and the lack of communications. True, these are formidable enemies and will not be overcome without the sustained effort, courage and grit of the men and women at this new front. These are enemies who will give us difficulties or setbacks and even moments of heartbreak, just as the Afrika Korps did six years ago, but they are enemies, again like the Afrika Korps, which will be overcome.[15]

He had to admit that progress had been slower than planned, and that work in 1947 was 'largely exploratory and experimental'. But he goaded the Tories with the fact that they would have left the Groundnut Scheme to the UAC, who would have done it solely for their own profit, and assured Parliament that the problems would be overcome and

---

[14] Brook to Attlee, 14 Jan 1948, PREM 8/923 (reprinted in Hyam, *BDEE*, vol. II, no. 121).
[15] *Hansard*, vol. 443, cols 2016–35, 6 Nov 1947.

real operations begin in 1948, with the first major crop reaching world markets in early 1949.

The Tories broadly welcomed the proposals, Col. Oliver Stanley even claiming some paternity for the CDC from his time as Colonial Secretary during the war. But it did not stop him criticising the 'cock-eyed set up' of two separate corporations. He also put his finger on one political reality:

> The fact is that the Minister of Food is the cuckoo in the nest. He got into the groundnut nest pretty early, and is a big and loud bird, and all the flustered flutterings of the hen birds from the Colonial Office have never managed to get him out.[16]

Overall, though, Strachey's line was accepted and the government's efforts welcomed, the Hon. Member for Stockton-on-Tees expressing his enthusiasm for the fact that 'the African people are being bulldozed into civilisation'.[17] The Bill was passed without trouble.

On 11 February 1948, the Overseas Resources Development Act received Royal Assent from King George VI and entered into force. Creech Jones had already informed his Governors about the CDC and proceeded to tell them about the OFC as well.[18] Strachey had also already moved fast to select and announce the OFC's Management Board.

The Overseas Food Corporation Board

For Strachey, people always came first, and he had known for some time exactly who he wanted as chairman of the Corporation.

Dick Plummer, a close friend since the heady days of the General Strike, was by 1947 the Assistant General Manager of Lord Beaverbrook's *Daily Express* group. This made him in practice the third most powerful man in the organisation, earning a salary rumoured to be around £12,000 a year (nearly £500,000 today) at a time when a Permanent Secretary, the most senior civil servant, earned £3,750 a year. Beaverbrook was no easy master, and Plummer had built up a formidable reputation as an efficient and energetic manager, having left school at 15 and worked his way up entirely by his own efforts. Strachey told Dalton that he thought Plummer the right man to ensure the scheme

---

[16] Ibid., cols 2042–3.
[17] Mr Chetwynd, ibid., cols 2086–7. Interestingly, Alan Lennox-Boyd, the future Conservative Colonial Secretary, objected to the phrase on the grounds that in Africa 'some of the virtues of the age of innocence still survive' and Africans should be allowed to find their own way to 'full economic and political liberty'. Ibid., col. 2111.
[18] Circulars from the Creech Jones to Colonial Governors, 17 Dec 1947 and 22 Mar 1948, in MAF 83/1880.

was 'run with real vigour and efficiency and completely in line with the Government's Colonial policy'.[19] A stout, bustling, good-humoured, forthright man with big, round horn-rimmed glasses, Plummer had not only private-sector experience, the confidence of the City, boundless self-confidence and courage, but also complete conviction in Strachey's vision of the scheme. In all circumstances, he would be 100% loyal. Moreover, the Beaverbrook press became – at least for a while – one of the most vocal supporters of Strachey's scheme. To induce him to leave Beaverbrook's well-paid employ, Strachey persuaded the Chancellor to provide the Chairman with a salary of £5,000 a year – a fortune in public service terms.[20]

The only drawback was that Plummer knew little of agriculture and even less of Africa. To remedy this gap, Strachey appointed both the agricultural brains behind the scheme, John Wakefield, and a veteran colonial administrator, Sir Charles Lockhart, to the board. Sir Charles had served as Financial Secretary (in effect minister of finance) in Northern Rhodesia, Nigeria and Kenya, then as Chief Secretary in Kenya, where he was made responsible for coordinating the war effort between all the East African colonies. Quietly and wittily acerbic, he knew Africa well and had 'a reputation for great ability with the Colonial Office', helping ensure their confidence in the Corporation.[21]

As well as Wakefield, two other founders of the scheme found their way onto the Board – John Rosa, as the member responsible for finance (despite his later admission that he was 'not an expert' on the subject), and Frank Samuel, who was to provide the link to the UAC as Managing Agents. One other non-executive was appointed to add some further heft, and an independent view, on the scientific side. Strachey selected another old friend and long-standing Labour Party supporter, Lord (Victor) Rothschild, the eminent biologist and former fellow of Trinity College, Cambridge.

As a foil to the energetic Plummer, Strachey chose as Vice-Chairman the solid and dependable James McFadyen. The pipe-smoking son of a Scottish labourer, McFadyen had left school at nine, even earlier than his chairman, but had made a successful career in the cooperative movement, becoming Director of the Cooperative Wholesale Society. A solid Labour man and already a member of the Government's Colonial Economic Development Council, his presence also

---

[19] Strachey to Dalton, 30 Apr 1947, T 161/1371.
[20] Wood, *Groundnut Affair*, pp. 105–9; Thomas, *Strachey*, p. 249 on the Board appointees, especially Plummer; *Hansard* vol. 443, col. 2051, 6 Nov 1947 for the salaries. Although Plummer took a pay cut, his salary was still roughly double that of most Colonial Governors. The disparity between pay of permanent civil servants and the salaries offered to imported private-sector 'experts' or 'managers' has been a long-standing civil service grievance. Nothing changes.
[21] Strachey to Dalton, 30 Apr 1947, T 161/1371 (and MAF 83/1748).

pointed towards the scheme's long-term goal of being an enterprise run by and for Africans. To complete the OFC's senior management team, Strachey appointed an executive General Manager. In tune with spirit of the enterprise, Strachey chose a military man. Of Anglo-Irish extraction, Major-General Desmond Harrison, CB, DSO, of the Royal Engineers, had served with distinction in France and Palestine during the First World War, Baluchistan in the 1930s, and as Mountbatten's Engineer-in-Chief in Southeast Asia during the Second World War, acquiring a reputation for leadership, judgement and sound organisation. Now Director of Works at the War Office, Strachey went straight to the Secretary of State for War to plead, successfully, for his release for this job of 'first class national importance'. Harrison too had never set foot in Africa before.[22]

Although ostensibly the Board was a balanced mixture of African, agricultural, technical and managerial expertise, it was quite clear that the whip hand lay with Labour Party loyalists and John Strachey's friends. Even when some began to have 'doubts' about the scheme's viability, they found themselves unable to force the Board into reviewing policies. But with the Bill and the Board both finally settled, the scheme was ready to be transferred into public management.

Handover to the Overseas Food Corporation

A few days after the Parliamentary debate, the Tanganyika's Provincial Commissioner of the Central Province commented:

> Mr Strachey may satisfy the public at home with assurances that there are no difficulties which cannot be overcome but those people who live on the scene of operations will not be satisfied so easily ... Men who a few months ago were full of hope and vigour are showing signs of despondency and even despair.[23]

One groundnutter, A.T.P. Seabrook, who arrived in Kongwa at that time, noted that others remained undaunted: 'Although it was already clear that things were not going according to plan, there was an almost fanatical faith in ultimate success and the setbacks experienced were only the teething troubles to be expected.'[24] It was a scheme drawn up by experts, so it was bound to work. Sheila Unwin also defended the scheme in her letters home: 'I don't think you'd find so many people at home working as hard as quite a lot of the people out here ... Don't people

---

[22] Strachey to Bellinger, 23 Apr 1947, MAF 83/1752. Announcement of Board members was made on 15 May 1947, MAF 83/1839. See also the message from L.A. Plummer in *Our World*, Dec 1948.
[23] PC Central Province to Chief Secretary, 21 Nov 1947, TNA 36826.
[24] Seabrook, 'Groundnut Scheme in Retrospect', p. 88.

want more margarine? Because they will get it, even if not so quickly as they'd hoped.'[25]

The fact of the matter was that the Managing Agent's 'headlong' pursuit of clearing land at any cost meant that the scheme was haemorrhaging cash. By early 1948, money was being spent at the rate of £500,000 a month, with the result that only a year after the scheme was launched nearly a third of its total budget had already been spent, with very little to show for it.[26] It was time to take stock. Strachey had promised to report back to Cabinet in January 1948, and it was time for the nominated chairman of the Board to pay his first visit.

Plummer travelled with Major-General Harrison and W.A. Faure of the UAC – Willie, Dick and Desmond as they called each other – to help demonstrate that the UAC and the OFC were operating as one. In Kongwa they saw the lines of unusable tractors and the primitive accommodation in which the pioneers were living, and recognised that morale was suffering as a result. The only good news was that the experimental plots of groundnuts near Kongwa, grown by Bunting's team, had yielded good results helped by the best rains for years. The team from London reached two conclusions: that effort needed to be diverted from clearing into improving the accommodation and facilities for those doing the work; and that the transition from the Managing Agents to the OFC should be accelerated as fast as possible. It was therefore agreed that this should take place in March 1948.[27]

The report that the Minister of Food presented to the Cabinet on 19 January 1948, and subsequently to Parliament, put a brave face on it. Problems were acknowledged, including the significant increase in the cost of clearing. But this was compensated for by the extent of activity and the continued rise in the price of oilseeds on the world market. The scheme was in any case insulated from judgement on commercial grounds: 'It becomes clear that the criteria to be applied are those by which the success of the initial phases of a modern military operation is judged, rather than those which are usually applied to a commercial enterprise.'[28] Strachey assured the Cabinet that most of the technical problems were now being solved, and though capital costs had increased by £5.7 million and operating costs by £1.6 million, they were more than compensated for by the rising world price. The Ministry of Food were already paying £50 a ton for Indian groundnuts. For Stra-

---

[25] Letter of 29 Dec 1948, Unwin Papers.
[26] Progress reports in MAF 83/1778 give the monthly spend figures.
[27] *PAC Evidence*, 9 May 1950, replies from Faure to qns 2001, 2211. The 1947 rains were exceptionally good. The DC of Nzega District celebrated: 'Glory be to God, the seven lean years are over and the seven years of plenty have begun. At least, it is to be hoped there will be seven.' Sadly, there weren't. Nzega District Annual Report, 1947, TNA.
[28] *Groundnut Scheme: Review of progress*, Cmd 7314, para. 25.

chey, as Minister of Food, it was a win-win situation: if the price rose further, the scheme made even more sense; if it fell, Britain would save on its import bill. Anyway, he reminded them, it 'is the application of Socialist public enterprise in a new and potentially most fruitful field'.[29]

The Cabinet 'considered that an encouraging start had been made with this project', and urged Strachey on.[30] Parliament, however, when it debated the report in March 1948, gave him a tougher time. Alan Lennox-Boyd, Conservative MP for Mid-Bedford (and a future Colonial Secretary) launched a well-informed attack on the delays, the poor quality of machinery, and the divergence of reality from the targets. Others who had visited the scheme, while praising the hard work of the pioneers, reported on the dereliction rate among bulldozers and argued for a smaller, cheaper pilot scheme. But Strachey had answers for them all. The money spent was only capital, an essential upfront investment, and in any case went back to the Exchequer for war surplus goods; lessons had been learnt and would now be applied; and, above all, the need for oils and fats still existed and the world price continued to rise. Moreover, he added, 'if there was an accusation in regard to an over-optimistic picture, it would lie against the United Africa Company', who had proposed the scheme in the first place. So it was as well that the OFC would take over the following month.[31]

The blame game had begun.

That did not stop Strachey and the management of the UAC exchanging warm letters of appreciation on the handover, praising each other for the 'unfailing support, perseverance and sympathetic understanding' on the one hand and 'unfailing helpfulness and enthusiasm' on the other.[32] The Resident Member of the Board, Major-General Harrison, took up residence – in a large marquee for an office, with a board bearing his name outside – and summoned the Managing Agents to account.

The first thing the OFC did on taking over was to look at the books, only to find there were none – the cupboard was bare. The Corporation had not yet recruited its own accountants, so a team from the Ministry of Food's Internal Audit department undertook a preliminary review in December 1947. They found almost none of the information they needed. When the Treasury got to hear of it, they were aghast:

> The report of the Internal Audit Division reveals that there was the most appalling muddle at the end of last summer. There had been serious delay in setting up any proper local audit and ... the stores

---

[29] Memorandum by Minister of Food, 14 Jan 1948, CP(48)18, CAB 129/23.
[30] Cabinet minutes, 19 Jan 1948, CM(48)5th Conclusions, CAB 128/12.
[31] *Hansard*, vol. 448, cols 1484–1529, 11 Mar 1948.
[32] Edwards (UAC) to Strachey, 1 Mar 1948, and Strachey to Edwards, 17 Mar 1948, MAF 83/1752.

accounting arrangements were totally inadequate ... I'm afraid we all rushed into the East African Groundnuts Scheme with such speed and enthusiasm that difficulties were bound to be overlooked and elementary precautions neglected. The O.F.C. have simply inherited a mess.[33]

Given that much of the first year had been spent buying almost anything that didn't move, until there was a proper account of the existing stores and their value, it was impossible to have any idea of what the Corporation's accounts should look like. Coopers Bros. were hired to review the accounting arrangements and recommended a more decentralised structure to ensure proper audit was undertaken on the spot in Kongwa and Dar es Salaam. The only trouble was finding people to do it. As Rosa explained later to the Parliamentary Accounts Committee, it was hard enough getting accountants willing to work in London, let alone East Africa. They had to push the salary on offer up to £2,000 a year to attract any recruits, and it still took time to get them out to Tanganyika. The lack of staff made Coopers' plan impractical, and Rosa reverted to a more centralised system to try and get the OFC's accounts straight. It took a full year before the MoF's Audit Division produced its final Audit and Account of the Managing Agency period, a damning document that described Kongwa as 'the negation of organisation' and chronicled the consequences of proceeding 'headlong' in the false hope of clearing the maximum acreage in the minimum time.[34]

As a corporation, the OFC had a degree of autonomy from the Treasury that limited the latter's right to intervene. Although forbidden from exercising 'undue influence', the Treasury nevertheless knew that, 'in the last resort, we can exercise the necessary control over the Corporation by limiting the advances and controlling supplies of materials.'[35] The Treasury itself also had a new master of unbending austerity.

Sir Stafford Cripps had been a prominent, if frequently maverick, member of the Labour leadership since the early 1930s. A thin, intellectual barrister of strongly left-wing views, he became the dominant figure in the Socialist League and was eventually expelled from the Labour Party in 1939 for his support for the anti-war Popular Front. Churchill nevertheless deployed him in a number of jobs during the war – as Ambassador to Russia (where, as a teetotal vegetarian, his penchant for dining off a plate of raw carrots puzzled his hosts), envoy to India, Leader of the House and eventually Minister of Aircraft Production. Having swung back from the far left to the centre, he was re-admitted to

---

[33] Minutes by Fisher (HMT), 5 Mar and 14 Jun 1948, T 223/120.
[34] 'Final Audit and Account of the Managing Agent Period', Mar 1949, T 233/121. See also Rosa's testimony in *PAC Evidence*, 23 Mar 1950, qns 149–395. The Coopers' team was led by a Mr Perfect: CP(48)175, 6 Jul 1948, CAB 129/28, para. 8).
[35] Minute by Fisher, 14 Jun 1948, T 233/120.

the party in 1945 and was appointed President of the Board of Trade in Attlee's Government. His powerful, religious sense of destiny and belief that he should be Prime Minister (Cripps was educated at Winchester) remained undiminished, and in 1947 he orchestrated a *putsch* against Attlee. This fell flat on its face when Bevin refused to back it and Attlee astutely bribed Cripps with the wider economic remit that Morrison had proved himself incapable of managing.[36]

Cripps was thus perfectly placed when Dalton was forced to resign after carelessly leaking details of his budget to a waiting lobby journalist as he entered the House of Commons to deliver the budget speech in November 1947.[37] Appointed Chancellor, Cripps swiftly proved he was the man for the hour. No-one took more relish in the serious task of tightening the nation's belt.

But for Strachey it seemed at first a change for the better. Dalton had never been a fan of Strachey, whereas Cripps had been a close ally and friend from the days both had been on the far left of the Labour Party. Strachey was included in the discreet private dinners that Cripps held on alternate Thursdays, alongside Hugh Gaitskell, Douglas Jay, George Strauss and, occasionally, Nye Bevan. This gave him the opportunity to chat to Cripps informally, outside the official ministerial channels.[38]

When the Treasury began to ring alarm bells about the Groundnut Scheme in early 1948, urging Cripps to 'put the brake on', he disagreed: 'A more orderly acceleration is a much better aim', he scribbled.[39] But by June that year, as the evidence mounted, he became more worried. On seeing the Ministry of Food's first audit report, he noted: 'This is a sorry story for which the M. of F. must carry the responsibility. Obviously there has been great waste which we can ill afford. We cannot remedy the state of affairs but the future must be guarded and I hope the suggested measures will be adequate.'[40] The Treasury passed the Chancellor's 'grave concern' on to the Ministry, and Strachey urged Plummer to speed up the recruitment of auditors.[41]

Strachey also decided it was high time for him to pay his own first visit to the scheme. He flew to Dar es Salaam in late May 1948 and thence to Kongwa before returning through Nairobi at the beginning of June. The photograph of his arrival at the Kongwa airstrip on 26

[36] Simon Burgess, *Stafford Cripps: A political life* (London, Gollancz, 1999), especially ch.18; also Peter Clarke, *The Cripps Version: The Life of Sir Stafford Cripps* (London, Allen Lane, 2002).
[37] Harris, *Attlee*, pp. 353–4.
[38] Chris Bryant, *Stafford Cripps: The first modern chancellor* (London, Hodder & Stoughton, 1997), pp. 408–10.
[39] Minute by Fisher, and Cripps' manuscript note, 17 Mar 1948, T 233/120.
[40] Cripps minute, 7 Jun 1948, ibid.
[41] Fisher to Huntley (MoF), 14 Jun, and Strachey to Plummer, 29 Jun 1948, MAF 83/1752.

Photo 6.1 John Strachey (in white hat) visiting Kongwa 1948, accompanied by (l. to r.) Dick Plummer, David Martin, Adam Noble and Major-General Harrison (in pith helmet) (Overseas Food Corporation/Crown Copyright)

May reveals the key figures in action – Strachey a tall figure, like The Man in the White Suit, wearing a white trilby, with Plummer looking uncomfortable beside him in a safari suit and briefcase, the solid David Martin sucking his pipe and a dour, pith-helmeted Major-General Harrison striding alongside. Strachey made speeches in all three places vigorously defending the scheme, emphasising how essential it was to Britain's post-war recovery as a complement to the Marshall Plan, and arguing that 'it would be a frightful error if we were to slavishly follow the original scheme'. Everyone was 'learning by experience, keeping their plans flexible and adaptable'. He lavishly praised the efforts of the pioneers and the talents of the Africans employed by the scheme, encouraging all to keep up the good work.[42] Accompanied by Mrs Plummer, he even found time to visit the sick, who at this moment happened to include Sheila Unwin: 'Both were charming', she wrote to her parents. 'Strachey is a huge man, very natural and jolly ... altogether [he] has given a very good impression. He is rather quiet, well-spoken and seems shy and studious.'[43]

What he saw was in many ways truly impressive. Out of nothing, in little over a year, the scheme had carved a vast area ready for farming. Some idea of the vastness was given by a visiting American, one of the foremost agricultural experts in the US, who, on looking out from the small hill at Kongwa, 'confessed that he was experiencing the thrill of his life because there was spread before him the largest continuous area of mechanised arable land in the world'.[44] But Strachey also saw for himself the chaos the OFC had inherited, and tough talking went on behind closed doors, not least with the Tanganyika Administration with whom relations were already becoming strained.

His report to the Cabinet on his return to London pulled no punches on the problems the scheme had encountered. But he made sure that all the punches landed squarely on the Managing Agents. While the UAC had performed its functions to the best of its ability, 'very serious mistakes' had been made, demonstrating that the scheme was indeed too large an undertaking for the private sector to manage. While it may now take six to eight years rather than five for the scheme to reach its full extent, the world's shortage of oils and fats had continued to worsen, and future projections (courtesy of Unilever) looked even worse. As a result, he concluded, 'if we had not launched the groundnut scheme 18 months ago it would be imperatively necessary for us to launch it

---

[42] Wood *Groundnut Affair*, p. 161; *Tanganyika Standard*, 26 and 28 May 1948 (in TNA 35147); Strachey speech to Nairobi Rotary Club, 10 Jun 1948, CAB 124/1090.
[43] Letter from Mills, 2 Jun 1948, Unwin Papers.
[44] *The Times*, 4 Oct 1950, quoted in S.H. Frankel, *The Economic Impact on Under-developed Societies* (Oxford, OUP, 1953), pp. 141–53.

now.'⁴⁵ The Cabinet took his word for it. They were rather more preoccupied in July 1948 with a little local difficulty the Russians were causing through their decision to blockade Berlin.

Once more, however, Strachey had to run the gauntlet of a Parliamentary debate, as the Conservatives now began using Commons Supply days, when a minister had to answer any oral question that was raised about the work of his department, to raise the issue. Strachey deployed the same arguments to this more sceptical audience, but added another: 'It does seem to me of vital importance that in a perhaps, rather humdrum, drab world, we should start some project, some enterprise, which strikes the imagination and this scheme has struck people's imagination.'⁴⁶ People were flocking to work on the scheme, declared Strachey. 'Because they want to get out of *this* country', interjected a Tory backbencher. They were beginning to scent political blood.

Sorting out

With the Minister back in London, the Resident Member, Major-General Harrison, retired to his tent to try to bring some order from the chaos.

Meetings began to multiply, as did the number of suede-shoed bureaucrats brought in to manage the accounts, the stores, the supply chain, the amenities, the public relations... It was at this stage that Alan Wood himself was recruited as public relations officer to the scheme. But like many OFC staff, he was based in their comfortable headquarters in the heart of Mayfair at 31 Hill St, just off Berkeley Square, along with 200 others. One thing people noted about the OFC – it never did anything by halves.

As we have seen, the Tanganyika Administration and older expatriate businesses still regarded the scheme as an alien intrusion. They hoped it would bring them some benefit, but as the mismanagement became more evident, tension began to appear. The OFC found it had to create from scratch much of the basic infrastructure a normal business would expect to find in place, or that would be provided by government. Not just roads and railways, schools and hospitals, but telephones and police forces. They even leased an aircraft from BOAC to provide

---

⁴⁵ Memorandum by the Minister of Food, 6 Jul 1948, CP(48)175, CAB 129/28, attaching a speech by Faure (Unilever) on the coming oils and fats famine. Morrison had received a critical evaluation of the scheme from the former Chief Agricultural Adviser to the Ministry of Agriculture, Sir William Gavin, in April, and thought Strachey's paper to Cabinet 'a bit wishful thinking and woolley [sic]'. But as usual he kept his thoughts to himself and did not speak up in Cabinet; manuscript note by Morrison, 8 Jul 1948, and Gavin to Morrison, 19 Apr 1948, CAB 124/1090.
⁴⁶ *Hansard*, vol. 453, cols 867–78, 12 Jul 1948.

regular flights between Kongwa, Lindi, Dar es Salaam and Nairobi.[47] The Administration resented the diversion of its resources, from the crying need for development throughout the country to a scheme that appeared to be going nowhere fast, at great expense. As we have seen, Tanganyika had been starved of finance for a decade, and was desperate to make up for lost time. The Introduction set out briefly the evolution of Tanganyika's development plans during the 1940s, culminating in a serious Ten Year Plan in 1946. But even once the plans were agreed, Tanganyika lacked the finance and the human resources to implement them. Some cash came from the CD&W funds, some from the Territory's growing revenue (partly a by-product of inflation, partly of healthy sisal prices), but the Administration loyally held off seeking new loans from the London market, at Treasury behest so as not to put further strain on sterling.[48]

It is therefore scarcely surprising that they viewed the well-staffed, spendthrift Groundnut Scheme with envy. Even so, it was striking that at no point during the 1940s, even in the revised plan of 1949, was the scheme seriously factored into the Territory's own development plans – an attitude of mutual disdain that was fully reciprocated by those working on the scheme itself. When a Ministry of Food official visited the scheme late in 1948, he observed that:

> Relations between Government Officers and the Corporation were not satisfactory. Government Officers were apt to regard OFC staff as a lot of 'know-alls' who were disinclined to seek or accept advice from experienced men on the spot, and were accordingly inclined to let them 'stew in their own juice'. The OFC staff, on their side, felt that Government Officers resented their incursion into the country and the inevitable dislocation and disturbance which their activities created.[49]

There was no formal machinery for consultation, so no means of resolving differences when they arose – as they did for example between the OFC and the East African Railways and Harbours over the Southern Province developments, a row that was reported in the *Financial Times*.[50] A Colonial Office official visiting the following year was 'very much struck while I was in Tanganyika by how very little the Tanganyika Government knew of what was going on'. The Acting Governor even admitted that they got most of their information about the scheme from its monthly publication *Our World*.[51] They

---

[47] OFC, *Second Annual Report*, p. 49.
[48] See material for 1946 in CO 691/200/42501 and CO 691/198/42303.
[49] Scott minute, 24 Feb 1949, CO 691/205/2; also Dodd to Lee, 30 Mar 1950, MAF 83/1940.
[50] Quoted by Lennox Boyd, MP, *Hansard*, vol. 448, col. 1490, 11 Mar 1948.
[51] Surridge to Colonial Secretary, 2 Mar 1949 and Eastwood minute, 7 Aug 1949, CO 691/204/4.

tolerated it because they had to. But they showed little interest in finding out more than the minimum necessary. When shown a copy of the November 1947 Progress Report from the Managing Agents, Tanganyika's Director of Public Works commented that they seemed to be building roads and airstrips he knew nothing about, and was 'concerned in connection with these activities that expensive haste is replacing sound consideration and the results will be prejudiced thereby.'[52] The locals wryly observed that the scheme had imported enough Angostura Bitters in 18 months to last the rest of Tanganyika's Europeans for 70 years.[53]

In fact, as morale on the scheme faltered, the consumption of alcohol went up. In 1948, it was estimated that half of all the liquor imported into Tanganyika was consumed at Kongwa. The staff there felt increasingly leaderless. By September, the heads of department on the scheme submitted a joint memorandum to Harrison expressing their deep concern at the way things were going. It was met with complete silence. The reason, as Rosa later admitted was that it was already apparent that the blueprint to which they were working, set out in Wakefield's report, was completely unrealisable. But there was as yet no alternative. There wasn't even a budget.[54]

So Harrison started work on a budget and a plan. He looked at the experience gained so far. Wakefield had proposed to clear 150,000 acres in 1947, but they had managed only 15,000. The 1947 target was transferred to 1948, but was gradually reduced until by December it was recognised that they would only clear barely 50,000 acres in the year. By the end of 1948, and the end of the planting season, only 35,000 of those were actually planted. It wasn't just the roots that slowed things. Once cleared, the ground turned quickly to the consistency of a hard tennis court after a single shower of rain – giving rise to the rumour that the tractor drivers had accidentally spread cement powder instead of fertiliser on the fields, the two being stored in similar sacks in the same hut.[55]

As the acreage shrank, the costs rose. Wakefield's estimate of £3–£4 to clear an acre had risen tenfold, to £30–£40; and the total cost of production, which Samuel had put at £7 13s 2d and Wakefield at double that (£14 5s 6d), was now around £60 a ton – the same as the world price. By the end of 1948, £16 million had already been spent, and not a peanut exported.[56]

[52] Minute by DPW, 24 Nov 1947, TNA 36826.
[53] *Picture Post* (London), 19 Nov 1949, p. 18.
[54] Seabrook, 'Retrospect', p. 89; Wood, *Groundnut Affair*, p. 168; Rosa in *PAC Evidence*, 23 Mar 1950, qns 259–60.
[55] OFC, *First Annual Report*, pp. 5, 17; Harrison, quoted in BBC Radio 4 'The Great Groundnut Scandal', 28 Jul 1982.
[56] OFC, *First Annual Report*, passim.

Photo 6.2 Ploughing the experimental plot at Kongwa (Hugh Bunting, courtesy of Edward Bunting)

Harrison was a methodical man. He took all the information they had, about clearing, yields, rotation and costs, rationalised the clearing plan to simplify transport, and calculated what it would now cost, and over how long, to deliver the targets in the White Paper. It came to around £100 million in total over 10 years, with a net borrowing requirement of £66.5 million once anticipated revenue from the crops was included.[57]

This was the plan that, in December 1948, Harrison took back to the OFC Board in London for their consideration.

---

[57] Harrison's plan and the costings in Wood, *Groundnut Affair*, pp. 187–90; Morgan, *Colonial Development, Vol. II*, p. 286; *PAC Evidence*, Annex 3, 'OFC Development Plans', p. 115.

7

1949: The Crisis

It was not a very Happy New Year for the OFC.

Dinner at the Café Royale

Harrison's plan, which acknowledged the true scale of the escalation of costs and the delay to the proposed timetable, came as a shock. Plummer and the OFC Board realised that anything along the lines he proposed would require more money than the Overseas Resources Development (ORD) Act provided, and therefore require Parliamentary legislation to amend the Act. Plummer and Strachey agreed that an informal approach direct to Stafford Cripps stood the best chance of success. A dinner was therefore arranged at the Café Royale, a legendary restaurant just off Piccadilly (beloved of Oscar Wilde and Winston Churchill), for Cripps, Strachey and the OFC Board on 4 January 1949.

Nobody knows exactly what was said at the dinner. But it is clear that when Plummer outlined the OFC's plan to Cripps, he categorically rejected any increase in the Corporation's spending limit of £55 million. Under no circumstances would the government introduce amending legislation. Any new plan for the scheme had to be found within that limit; they must 'cut their coat according to their cloth'. The OFC Board were given until September to draw up a new plan within these limits, to allow it to take account of the 1949 harvest. But for now it left the scheme – once more – without a plan.[1]

What made Cripps so intransigent? Three things would have been weighing on his mind. The scepticism of Treasury officials had been growing throughout 1948, and was increasingly borne out by the facts reported by the OFC itself. It was therefore only prudent to limit the

---

[1] The conclusions of the dinner are recorded in Strachey to Cripps, 5 Jan 1949, MAF 128/11; quote from Fisher to Gregoire, 1 Jun 1949, MAF 83/1940; and see Wood, *Groundnut Affair*, pp. 197–8.

government's liability. Secondly, though Strachey was right that the world price for oils and fats remained high, the Cabinet was no longer as obsessed with food as it had been the year before. Strachey's success in other areas, arranging long-term bulk contracts with producers for major staples, along with an easing of world shortages, had improved the position considerably. Thirdly, Attlee's Cabinet were increasingly preoccupied with other problems, above all the deteriorating international climate with the onset of the Cold War, and the deteriorating economic situation as the pressure on the pound continued to mount.

Though Marshall Aid was beginning to bring an increased flow of dollars into the country, there was still a huge dollar gap. Britain's foreign exchange reserves and the balance of payments both remained precarious. Cripps was therefore forced to maintain strict spending controls at home in order to avoid unmanageable pressure on sterling. He could scarcely slam the brakes on for the rest of the government while stepping on the accelerator for the Groundnut Scheme. He was willing to see the scheme continue, but only within the financial limits already set. That was as far as the Treasury was willing to compromise.[2]

Depression and drought

Things were no better in East Africa.

Whether it was the strain of putting together the new plan, or the frustration of hearing it had been blocked, or simply that the climate in Kongwa did not agree with him, was never clear. But at the end of 1948 Major-General Harrison fell ill with anaemia, left for Britain on sick leave, and never returned. His deputy similarly fell ill and left. In their absence, Plummer himself moved out to East Africa and for three months ran things on the spot. By Strachey's later account, Plummer had had no choice but to take over personally at a time, 'when the scheme was almost in ruins'. Only thus, Strachey told Attlee, was he able to implement a series of tough organisational and cost-cutting reforms that salvaged the operation and put it on a viable footing.[3]

But that was not the view on the spot at the time. Plummer seems to have been almost universally loathed by the scheme staff. No-one had a good word to say for him. It may have been his efforts to rebut rumours about Harrison and his plan that subsequently turned out to be true; it may have been his lack of communication skills, his direc-

---

[2] Burgess, *Cripps*, pp. 270–5; Kynaston, *Austerity Britain*, p. 347, Harris, *Attlee*, p. 429.
[3] Strachey to PM, 22 Dec 1949, CAB 124/123.

torial, Beaverbrook-style management, and his determination to root out waste; or it may have been his ignorance of African agriculture and the practicalities of the work that was being done. But, whatever it was, his reputation with those whose job it was to deliver the scheme never recovered from this time in Africa. 'He has been out here for five or six months now, and I think everybody is wishing he would go home ... as he has really made rather a fool of himself by interfering in things he ought to have left alone', reported Sheila Unwin in June 1949. She later added: 'Although I know little of the man personally, he is heartily disliked, and I believe his dealings regarding the scheme have often been verging on the crooked. I think there's little doubt that he has given things a twist to serve political ends.'[4]

On his arrival in January, the heads of department re-submitted their memorandum complaining about the lack of a plan, constant changes in instructions and consistent neglect of the views of the men on the spot. One of the problems was that the man on the spot kept changing too. Alan Wood recalled:

> When I made my second visit to East Africa in March 1949, I found scarcely a senior executive left whom I had met in July 1948. Nobody knew when a plane would arrive from England with somebody on board to take over their jobs; and men went on holiday half expecting to find someone else sitting at their desks when they got back.[5]

Two of the new arrivals were Professor John Phillips and George Raby. The South African agronomist Phillips was one of the most prominent agricultural scientists in the Commonwealth. He was only persuaded to leave Witwatersrand University, where he had taught Bunting, to join the scheme when the South African Prime Minister, General Smuts, himself gave his permission. He arrived in Kongwa as Agricultural General Manager following David Martin's departure back to the UAC at the end of 1948. He was subsequently promoted to joint General Manager alongside Raby, a British engineer brought in to replace Major-General Harrison, who came straight from managing the construction of steel mills in South Africa.[6]

But no changes in management could do anything about the 1949 harvest. It was a disaster. The 1948 rains were late in coming, so that no planting was possible until Christmas, instead of October/November.

---

[4] Letters of 12 Jun and 8 Dec 1949, Unwin Papers; Listowel, *Making of Tanganyika*, p. 150, who claims Plummer was known in Kongwa as the "Plum tart". This local view was corroborated by Le Maire, interview 12 Oct 2007.

[5] Wood, *Groundnut Affair*, p. 201; *Our World*, Dec 1948, p. 3; Seabrook, 'Groundnut Scheme in Retrospect', p. 90, who quotes one frustrated head of department complaining: 'You cannot recast the plan and re-plan the caste at the same time!'

[6] Wood, *Groundnut Affair*, pp. 157, 220.

Photo 7.1 Aerial view of Unit I farm at Kongwa (Overseas Food Corporation/Crown Copyright)

Rain was then at best patchy until Easter, after which it dried up completely. Throughout Tanganyika, 1949 saw the worst drought for 30 years. At Kongwa, total rainfall for the season was barely 12 inches rather than the 20-plus needed, and at harvest time the crops were so scorched and desiccated that yields were far below estimates, and some fields not even worth harvesting.[7]

The small 1948 harvest had, with good rains, delivered average yields of 500 lbs per acre, though this was partly a result of testing several varieties of seed with yields ranging from 200 to 900 lbs per acre. Despite selecting only the best varieties, the average yield in 1949 was only 245 lbs per acre. True, the area planted was eventually 47,000 acres. But of that only 25,000 acres was actually planted with groundnuts. The rest had been sown with sunflower, for which the yield was a bare 99 lbs/acre. This crop had been experimented with in 1948 and seemed amenable to the conditions. It was also much quicker to sow and could be planted without as much preparation of the land, even if it did require bees for pollination, which groundnuts did not. As the planting of groundnuts proved too slow – the available time was too short for the vast area to be covered – the order came from the OFC Board to plant up the maximum possible acreage with sunflower so that a decent area could be broadcast to Parliament. These areas were called 'political sunflower' by the groundnutters. But faced with a failure of the rains, the sunflower proved even less drought resistant than groundnuts, and the decision simply compounded the awfulness of the 1949 harvest.

[7] Tanganyika Territory, *Agricultural Report*, 1949, TNA.

There was virtually nothing to export to the hard-pressed, fat-starved 'housewives of Hounslow'.[8]

Not even the ceremonial arrival, complete with police band and plumes, of the new Governor of Tanganyika, the bluff, boisterous and rotund Sir Edward Twining (a son of the famous tea family of that name), could hide the stark problems the scheme faced.[9] At the end of its first year of operations, the OFC had little to report to Parliament except massive endeavour for little product. On top of which, the scheme's costs were now running at £1 million a month.[10]

Parliament

Not surprisingly, Parliament was getting restive. By December 1948, the Opposition were already giving Herbert Morrison a roasting in Parliament over the lack of accountability of the OFC. Not only the OFC Board, but the Minister of Food refused to answer straightforward questions about the Corporation's operations. Morrison did his best. The men running the scheme were businessmen, he said, 'and if we suddenly plunge them into the middle of the Floor of the House and knock them about, we may well retard their business efficiency.'[11]

The knock-about stuff was led by the shire Tories: Colonel Stanley, Colonel Ponsonby, Captain Crookshank and their ilk. They sensed a chink in Labour's armour, a point where their scepticism about state enterprise would prove to be well-founded. Starved of formal debating time, they continued to use the MoF Supply days and oral questions to mount their assaults. At the end of one futile attempt to get Strachey to make a statement on the scheme, the Conservative MP, Sir W. Smithers, was reduced to spluttering rage:

> *Sir W Smithers*: [the Minister] is adding another colossal blunder to his already long list. May I ask him how much longer he is going to pour the good money of the taxpayers of Britain down the Socialist sewer? May I –
>
> *Mr Speaker*: This supplementary question is getting very, very lengthy.
>
> *Sir W Smithers*: May I say that it is not Africa that has got nuts: it is this Government.
>
> *Mr Strachey*: I am extremely sorry to hear the hon. Member call a part of the British Empire a sewer.

---

[8] OFC, *First Annual Report*, pp. 18–21; *Hansard*, vol. 466, cols 1769–70 (14 Mar 1949) and vol. 467, cols 10–14 (11 Jul 1949); Wood, *Groundnut Affair*, pp. 158–63.
[9] Le Mare interview, 12 Oct 2007.
[10] OFC, *First Annual Report*.
[11] Morrison in *Hansard*, vol. 459, col. 1541, 17 Dec 1948.

Sir W Smithers: I called you a sewer.

Mr Skeffington-Lodge: Is it in Order, Mr Speaker, for an hon. Member to refer to you as a sewer?[12]

And so it went on.

On 14 March 1949, the Opposition launched their first full frontal attack on the scheme. Captain Crookshank castigated the lack of official information on the scheme's progress. Despite this, a certain amount of information had leaked out in the press and from visiting MPs, painting 'a picture of muddle, mismanagement, miscalculation and waste of all sorts and, up to now, of no appreciable results.' Clearing had been so slow and the eventual yields so low that it 'knocks the bottom out of all the forecasts.' Surely the mistakes could have been avoided if the scheme had proceeded more slowly. Henderson Stewart, MP for Fife, argued that the 'mad tempo' of development had been entirely dictated by Whitehall, not the Managing Agents themselves. Others pointed out that Wakefield's original estimates were already proven to be wildly wrong, that clearing was well behind schedule, that rainfall at Kongwa was wholly inadequate, that most of the chief officers had already resigned or left, and that the total cost of the scheme looked like escalating to at least £80 million. 'We are losing not only money, but skill, raw material and capital goods' that were sorely needed at home. The government might as well have spent £25 million on growing arctic plants in the middle of the Sahara, declared Lt-Col. Sir Walter Smiles.[13]

Strachey fought back. The original estimates had been the subject of scrutiny by the best experts of the time, not just Wakefield, and had been endorsed by the Ministry's Special Section. He 'categorically' denied that he had imposed unreasonable speed on the scheme's development, and defended the use of sunflower as a supplementary crop. But he acknowledged that adjustments were necessary in the light of experience. The OFC now believed that it could produce the target of 600,000 tonnes of oilseeds a year from 2 million acres rather than 3 million, by revising the rotation and cropping plans. Admittedly 50,000 acres under cultivation was less than had been anticipated, but it was already a vast area, equivalent to farming a mile-wide strip from Westminster to Portsmouth. Future expansion would nevertheless be mainly in the south, a 'smiling and attractive land' where rainfall was more reliable. Costs, he admitted, would increase to 'anything up to double' the original estimate, but would remain within the ceiling set by the ORD Act. What he did *not* tell Parliament, that he had shared three days before

---

[12] *Hansard*, vol. 459, cols 819–20, 13 Dec 1948. It is the British Parliamentary custom that all remarks are addressed to the Speaker, not the speaker.

[13] All the quotations in this paragraph are from *Hansard*, vol. 466, cols 1755, 1759, 1838, 1849, 14 Mar 1949.

with Cabinet, was that the effective start of the scheme had been delayed by two years, and he now expected the scheme to take 10 years to reach full production rather than five.[14]

Put to the vote, the Government won easily by 231 to 113.

Nevertheless, the Public Accounts Committee were beginning to pay more attention to the scheme. In June they grilled the Government Auditor General, Sir Frank Tribe, and the new Permanent Secretary at the Ministry of Food, Sir Frank Lee, on who exactly was taking responsibility for the financial conduct of the OFC. To whom were they answerable: Parliament, the Government, the Minister or just their own Board? They got no clear answer from the mandarins.[15]

Strachey decided it was time to visit East Africa again to see for himself what was happening on the ground. He left on 19 June 1949 by flying boat, and returned on 3 July. On 28 June, he and Plummer had a meeting with the senior management at Kongwa. As well as Phillips and Raby, this now included the OFC's new Financial Controller, Jack Troughton. Financial Secretary in Kenya from 1946–49, the balding Troughton came with a reputation for toughness and blunt speaking that the OFC felt they needed in order to get their finances under control. He was horrified at the financial arrangements he found in place ('My old grandmother always warned me against cost plus', he was heard to say), and immediately put in place plans for retrenchment to bring costs down below £12 million for the current financial year. This did little for the already fragile morale of staff on the scheme, and Strachey was told that some guarantee of continued employment and continuity of management was desirable to steady the troops.[16]

By the time he got there, the scale of the disaster of the 1949 crop was fully apparent, and Strachey asked what the realistic future prospects were for the following year. Phillips gave an honest assessment. At Kongwa, groundnuts should be confined to the land with good yields and easy lifting, and he was looking to turn the rest of the cleared area into pasture for cattle. Urambo was making better progress and should continue according to plan. But development of the Southern Province areas was proving slow and expensive, with a serious lack of available water. Following his words to Parliament, Strachey argued hard for persevering with the southern areas: a big investment had already been made, and it should be given a chance to prove its worth. Raby, the relative newcomer, still full of optimism, supported.[17]

---

[14] Ibid. Also Memorandum by Minister of Food, 11 Mar 1949, CP(49)63, CAB 129/33.
[15] See the extracts from Jun 1949 in T 223/121.
[16] Wood, *Groundnut Affair*, p. 148. On Troughton, see David Throup, *Economic & Social Origins of Mau Mau* (London, James Currey, 1987). p. 283.
[17] Note of meeting at Kongwa, 28 Jun 1949, MAF 83/1905.

Speaking to the staff at Kongwa and the press in Nairobi, Strachey did his best to rally morale and respond to the critics. He was reported by *The Times* as admitting that the Groundnut Scheme was evolving into 'a food producing scheme in which groundnuts, though a principal crop, will no longer be the main objective. The original White Paper is now regarded more as an idea than a rigid programme.' He scotched rumours that the Conservatives would close the scheme down if they won the next election (already not much more than a year away): they were unlikely to win, and even if they did, though critical of the scheme, had not threatened to close it.[18] Back in the UK, he told Parliament that the drought had proven a bitter disappointment to the staff of the scheme, and exports to the UK would be no more than a few thousand tons. But he promised the following year would be better.[19]

Strachey was not the only visitor to the scheme that summer. Sir John Barlow, Conservative MP for Eddisbury, paid his second visit to the scheme in June, just before Strachey. He too publicised his impressions, both in the *Manchester Guardian* and in the next Parliamentary debate on the Ministry of Food's Supply on 27 July. These impressions were rather less upbeat than Strachey's. In a catalogue of waste, Barlow listed the enormous inputs the scheme had consumed and the minimal output it had achieved: 400 bulldozers, a quarter of which had never even moved, the 1,000-odd vehicles, the hundreds of European staff and 11,000 African workers now employed on the scheme, the lack of water, the waste of precious dollars, and the disappointing yields. He concluded the scheme needed serious overhauling. Backed up by other Tory MPs, it was the most serious attack on the scheme so far. The debate was also beginning to take on an increasingly party political and ideological tone. The Conservatives blasted Labour mismanagement and accused the Government of the very exploitation of imperial resources they denied. Labour MPs replied again that the Tories would have left it all to private enterprise, or not even made the honest attempt to develop African resources in the first place.[20]

On this occasion, for once, Strachey left the hatchet work to some of his Labour colleagues, including a young Jim Callaghan. Confident in the Government's majority (they won the vote again by 257 to 111), Strachey kept his remarks to a minimum and said little about the future. He pinned great public hope on Professor Phillips's agricultural expertise and opinion that the scheme remained viable, particularly with the opening up of the south, where 2,000 acres should be planted for the next year, on top of the 19,000 acres in Urambo and 100,000 acres at Kongwa,

---

[18] *The Times*, 30 Jun and 1 Jul 1949.
[19] *Hansard*, vol. 467 cols 10–13, 11 Jul 1949.
[20] Barlow's article in the *Manchester Guardian*, 9 Jul 1949; debate in *Hansard*, vol. 467 cols 2485–2554, 27 Jul 1949.

which would be the limit of development there. In public at least, Strachey remained robust and confident. The scheme would go on.

Behind closed doors

But debate over the scheme's future was also raging behind the closed doors of Whitehall. Creech Jones, the Colonial Secretary, was increasingly nervous, worried no doubt by the Opposition demand that the scheme be transferred to Colonial Office control.[21]

In the Treasury, concern was becoming alarm. By the end of March 1949, £20.3 million had been spent, £7.3 million of it going to the Managing Agents, and an estimated £12.6 million was needed for the next financial year. The Treasury put a cap of £1 million a month on advances to the scheme. But by June 1949, all the key Treasury officials – Compton, Fisher and Sir Bernard Gilbert – were aware of the grave crisis in the scheme and demanded that drastic action be taken to prevent it ploughing to financial disaster. Some even demanded an independent enquiry into how the OFC got into such a mess. The Chancellor was briefed to propose one, but once more they found that Strachey had got to him before they had. On 6 June that year, Labour held a Party conference in the seaside town of Blackpool. Officials, as usual, were excluded from the event, so Strachey was able to speak unhindered to Cripps and persuaded him to allow the OFC and Ministry of Food to come up with their own proposals for the future of the scheme. This at least bought them some time.[22]

But as July moved into the dog days of August, Treasury opinion hardened. Their long-standing suspicion of Rosa and Wakefield turned into a determination to change the OFC Board and bring in some more independent voices.[23]

Their champion, however, had retired from the field. Cripps had taken refuge during the summer in a Swiss sanatorium, having worked himself into the ground and begun to suffer a serious gastric ailment that made it difficult for him to eat or sleep. From there, he was, like the rest of the Cabinet, preoccupied with the growing pressure for a devaluation of sterling. As in 1947, Britain's foreign exchange reserves were rapidly dwindling, but this time the only escape was a drastic cut in the sterling-dollar exchange rate. In early September Cripps and Bevin travelled to Washington, two ailing men in defence of an ailing currency. There they finally agreed on a cut in the exchange rate from $4.03 to $2.80 to the

---

[21] Creech Jones minute, 9 Aug 1949, CO 691/204/4.
[22] Correspondence and minutes for Jun 1949, T 223/84; note of meeting on cash advances, 30 May 1949, MAF 83/1938.
[23] Notes from Jul–Aug 1949, T 223/84.

pound, a rate that kept the price of a loaf to no more than 5½d, which Bevin deemed the most the working man could bear (provided it was a white loaf, not the grey-brown 'national loaf' that he disliked so much). Food remained at the heart of even exchange rate decisions.[24]

The devaluation was announced on 18 September 1949. On 30 September, the Ministry of Food finally communicated the OFC's revised plan for the Groundnut Scheme, together with the draft Report and Accounts for its first year of operation, to Whitehall colleagues.[25]

The Report and Accounts set out in 160 pages of detail the labours of Hercules that the OFC had undertaken: gathering equipment, building infrastructure, clearing the land and cleaning the Augean stables that were the stores and accounts. Despite all the work that had been done, however, the OFC's auditors, Cooper Brothers, felt obliged to insert a qualification in the Accounts:

> We are unable to report that in our opinion proper books of accounts have been kept by the Corporation and that we have obtained all the information and explanations which, to the best of our knowledge and belief, were necessary for the purposes of our audit because –
>
> (1) for the reasons set out in the Explanatory Notes, proper records of expenditure relating to the Fixed and Current Assets were not maintained,
>
> (2) there have been many instances where documents in support of transactions recorded in the books have not been produced to us.[26]

In the private sector, such words would produce alarm and despondency among the shareholders and normally ring the death knell for a Board of Management. But the Groundnut Scheme was different.

For the future, the OFC examined two options: abandoning the scheme completely, or limiting it to 600,000 acres. The former, it argued, would produce a 'dead loss' of £32 million with no effective benefits. The latter, on the other hand, could produce a viable scheme that would deliver a profit on operations from 1954, at a maximum borrowing requirement from the Exchequer of £44.6 million in 1953. This left £3 million in reserve under the ORD Act, plus £2 million for the Queensland pig farming scheme (another story in itself). It recommended the second option – continuing with a more limited scheme.[27]

---

[24] Hennessy, *Never Again*, pp. 372–6; Harris, *Attlee*, pp. 436–8; Alec Cairncross and Barry Eichengreen, *Sterling in Decline: The devaluations of 1931, 1949 and 1967* (Oxford, OUP, 1983), ch. 4. On 18 September, staff on the Groundnut Scheme were given 'an unexpected holiday, owing to the devaluation of the pound'. Letter of 22 Sep 1949, Unwin Papers.
[25] Bishop (MoF) to Fisher (HMT), 30 Sep 1949, T 223/84.
[26] OFC, *First Annual Report and Accounts*, p. 66.
[27] Bishop (MoF) to Fisher (HMT), 30 Sep 1949, T 223/84.

Strachey lost no time in putting the case to his fellow ministers. On 10 October he wrote a 12-page letter to Cripps and Creech Jones attaching the proposals and arguing for the 600,000 acre scheme.[28] He admitted that the fundamental error had been the initial under-estimate of the cost of clearing, but emphasised that the OFC was now proposing a major curtailment of the scheme, including an immediate cut in the current year's spending from £12.6 to £10.6 million, with the winding up of the cost-plus contracts with Mowlems and Paulings. In support of continuing, he drew on the views of the two East African Governors, Mitchell and Twining, who were both 'of the emphatic opinion that the abandonment of the Groundnut Scheme at this stage would be a catastrophe from every point of view: '[it would be] a national setback and indeed humiliation, which would have very widespread consequences both in Africa and throughout the world'. He even cited the reported view of the South African Prime Minister, Jan Smuts, that it 'would deal an almost irreparable blow to British prestige in Africa'. Finally, he appealed to the spirit in which 'we, as a Socialist Government' had entered into the scheme:

> Surely it is because we believe that projects with risks too heavy to be borne by private enterprise single handed could bring untold advantages to the whole nation and, indeed, the whole world, that we feel it right to bring the resources of Government to bear. If we are to abandon a scheme simply because it turns out not to be a commercial proposition, in the sense that it doesn't pay interest in full on the capital invested, are we not denying the very reason which prompted us to undertake such large-scale investment in the first place?[29]

The decision, in other words, should not be based on economics, but on politics.

His bravado, however, concealed a deepening split within the Ministry of Food itself. While the policy side of the Ministry, now under Strachey's former Private Secretary, George Bishop, was wholly behind the OFC proposal, the Finance Division, still under the tough-minded Dr E.E. Bailey, was not. Bishop argued: 'It is not possible to prove conclusively that they [the OFC] are right, but on the other hand, on the evidence which has been supplied it would be the height of scepticism to suggest that they are wrong.'[30] The sceptics, however, took a very hard look at that evidence. In a detailed memorandum on the OFC's financial estimates dated 17 October, Bailey's finance colleagues Huntley and Dyson concluded that:

---

[28] Strachey to Cripps, 10 Oct 1949, T 223/84
[29] Ibid.
[30] 'Technical Feasibility of the Groundnut Scheme', Note by Bishop, 15 Oct 1949, MAF 83/1938.

there are no grounds for believing that continued agricultural operations could be conducted profitably on a cleared area of 20 units [600,000 acres] after 31 March 1954. On the contrary ... revenue would fall far short of production costs in a year when yields of 750 lbs/acre were harvested. [Unless prices rose] an increasing aggregate deficit would result from adoption of the Plan.[31]

The argument was settled at an internal meeting on 18 October chaired by Frank Lee, who, as the new Permanent Secretary, carried the responsibility as Accounting Officer before Parliament. Originally from the Colonial Office and recently in Washington, Lee was a stocky, florid man with crew-cut black hair. Intelligent, humorous, widely read, and a lover of cricket, he was a man altogether more to Strachey's taste than the rather dry Liesching whom Lee had replaced only a month or two before. At the meeting, both sides argued their corner, but Lee made clear that 'there was no doubt in his mind that the future of the groundnut scheme could not be settled on grounds of pure reason, logic or finance'. He set out his conclusions at length in a formal minute to the Minister of Food. It admitted that, 'there is no expectation that the scheme as now envisaged by the Corporation will prove "economic" in the ordinary commercial sense', but any smaller scheme would be even less viable, and abandoning the scheme, as Strachey himself had said, would have disastrous consequences. So he recommended accepting the OFC's proposals. Dr Bailey formally dissented.[32]

In the Colonial Office, Creech Jones's initial reaction to the report and proposals was one of despair:

> This is a very distressing picture on the vast preparations for little result either now or in the future, the slow progress of the scheme and the heavy deficiency in area of acreage under cultivation now and in the future and the remarkable difference with the expert estimates originally submitted. What is alarming is that after all the capital expenditure the scheme will not be able to wipe out the debt and redemption charges and so far as one can read the guarded forecasts will not be profitable.[33]

His officials, however, were strongly – almost unanimously – in favour of the OFC proposals. On grounds of prestige and strategic interest, Britain must fulfil its trust to African people, build up its agriculture and protect its other development schemes by saving something from

---

[31] 'Memorandum on the Financing of the Groundnut Scheme', Huntley and Dyson, 17 Oct 1949, attached to Bishop (MoF) and to Cohen (CO), 5 Nov 1949, CO 691/204/4.
[32] Note of meeting, 18 Oct, and Lee's minute to Strachey, 21 Oct 1949, MAF 83/1938. For Sir Frank Lee, see his entry in the *Dictionary of National Biography*.
[33] Creech Jones manuscript note on Strachey's letter of 10 Oct 1949, CO 691/204/4.

the 'threatened shipwreck at Kongwa'. Andrew Cohen (who had struck up a good working relationship with Bishop) believed the Colonial Office 'must vigorously support the MoF in securing the necessary money to continue the groundnut scheme' and, after a meeting of officials on 25 October, Sir Hilton Poynton, the Deputy Permanent Secretary, advised Creech Jones that 'we all agree most strongly that the Scheme must go on in some form'. The only dissenting voice was, once more, from the agricultural advisers who thought the speed of clearing and proposed crop rotation were both still over-ambitious.[34]

Creech Jones, however, had already been won over by Strachey himself. They met in the House of Commons on 19 October and the Colonial Secretary returned convinced that the drastic cut proposed was sufficient to allow the scheme to continue and thereby preserve all the ancillary benefits which Tanganyika was accruing from its operations. He even agreed to put a separate paper to Cabinet supporting the OFC proposals on colonial policy grounds.[35]

Which left only the Treasury to convince. Officials there were deeply disappointed in the OFC proposals, and were thoroughly convinced that the scheme would never make money. By the end of October, however, Sir Bernard Gilbert recognised that the political argument made it hard to close the scheme down, and the Treasury therefore sought to limit the liability as much as possible by insisting the scheme be reduced to 300,000 acres over two to four years with a review at the end, and that it should be financed from annual Departmental Votes, preferably the Colonial Office's, not direct to the OFC from the Consolidated Fund, so that Parliament would have better scrutiny of the spending. On 1 November the Treasury put these arguments to a meeting called to discuss the draft Cabinet paper. The meeting however, concluded that a further cut in acreage would be 'disastrous' and a transfer to the Colonial Office 'most undesirable'. It was agreed, nevertheless, that both the Colonial Office and the Tanganyika Government should be more closely involved.[36]

Strachey then, on 2 November, sent the Chancellor directly a copy of Lee's minute to him setting out the case for continuation. Cripps passed it to his officials with the comment: 'Does any of this alter the views of the Dept.?' It didn't. But Cripps nevertheless found Strachey's arguments more convincing than those of his officials. On 8 November, he told them that he believed the extra 300,000 acres in the Southern Province were essential to make the new railway and port pay. Fisher's

---

[34] Minutes by Dawson, 6 Oct, Cohen, 8 Oct, and Poynton, 26 Oct 1949, CO 691/204/4.
[35] Undated manuscript minute by Dawson (CO), Oct 1949, CO 691/204/4.
[36] Gilbert minute, 28 Oct 1949, T 223/84; 'Note of meeting at Dean Bradley House' [Ministry of Food], 1 Nov 1949, CO 691/204/4.

note rebutting this point merely produced a set of Chancellorial doodles. Cripps also refused to change the means of financing the scheme because 'it does not seem to me to be practical in this Parliament'.[37] The political arguments, more than ever, were coming to trump the practical ones.

On 11 November, Strachey and Creech Jones circulated their papers to Cabinet.[38] Strachey admitted that the OFC Annual Report would come as 'a disappointment and a shock' to many, and that by the end of March 1950 only 112,000 acres would have been cleared. He then rehearsed the proposals and alternatives, dismissing a 300,000 acre scheme as costing nearly as much without giving the scheme a chance of proving viable. He argued that closing down would mean admitting the waste of £30 million and that 'it would be disastrous for the prospects and prestige of public enterprise if we were to abandon the East African Groundnuts Scheme because some of the risks in the opening years had gone against it.' For Bevin's benefit he noted that the scheme was also a vital part of demonstrating to the Americans that Britain took the development of its colonies seriously. Creech Jones set out the risks to Britain's colonial reputation, agreeing that abandonment would be 'a major disaster for East Africa', stripping it of much of the technical expertise and experience that the scheme had brought. He also argued against the suggestion that the scheme be transferred to the CDC, which had enough on its plate.

Elsewhere in Whitehall, that constant voice of reason, Max Nicholson, did not temper his advice to Morrison. Noting Strachey's acknowledgement in his letter to Cripps that the report would be a shock, he commented:

> It will also shock many who have taken seriously the various reassuring explanations given by the Minister in the past two years, which have turned out to be so abysmally ill-founded ... it is definitely throwing good money after bad to put substantial further resources into this scheme, and unless we can get the United Nations, the World Bank, the United States government or someone else to carry a large share of the baby, it would pay to cut our losses even at this stage and not to break in further new territory.[39]

A few days later, when he saw the joint Cabinet papers, he was even more forthright:

---

[37] Strachey to Cripps, 2 Nov and Cripps manuscript note, 4 Nov 1949, T 223/84; Gilbert minute, 7 Nov, Cripps minute 8 Nov and Fisher minute 9 Nov 1949 (with doodles), T 223/85.
[38] Memoranda by the Minister of Food, 19 Oct, CP(49)210, and 11 Nov, CP(49)231, and by the Colonial Secretary, 11 Nov 1949, CP(49)232, CAB 129/137.
[39] Nicholson minute, 28 Oct 1949, CAB 124/126.

> The Minister of Food reviews the groundnut scheme in a large number of words, but not very comprehensively. As on previous occasions, he glosses over snags and difficulties and often produces a misleading impression ... the Minister has consistently ignored some of the risks and minimised others, and he continues to do so. For instance, in paragraph 11(a) he writes airily, 'Of course, like all other farmers they have to accept the hazards of the weather' as if growing crops in the East Africa highlands were just like farming in Essex. There is nowhere even yet any hint of the fact that on the most optimistic assumptions some total crop failures must be expected ... It is not until 1960 at the earliest that enough experience can possibly have been gained to make unpleasant new surprises anything unusual.[40]

Nicholson recognised that 'on political grounds the closing down of the scheme is ruled out'. But, '[t]he longer the Minister persists in misleading Parliament and the public about the commercial and supply possibilities, the more the scheme will become discredited'. He recommended that it be turned into a purely agricultural research project, and that US support be sought to make it financially viable.[41]

The criticality of the decision for the Government was also reflected in a long minute that the Cabinet Secretary, Sir Norman Brook, submitted directly to the Prime Minister. He set out the three options: to abandon the scheme; go ahead with a more limited scheme, on Nicholson's lines; or accept the OFC proposals. 'I assume', he wrote, 'that there would be no support for a proposal to abandon the scheme. This would mean the complete loss of the money so far spent; it would have major political consequences; and it would involve great loss of prestige.' But he too had no confidence in the OFC's predictions, except that they would never be able to repay the capital. He recommended the Minister [Strachey] take the House and public 'completely into his confidence', and immediately find ways to strengthen the OFC Board.[42]

Both Nicholson and Brook put their finger on the damage done to the Government by the Minister's tendency to be what later came to be called 'economical with the truth'. It was simply storing up trouble for the future.

But when Cabinet finally met on 14 November, it again had other things on its mind. Discussion about the date of the next general election, due by August 1950 at the latest, had been under way since July. Proponents of an early election, including Cripps, lost out to those preferring early 1950, and a February date was finally agreed. This was a Cabinet gearing up to go once more into the electoral lists.[43]

[40] Nicholson minute, 11 Nov 1949, CAB 21/1688.
[41] Ibid.
[42] Brook minute to PM, 12 Nov 1949, CAB 21/1688.
[43] Harris, *Attlee*, pp. 435–41; Bew, *Citizen Clem*, p. 475

The Groundnut Scheme put it in a bind: to retreat would be to hand a significant victory to the Opposition only a few months before the general election; but to advance created the risk of greater financial loss and political exposure in the future. The majority, however, clearly felt that the latter was the lesser of the two evils, and were not willing to admit defeat in the face of Tory attacks. 'The Cabinet agreed ... there could be no question of abandoning the Ground-nuts Scheme', according to the Cabinet minutes. The Foreign Secretary, noted one official, 'gallantly found a defence reason for going on with the scheme, but unfortunately this was not really valid'. Nevertheless, searching questions were asked about the realism of the OFC's estimates and it was agreed to review the situation in a year, when there was more evidence of progress in the Southern Province, on which such hopes were pinned. Most time was spent, however, on how to handle the forthcoming Parliamentary debate on the Report and Accounts. Mistakes had to be admitted, mainly in the original estimates and by the Managing Agents, but it was accepted that the OFC itself could not be exempt. The Treasury demand to strengthen the Board was therefore accepted, and Strachey was asked to agree changes with the Prime Minister.[44]

This one week, from Cabinet on 14 November to the Parliamentary debate on 21 November 1949, is the fulcrum on which the political fate of the Groundnut Scheme swung. It was clear the project was failing; it was clear that it would never make a profit; it was clear Strachey had misled both colleagues and Parliament. Yet they carried on.

A week is a long time in politics

The first step after Cabinet was to strengthen the OFC Board.

Strachey wrote to Attlee setting out his views in blunt terms. Wakefield and Rosa had to go. Wakefield had 'shown very little grasp ... or grip upon the day-to-day agricultural or scientific problems with which the Corporation is faced', while Rosa had 'completely failed to measure up to the responsibilities of his post'; he had 'a lack of grasp and energy' and the auditors had 'made it plain they have no confidence in his ability to get things put right'. As authors of the original report which had proven so disastrously wrong, he argued, they inspired no confidence among men on the spot and should carry the can. McFadyen had proven 'inadequate' and should be demoted from Deputy Chairman, while Frank Samuel had 'undoubtedly failed in certain conspicuous respects', and should not have his appointment renewed when it expired

[44] Cabinet minutes, 14 Nov 1949, CM(49)66th, CB 128/16 (reprinted in *BDEE*, II, doc. 134); Note by Lee, 11 Apr 1950, MAF 83/1938.

in February. But despite all this, the (recently knighted) Chairman of the Board, Sir Leslie Plummer, 'retains my full confidence'. Though he too had made some mistakes, he had shown loyalty, cooperation, imagination, resilience and energy, and had done the best he could with a weak Board. That, at any rate, was Strachey's view.[45]

To strengthen it, he proposed to import a 47-year old Under-Secretary from his own Ministry of Food, Sir Donald Perrott, 'an administrator of sound judgement and great experience … full of drive', and Sir Eric Coates, the last British Financial Secretary of the Indian Empire. In Coates, the scheme finally found someone equal to the financial challenges it faced – smart, experienced, economically literate and no-nonsense in his approach, he had efficiently run the finances of what even then was one of the biggest economies in the world. To provide some kind of agricultural experience following Wakefield's departure, Strachey added the Professor of Rural Economy at Oxford, Professor G.E. Blackman.

Commenting on the letter, Creech Jones meekly protested that he did not entirely agree with the comments on personalities. Morrison too had earlier scribbled to his staff that the solution might be '?Eliminate the Chairman'. But the laconic Attlee simply wrote 'I agree' on Strachey's note, and the deed was done.[46]

Strachey spoke to Wakefield on 16 November, inviting him to resign. Wakefield refused unless Plummer also resigned, and was therefore summarily sacked. So was Rosa. The changes to the Board were announced late on Thursday 17 November, and uproar ensued. Furious at his treatment, Wakefield released the exchange of letters to the press on the Saturday following, and the Sunday papers had a field day with the story – the day before the keenly awaited Parliamentary debate. Wakefield claimed he had proposed a greatly scaled-down scheme in February 1949 to take account of the difficulties in clearing the land, but that Plummer had rejected it. Rosa too defended himself later to the PAC, arguing that Plummer had ignored his earlier suggestions for putting the finances right. But they were Strachey's sacrificial lambs, the scheme's scape-goats, and they knew it.[47]

Strachey's own bitterness towards the authors of the scheme to which he had become such a devoted convert went deep. He told a journalist years later:

> John Wakefield could not have been more wrong in choosing the area he did. Kongwa was utterly unsuited for it. Everything else, expensive machinery, erroneous accounting, numerous mistakes, etc. would

[45] Strachey to PM, 10 Nov 1949, CO 691/204/4
[46] PS/Creech Jones to Dawson, 14 Nov and Attlee to Strachey 16 Nov 1949, CO 691/204/4; Morrison manuscript on Pimlott note, 28 Oct 1949, CAB 124/126.
[47] *Sunday Chronicle* and *The Observer*, 20 Nov 1949. *PAC Evidence*, Rosa's presentation, 23 Mar 1950.

have eventually righted themselves had groundnuts grown in reasonable quantities there.[48]

But the press were also turning against Strachey. Oliver Stanley had warned in 1947 that the Government should beware of the approval of Lord Beaverbrook: 'It is comforting while it lasts, but is apt to be transitory.'[49] Sure enough, even the *Daily Express* joined the public criticism. As early as March 1948, the journalist James Cameron had raised some searching questions in an article in the *Sunday Express*.[50] In October 1949 came the first of two heavy blows: Alan Wood, the scheme's own public relations officer, resigned and went public with his reasons. In an article headed 'The Facts about the Groundnut Scheme' in the *News Chronicle* on 21 October, he praised the efforts and ingenuity of the groundnutters, believed the experimental work was genuinely worthwhile, but concluded that

> the real fault was in still trying to press on full tilt when errors were already apparent ... The Groundnut Scheme to date has been a first class lesson in How Not To Do It, in which one feels at times that almost any conceivable mistake must have been made. If the lessons learnt are not used, then, indeed, £25,000,000 has been spent to very little purpose.[51]

The second blow inflicted an almost mortal wound. The *Picture Post* was a national institution in Britain in the 1940s. It combined the circulation and popular appeal of today's glossy weeklies (like *Hello!* in the UK) with the photographic excellence of *Life* and the journalistic impact of *Time*. It sent photographer Raymond Kleboe and a young Scottish journalist called Fyfe Robertson to Tanganyika for three weeks to find out exactly what was going on. They filed their report in the edition of 19 November 1949 (two days before the debate) under the headline, 'We investigate the Groundnut Scandal'.[52] It was unsparing in its openness and honesty, both about the heroism of the groundnutters, the difficulty of the challenge, the benefit to African workers, and equally about the appalling blunders that had been made and the dissimulation of Strachey, Plummer and the OFC in trying to hide them from public gaze. For a newspaperman, it was apparent that Plummer was peculiarly averse to open government or freedom of information. The article was explicit that 'the finest single thing that could happen would be the resignation of Sir Leslie Plummer'. More-

---

[48] Listowel, *Making of Tanganyika*, p. 153
[49] Stanley in *Hansard*, vol. 443, col. 2037, 6 Nov 1947.
[50] Wood, *Groundnut Affair*, p. 228; Sheila Unwin had met Cameron during his visit to Kongwa and been unimpressed, letter of 15 Mar 1948, Unwin Papers.
[51] Wood's article in *News Chronicle*, 21 Oct 1949.
[52] *Picture Post*, 45: 8, 19 Nov 1949, pp. 13–21. Fyfe Robertson went on to a distinguished career as a journalist and presenter at the BBC.

over it put its finger on one of the core problems, that the staff of the OFC, from top to bottom,

> have no *direct and defined* personal responsibility. They can shelter behind civil service anonymity. The money they spend is not theirs, nor have they any direct financial inducement to spend carefully. The machine is too big and impersonal, and local authority is too hedged about for effective sobering discipline.[53]

When the editor obligingly sent Morrison an advance copy, Max Nicholson noted ruefully: 'They seem to have got dangerously near the truth'.[54] The report made Fyfe Robertson's name and did more than anything else in the popular mind to puncture the balloon of optimism that Strachey had so assiduously inflated.

It was therefore not just the politicians who watched as MPs assembled in the House of Commons on Monday 21 November 1949, but the whole Parliamentary press corps and, beyond them, the British public. At 3.30 pm on a cold, wet November afternoon, John Strachey rose to open the debate. Unusually, the Prime Minister, Clement Attlee himself, sat beside him with what was described as 'a judicial air', visible evidence of the importance of the debate to the Government as a whole, and to Strachey's personal future. It was not until 9.30 pm that night that Creech Jones rose to wind up at the end of a coruscating six-hour debate.[55]

The debate

The purpose of the debate was to take note of the OFC Report and Accounts. The Opposition had tabled an amendment calling for a full independent enquiry into the Scheme.

With his customary eloquence, languid self-assurance and skill at debate, Strachey began with the weakest point – the auditors' qualification of the accounts. He defended the mass purchase of war surplus equipment on the familiar grounds that they were all that was available, were very cheap, and simply re-cycled the money back to the Exchequer. But he admitted that 'the arrival of war stores on a mass scale swamped all the existing arrangements they had at the time'. He acknowledged that Wakefield's original targets had been missed and the difficulties under-estimated. The whole enterprise was high risk, but was not the whole purpose of public enterprise to take such risks

[53] Ibid. (emphasis in the original).
[54] Note by Nicholson on Hopkinson to Morrison, 15 Nov 1949, CAB 124/123.
[55] As well as *Hansard*, vol. 470, cols 36–166, 21 Nov 1949, the following account draws on reports in the *Manchester Guardian*, *The Times* and the *Daily Herald* of 22 Nov 1949.

in the public interest? The Opposition's demand for an enquiry was motivated by party political manoeuvring rather than the needs of the situation. He defended the sacking of Wakefield and the replacement of Rosa by Coates as necessary to get the books in shape. He expressed confidence in the new Board and the management in East Africa, and such confidence in the OFC Chairman that he was thereafter referred to as the 'Plummer's mate'.

Strachey set out the plans for future expansion in the south from 2,000 acres in 1949 to 600,000 acres by 1954. The scheme would then pay its way, though not repay the £45 million capital spent. Still, he argued, if the Government subsidised the British farmer, and subsidised imports, why not subsidise the colonial producer for food that was needed? He quoted Francis Bacon's 17th-century defence of plantations as a long-term investment. 'Let us not falter!' he urged the House, sitting down to a rousing cheer from the Labour benches.

The Opposition had clearly been briefed by Wakefield and launched a wholesale attack on the scheme. Led by Col. Stanley, the shadow Colonial Secretary, they focussed on the dismissal of Rosa and Wakefield. Why now, just before the debate, when it was clear things had been going wrong for months? Why them and not the Chairman of the OFC? There was a sustained attack on Plummer personally, Stanley commenting that it was obvious 'it would take dynamite to move him', as all the other signatories of the memo that criticised him had been dismissed, moved or forced out. Using Strachey's own military analogy, he argued that when an army lost a battle, it was the general who should carry the can.

The dismissals were also blamed for plummeting morale among the staff of the scheme. In response to a direct question from the Liberal spokesman, Wilfred Roberts, Strachey made a categorical statement that was to come back to haunt him:

> *Mr Roberts*: I ask the Minister ... whether he has any information to confirm or deny ... that there is no confidence in the Chairman of the board among the executive staff in East Africa?
>
> *Mr Strachey*: ...As the hon. Member knows, I went out to East Africa last June, and I was very careful to interview, privately and alone, all the senior members of the executive out there and to ask them their opinion and attitude, because these allegations have been made about the Chairman and the leadership of the Corporation, and their replies were that the allegations which the hon. Member has just made were not in fact true.
>
> *Mr Roberts*: I have had other information.[56]

The attacks went further. The Overseas Food Corporation, which should be brought under the Colonial Office, was accused of being just

---

[56] *Hansard*, vol. 470, col. 78.

as hand-to-mouth in their approach as the managing agents, and of suffering from having the Board in London rather than in East Africa. The Southern Province was believed to be not quite the bright and pleasant land Strachey made it out to be, but trying to get any information about the scheme out of the government was like getting blood out of a stone. Mr Anthony Hurd, Conservative MP for Newbury, pointed out that a 600,000 acre scheme may be affordable, but was still not commercially viable. The scheme had already cost 12/- per head of the whole British population.[57]

The debate became increasingly heated, and increasingly partisan, with Labour MPs attacking the Tory record of colonial development (or lack of it) in the 1930s. Conservatives responded by arguing that socialism was doing no better. This culminated in a strong personal attack on Strachey by Alan Lennox-Boyd, a future Conservative Colonial Secretary. Creech Jones did his best in reply. He argued that the attacks on the scheme were overwhelmingly political, particularly those on the Chairman. The scheme had been started from scratch, and three years was too short a time in which to judge it. The United Africa Company had done its best, but left a mess that the OFC was succeeding in clearing up; and the OFC itself should remain under the Ministry of Food, where it belonged.

At the division, Labour won comfortably by 315 votes to 161. But it was a Pyrrhic victory. The scheme was becoming an object of ridicule, and as Manny Shinwell, a minister in that Government, recalled many years later: 'The worst thing for a government is to be laughed at. You never recover from that.'[58]

Going on...

Why did the Government go on with the scheme when all the evidence seemed to point towards cutting its losses and closing it down? There were four reasons.

Firstly, the basic premise underlying the scheme excluded its costs. The scheme was necessary because the food was necessary, and as long as the latter remained the case, the cost was deemed irrelevant.

Secondly, Strachey had made it a flagship socialist enterprise, and there was a political imperative that it had to succeed. It must therefore continue until success could be declared. Imperial, as well as Socialist, prestige was equally bound up in it, with even the Opposition recog-

---

[57] Nominally 12 shillings is equivalent to 60 pence, but in real terms it would today (2020) be worth about £25.
[58] Shinwell interview, broadcast as part of the BBC Radio 4 programme, *'The Great Groundnut Scandal'*, 28 Jul 1982.

nising that 'this scheme has been blazoned all over the world as a great British effort.'[59] It was, as we say now, too big to fail.

Thirdly, there was too much at stake politically. With an election barely three months away, the Labour Cabinet was not willing to make a gift to the Opposition by admitting such an enormous failure. It was clear that the Cabinet was united in trying to brazen it out.

Fourthly, the decision-makers understood too little, or nothing, of Africa, of agriculture or of business. The caution of Whitehall officials was trumped by their political priorities, and they were willing to rely on OFC experts, who were too often no such thing, or were experts in something other than what they were now doing (building steel mills in South Africa was very different from building a groundnut scheme in Tanganyika, as George Raby found).

During this week too, like good civil servants, aware of the PAC breathing down their necks and the inquests and inquiries likely to come after, Treasury officials put in writing, on file, their apologia for the decisions taken. They, or at least the diligent Fisher, were making sure to get their defence in first. The official note listed all the efforts the Treasury had made to put the brakes on or get decisions reviewed, and concluded:

> a major mistake has been the excessive scale of the operations and the speed at which they have been put forward in an effort to reach the original targets as quickly as possible. This has placed an impossible strain on everyone concerned, and is the main reason for everything that has gone wrong.[60]

But for now, the scheme went on.

[59] Col. Stanley, *Hansard*, vol. 470, col. 70, 21 Nov 1949,.
[60] 'The East African Groundnut Scheme', unsigned note by HMT, 18 Nov 1949, T 223/121.

8

The Last Chance

When news of the debate reached Kongwa, there was uproar in the camp.

Mutiny on the *bundu*

Local managers were outraged that Strachey had explicitly claimed their full support for Plummer when they had already put on record, twice in the last 12 months, their lack of confidence in him as Chairman of the OFC. Following rowdy discussions, a collective telegram was despatched to London demanding that Strachey withdraw the statement. If he did not, it was threatened, there would be a mass resignation of all departmental heads. The telegram was signed by four of them: Dr Bunting, the chief scientist, Dr Porter, Dr Welch the Chief Welfare Officer, and Colonel Marchant the Chief Labour Officer.[1]

Morale had always been a bit fragile at Kongwa. The prolonged uncertainty about the future of the scheme in 1949, following the rejection of the Harrison plan, had fuelled concerns among the staff who, closeted together miles from anywhere or anyone, had little to talk to each other about except the scheme itself. Plummer had left a bitter taste in their mouths when he left in June, which Fyfe Robertson and visiting MPs had clearly picked up. Staff were equally aware that an election was in the offing, and the ferociousness of Conservative attacks on the scheme led many to fear that it would be closed down immediately should they win the election. In Urambo and the Southern Province, further from the corporate headquarters and still focussed far more on their pioneering efforts to clear the land, staff were working away happily enough. But the atmosphere at Kongwa was tense. Sheila Unwin reported: 'We are all very annoyed that Plummer hasn't had the sack and would have welcomed a public enquiry. After

---

[1] Papers, including the telegram of 22 Nov 1949 in MAF 83/1968.

all, we have all worked hard and it would show up those who didn't – especially those in high positions who were constantly making mistakes.'[2]

When it arrived in London, the telegram caused acute concern. Misleading Parliament, in those days, was a sackable offence and, in the febrile political atmosphere of an approaching election, withdrawal of the statement would be not just embarrassing to Strachey himself, but hugely damaging to the Labour Party as a whole. Attlee therefore reacted swiftly, summoning Strachey and sending him immediately to East Africa to sort out the problem. Sir Donald Perrott, already out there, dropped everything and flew back to brief Strachey on the insurrection before he went. He was tracked down by a *Manchester Guardian* reporter on 11 December on the links at Tyrrell's Wood Golf course, but was giving nothing away.[3]

A flying visit

Strachey had left, unannounced, the night before by flying boat from Southampton. The tickets for himself and George Bishop had been booked anonymously, on behalf of 'two OFC officials'. But with the press at their heels, it did not stay secret long. They landed the following day in Nairobi and Strachey in turn summoned the two General Managers, George Raby and Professor Phillips, to Kenya. He discussed with them his previous conversations, on which his statement to Parliament was based, and sought their agreement to a 'clarifying statement' to be given in the House of Lords debate on the OFC accounts, scheduled for 14 December. They accepted his explanation, and Strachey reported encouragingly to London that night – a report immediately circulated to Attlee, Cripps and Morrison, and to Lord Hall, who would have to lead for the Government in the Lords' debate.[4]

---

[2] Letter of 24 Nov 1949, Unwin Papers. See also Wood, *Groundnut Affair*, p. 203. It was at this time that the 'Song of Retrenchment' was written (still to the tune of Lilli Marlene):
   Now then up in Kongwa
   On the 'Gogo Plains
   They are checking lists
   And crossing off our names:
   There every day you hear the shout,
   The Troughton shout 'Get out! Get out!'
   You're in the retrenched army
   No longer Strachey's Own.
[3] *Manchester Guardian*, 12 Dec 1949.
[4] Telegrams marked 'Emergency' from Bishop and Strachey to Lee (MoF) 15 Dec 1949, CAB 124/123.

On 13 December, Strachey travelled from Nairobi to Kongwa and, the next day, confronted the mutineers themselves. We have two contemporary accounts of the meeting that took place, one from Alan Wood in his book, *The Groundnut Affair*, and the other a telegram from George Bishop to his Permanent Secretary, Frank Lee, written the same night. They tell a similar story. Hugh Bunting appears to have acted as spokesman for the rebels and, in effect, accused Strachey of lying. He repeated the demand for Plummer's resignation. Strachey lavished praise on the efforts of all involved with the scheme and made clear that the Government was determined to press on with it. But it had just expressed its confidence in Plummer, and been supported by Parliament. He would clarify his statement, but not ask Plummer to resign – though who knew what would happen after the forthcoming election. Phillips and Raby spoke up in support. According to Bishop:

> The executives then made it absolutely clear there was now no question [of] any resignations or threat of resignations. They were aware [of] constitutional problem. They affirmed their loyalty to the project and expressed their determination to do their duty in this critical year ... They expressed their full confidence in present management *in East Africa*.
>
> Later Minister had full and frank talk with two General Managers ... They explained some of the difficulties which they had experienced with the Chairman. It was a helpful talk.[5]

When the meeting broke up, staff gathered in the mess, clustered round the wireless listening, through the crackling ether, to the BBC World Service report of the debate taking place in the Lords that afternoon.

The Lords debate on 14 December was another five-and-a-half-hour marathon. The Opposition made hay not only with the shambles of the scheme but with its increasingly *Alice in Wonderland*-like quality. Lord Swinton, leading for the Conservatives, noted the fact that the Minister had 'softly and silently vanished away' to East Africa and, 'curiouser and curiouser', had not taken the scheme's indispensable Chairman with him. The Tories were provided with additional ammunition in the form of the resignation of the Chairman's own special adviser, Mr J.N. McClean, on 2 December because he had lost confidence in the Chairman himself; and of an exculpatory letter from John Rosa in *The Times* that morning arguing that: 'Large-scale operations carried out at speed are doomed to costly failure, as past experience has shown, and for the same reasons as in the past'. Lord Salisbury joined in, landing some telling blows on both Strachey and Plummer. The Opposition were enjoying themselves.[6]

---

[5] Bishop to Lee, 15 Dec 1949, CAB 124/123 (emphasis added); Wood, *Groundnut Affair*, pp. 220–21.
[6] *Hansard, Lords*, vol. 165, cols 1522–1610.

Lord Hall did his best for the Government to defuse the crisis by delivering the 'clarification' that Strachey had agreed:

> The Minister realises that people outside Parliament and in East Africa might have read this statement as an assertion that he solicited the positive expression of confidence in the Board and the Chairman of the staff in East Africa. This was certainly not what the Minister wished to convey. He would not, of course, have put a direct question to the staff in the form 'Have you confidence in the Board and Chairman of the Corporation?' It would have been quite wrong of him to do that ... His object was to ascertain the general condition of the morale and he took full note of a meeting with the executives and the Chairman collectively in which Professor Phillips expressed himself along the following lines. Although there had been a period of strain, things were settling down considerably ... As the management settled down to plan with a clear consistency of purpose, morale would continue to improve. The management were agreed that it was works and works alone that made morale. He thought that if the Minister could make a definite statement about continuity of employment, the improvement in morale over recent months would continue steadily.[7]

Hall claimed, to general hilarity, that Strachey had gone to East Africa simply to reassure staff about the future of the scheme. At the end of it all, the Government again defeated Opposition calls for an enquiry by 57 to 27. But the damage to the Government was continuing.[8]

In East Africa the next morning, Strachey confronted his nemesis, Bunting, directly. The two were seen pacing up and down in Bunting's office for over an hour, passers-by studiously pretending not to look in. Strachey left immediately after to speak to staff in Urambo and Nachingwea, accompanied by the General Managers and Tom Unwin. Tom's wife, Sheila, close to the action, reflected the local view:

> We have Strachey here at the moment. Great rumpuses unbeknown to everyone at home are going on, but the battle has been won – by Strachey! Nobody here likes Plummer, or has confidence in him, and a real, political game has been going on, whereby we, the people and the Scheme in Africa, are pawns ... We here have the greatest confidence in Phillips and Raby, but no-one cares a tuppenny damn about Plummer.[9]

Strachey flew back via Nairobi, landing in London on 21 December, and travelled directly from Southampton to No. 10 to report to Attlee in person. He set out the substance of that report in a note to the Prime Minister the next day. It is one of the most remarkable documents in the whole extraordinary story.

---

[7] Ibid., col. 1540.
[8] *The Times*, 14 and 15 Dec 1949.
[9] Letter of 17 Dec 1949, Unwin Papers.

Strachey reported that he had achieved the mission on which Attlee had sent him, to defuse the crisis over his 'badly expressed statement in the House', without retraction and without any resignations. He praised Raby's firmness and support and, 'though not so strong a man', believed Professor Phillips' loyalty had been re-established. He acknowledged the hostility to Plummer, but attributed it to the difficult role he had had to play retrenching staff and cutting costs early in the year, without which he was sure 'the scheme would have broken down during the first half of 1949'. He was sure the hostility to the Chairman would have abated once he returned to London, but for one factor – Dr Hugh Bunting.

> Dr Bunting, I already knew, had been a member of the Communist Party, at any rate until he joined the Scheme in 1947. He played an active part in the Communist Party's scientific work and was chairman of the Party's Scientific Policy Committee. He knew that the Chairman of the Board of the Overseas Food Corporation and I were aware of this. He had represented to us that the Party had been opposed to him taking a job with the Groundnut Scheme and that he had broken with them on the issue. I thought that his unquestioned scientific ability might be used and that Plummer and myself, together with the Security Services, would be able to watch for any trace of subversive activities: so I made no objection to his employment by the Corporation. I fear that this may have proved a serious mistake.[10]

He then accused Bunting of fomenting a conspiracy against Plummer and himself, mobilising the other senior managers, whom Bunting referred to as 'the Tories', to send the threatening telegram at the most politically damaging time. While Bunting admitted that it was a deliberate attempt to force Plummer to resign, Strachey told Attlee that he believed it was in reality a Communist conspiracy to discredit the Labour Government as a whole:

> there is no proof that he was working as a Communist Party member carrying out party directions. It is just possible that he was acting on his own for love of personal power. But I do not think so. In my view Bunting never in fact left the Communist Party and is now carrying out a clear party directive designed to ruin the Groundnut Scheme and to do the maximum possible amount of damage to the Government.

'By a curious coincidence', Strachey said, three of the four signatories of the telegram were leaving the scheme to take up other appointments, and Bunting himself was just proceeding on six months' leave in Britain. He could therefore be thoroughly investigated before returning to the scheme. In the meantime, the Opposition and the 'major part

---

[10] Strachey to PM, FM 49/12 (Top Secret), 22 Dec 1949, CAB 124/123 (emphasis in the original).

of the press which is hostile to the Government' would continue to attack Plummer. Like all men, Plummer had weaknesses; but Strachey re-affirmed how crucial he regarded his presence to the successful outcome of the scheme. The Chairman had to stay.

What did Attlee make of all this?

There is no doubt that Attlee liked and admired Strachey. He was articulate, intelligent, economically literate, a good Parliamentary performer and clearly ran his department effectively. Attlee himself later recalled that Strachey had 'done fairly well' at the Ministry of Food – high praise from the Prime Minister.[11] In August 1949, the PM's political adviser, Philip Jordan, briefed Strachey's press officer, Shelton Smith:

> I think that your boss [Strachey] has done a fine job of work and I'm glad that my boss thinks so too. My boss is ... deeply interested in the way your boss has run his department. If the Government get back your boss is certain to get promotion.[12]

But just sometimes – at least on the Groundnut Scheme – Strachey seemed to have a slightly slippery attachment to the truth. He may have been honestly blinded by his vision, by his commitment to make the scheme work. But Attlee could ignore it no longer. It was beginning to damage the Labour Party, and that mattered. There is no evidence whether or not Attlee believed the Communist conspiracy theory, which would have been more plausible in those days than it may appear now, and on which Strachey's own experience in the 1930s might have given him some authority to speak. But it was probably at this moment that Attlee decided, in a new government, Strachey should move departments, and not on the promised promotion. In the meantime, he would do nothing. The fire had been doused, and there was an election to be fought. But it didn't stop the Tories joking that Mr Attlee would be having peanuts for his Christmas dinner.[13]

Was Bunting really a Communist? His father certainly had been involved with the anti-apartheid struggle in South Africa. His son is not aware that he was, though acknowledges he had sympathies in that direction. His former scientific colleague in Kongwa, however, believes that he was, certainly for a while. Sadly there is no chance to put the question directly to Bunting himself. Whatever the truth, he was allowed to return to work on the end of his leave, though the Colonial Office later briefed the new Colonial Secretary that he was: 'Very able, but politically conscious. Have no reason to doubt his loyalty to the Scheme, but a little difficult to handle. Clever as well as able.'[14] But as for

---

[11] Attlee's draft autobiography, chapter on 1945–51, p. 8, Attlee Papers 1/17.
[12] Shelton Smith to Strachey, 6 Aug 1949, Strachey papers, Box 9.
[13] Bew, *Citizen Clem*, p. 479.
[14] 'Personality notes for the Secretary of State's dinner with the OFC', 22 May

the conspiracy, there is not a shred of other evidence to support it. The only person whose interests were served by such a tale of conspiracy was John Strachey.

Elections

On 10 January 1950, Attlee announced that the general election would be held on 23 February, the first winter election since 1910. The 1950 election had 'a curious, fuzzy aura of unreality about it', according to Mollie Panter-Downes, one of the Mass Observation regular reporters.[15] The two parties' campaigns were about as gripping as the titles of their manifestos: *Let Us Win Through Together* (Labour) versus *This Is the Road* (Conservative). The former focussed on consolidating the achievements of the past five years, the latter on breaking away from Socialist controls and bringing freedom back to the individual. Labour's record was the main focus of attention by both.

Attlee embarked on a 1,300 mile tour of the country in an old black Humber, driven with legendary ferocity by his wife Violet (reputedly leaving the escorting police vehicle far behind). But many of his senior ministers – Bevin, Cripps, Dalton, Morrison – were exhausted, sick or absent. For nearly a decade, since the early years of the war when they were brought into government, they had been working flat out first to save the country and then rebuild it. But they were proud of their many achievements – from the National Health Service to full employment – and confidently expected to be returned with a healthy majority.[16]

The Conservative manifesto was interesting in at least one respect. It marked a major shift in Tory thinking by, if only implicitly, accepting the welfare state reforms of Labour and the Keynesian economic policies that had achieved full employment. While they pledged to stop further nationalisations, a major plank in their campaign was the attack on Labour's 'socialist' inefficiency and waste in government, the kind of bureaucratic meddling that was pilloried in the contemporary film *Passport to Pimlico*. The Groundnut Scheme was a gift for them, an ideal stick with which to beat the Labour Government – which they proceeded to do with gusto.

1951, CO 691/211/III. Interviews with Edward Bunting and Peter Le Mare, 12 Oct 2007.

[15] Kynaston, *Austerity Britain*, p. 380. Mass Observation was a form of continuous public opinion monitoring by the Government begun during the War and continued afterwards.

[16] Hennessy, *Never Again*, pp. 387–9; Bew, *Citizen Clem*, p. 482; Harris, *Attlee*, pp. 442–5, according to whom Attlee's swopped his usual Hillman for a larger Humber during the election campaign.

The fact was that the Groundnut Scheme had become a byword for all that was wrong with Labour and the country. In May 1948, a poll had shown that only 16% of British adults had heard of the scheme.[17] Now, however, there was no question that it was a name familiar to almost every adult throughout the country. Everywhere Conservative candidates never failed to mention it, and it was a challenge thrown in the face of many Labour candidates. Frederick Willey, a Labour MP who became a junior minister at the Ministry of Food, recalled a member of the public, 'whose general demeanour indicated that he was obviously politically hostile, popping his head through the window and shouting "Groundnuts". From that, I presumed that "Groundnuts" was a term of political abuse.'[18] Strachey himself felt it necessary to defend his record in his address to his constituents in West Dundee. 'In four or five years time', he predicted, 'when the present development phase of that scheme is completed, I shall be prouder of having been associated with the Groundnut Scheme than with anything else I have done in my life ... and I trust the Conservative Press will be heartily ashamed of the way in which they have attacked it.'[19]

They were not. Like a dog with a bone, they would not let it go. Grist was added to the mill when one of the main contractors, Taylor Woodrow, announced in January 1950 that they were pulling out of the Scheme because they no longer wished to be associated with such a cock-eyed fiasco:

> Neither directors, executives nor staff have any confidence in the policy and ultimate success of the Groundnut Scheme ... Millions of pounds are still being wasted. After three years' experience the OFC is still making the same mistake over again and my company would rather not be a party to it,

announced the Managing Director.[20] It is ironic that the success of Strachey's other policies meant that rationing had been reduced and food shortages were scarcely an issue in the election – but that counted for little.

In the event, Labour hung on, but only just. Despite the record turnout of 84%, their majority in the House was reduced to five as the Conservatives gained 88 seats. There would no longer be a free ride in Parliament on contentious issues. Every vote would be hard fought.

Attlee reconstructed his Government. The big beasts of the party stayed in their posts, though Hugh Gaitskell, as Minister of State for Economic Planning became effectively deputy to the increasingly sickly

[17] Kynaston, *Austerity Britain*, p. 272.
[18] *Hansard*, vol. 477, col. 2161, 18 Jul 1950.
[19] 'To the Electors of West Dundee', Feb 1950, Strachey Papers, Box 10.
[20] *Tanganyika Standard*, 26 Jan 1950; Frank Taylor quoted in Jenkins, *On Site*, p. 53.

Cripps at the Treasury. Strachey retained his Parliamentary seat in Dundee (unlike Creech Jones who lost his), though with a much reduced majority of 4,701, but was, sure enough, moved from Food. Attlee wanted to make him Minister for Air but the incumbent, Henderson, refused to move, so he became Minister for War under Manny Shinwell, the new Secretary of State for Defence. He was philosophical about the move, but was sorely missed by his senior officials who had, despite everything, been charmed by their Minister. As Frank Lee, the Permanent Secretary, wrote to him: 'Let me say at once how greatly you are still missed among us as our Minister. "Never glad confident morning again"'.[21]

It was harder to find someone to take on the poisoned chalice of the Groundnut Scheme. As we have seen, it involved not only the Minister of Food, but increasingly entangled the Colonial Secretary as well. Following Creech Jones' defeat, Attlee offered Dalton the Colonial Office. According to Dalton's diary, 'continuing difficulties over groundnuts' was one of the litany of reasons why the job did not appeal to him.[22] He was happy to stay at Home and Country Planning, and Attlee appointed the practical Welsh trade unionist, Jim Griffiths, to the Colonial Office. Even Creech Jones himself went public soon after with his doubts about the scheme: 'I have always been sceptical about quick results and unplanned development in Africa and have never had time for loose talk about the great open spaces of Africa waiting to be cultivated'.[23]

But the Groundnut Scheme remained for now with the Ministry of Food and, in the end, it fell to Maurice Webb to take up the challenge. A Methodist preacher from Lancashire and Labour Party member from the age of 16, Webb was a long-time journalist and, from 1946, chairman of the Parliamentary Labour Party. Reduced to one leg following an accident at a children's party in 1944, he seemed just the popular, astute, safe pair of hands Attlee was looking for.[24]

Strachey, the visionary leader, was gone. But the Groundnut Scheme continued. The question was, how long could it last?

A new Board, a new budget

It was clear that the Cabinet agreement of November was the last chance to redeem the scheme and its reputation. But even before Webb

---

[21] Lee to Strachey (Private and Personal), 31 Mar 1950, Strachey Papers, Box 10. Thomas, *Strachey*, p. 258; quotation from Robert Browning's *The Lost Leader*.
[22] Dalton Diary, 28 Feb 1950, LSE. His full litany of reasons is quoted in Pearce, *Turning Point*, p. 94.
[23] Quoted by Lennox Boyd, *Hansard*, vol. 477 col. 2044, 18 Jul 1950.
[24] *The Times*, 'Obituary of Maurice Webb', 11 Jun 1956.

had his foot under the desk, it was already clear that things were *not* going to plan, any more than they had previously.

At the end of March, Webb received the proposed OFC budget for 1950/51. In line with the revised scheme, expenditure was cut back from £12 million p.a. to under £6 million, all cost-plus contracts were ended, and development was focussed on the Southern Province. But as officials noted when they discussed it with the Minister of Food, there were

> some ominous pointers as to what was to be expected in the future ... The Corporation had failed to achieve their clearing and planting targets for 1949/50 and did not expect to reach the 1950/51 targets in their long term plan approved by the Cabinet in November 1949.

Actual yields had fallen to 400 lbs/acre, and future yields were estimated only at 525 lbs/acre. Clearing would cease at Kongwa and Urambo and go more slowly in the Southern Province, where part of the new railway had been washed away in the rains and taken three months to restore. More resources were to be devoted to buildings and water supply than to clearing.[25]

Such depressing news must have persuaded Webb – if any more evidence was needed – that Plummer must go. Oliver Stanley had predicted in November that it would take dynamite to move him, and that was more or less what it did. Webb asked the Permanent Secretary, Frank Lee, to deliver the bad news. On 4 April Lee told Plummer that the Minister had decided his services were to be terminated because the country needed a change. Plummer protested that he was being sacrificed to political expediency, and demanded £10,000 and a statement of praise and thanks from the Minister. Lee told him that the Minister had made clear he had no confidence in the Chairman, and was not prepared to use words of fulsome flattery. After some bandying of threats of dismissal and counter-threats of writs, Plummer settled for a tax-free £8,000 and a neutral statement.[26]

Given the close personal friendship between Plummer and his predecessor, Maurice Webb felt he had better break the news personally to Strachey. Though now lodged in the War Office, Strachey still followed the fate of the scheme with a paternal eye, receiving the regular monthly reports from the OFC about progress on the scheme as he always had. Webb's nervousness in broaching the subject, as well as Strachey's passion for the scheme, is clear in his handwritten note to Strachey, dated 17 May:

> I deeply and sincerely appreciate the way in which you received the news I had to give you.

---

[25] Notes of meetings on 28 and 30 Mar 1950, MAF 83/1940; note by Lee 11 Apr 1950, MAF 83/1938.
[26] Letters from Plummer to Strachey, Apr–May 1950, Strachey Papers, Box 9.

> I realise to the full quite what it means to you. Indeed a large part of my anxiety since I approached this question has arisen from my knowledge of your personal position in the matter. I cannot tell you how much I am grateful for your forbearance, and from your not seeking in any way to oppose or complain about the decision which I know must be deeply painful to you.
>
> This is the hardest thing I have ever had to do. I wish I could have avoided it. But there was no escape, given my judgement on what the situation required.
>
> You may be sure I shall do my utmost in the future handling of the change to reduce to the minimum anything which might not be pleasant for you.[27]

A week later, on 24 May, Webb made the agreed statement to Parliament. Plummer was gone. The mutineers had got the captain's head at last.

His place was taken by Sir Eric Coates, who had been the Deputy Chairman on the new Board. His rigorous, dispassionate and effective approach at last brought some sanity to the scheme's finances. As soon as he was appointed to the Board the previous November he had begun a thorough review of the financial situation. He concluded: 'Up to December 1949 the accounts were in a state of uncontrolled disorder ... there remained no easily recognisable system or organisation of administration of the scheme as a whole.'[28] The new budget reflected his best efforts.

But it was not enough for the Treasury. They felt thoroughly vindicated, the new budget confirming everything they had said the year before. 'There is the usual hard-luck story about exceptional drought and famine conditions', commented Fisher, but the numbers simply didn't add up. This time they were not to be circumvented by the politicians. They refused to sanction the budget, and demanded a new long-term plan that could actually be implemented. On the same day he informed Plummer of his dismissal, Lee wrote to the OFC to tell them to go back to the drawing board.[29]

Coates' response, in consultation with the Colonial Office, was to set up the Kongwa Working Party. Their remit was clear: to ascertain whether groundnut production at Kongwa would ever be a profitable venture, and if not, what to do with the scheme there. At last, for the first time, some genuinely independent experts were sent to look at the situation: Sir Charles Lockhart and Professor Phillips represented the OFC; the Tanganyika Administration was at last brought fully into the deliberations through J.C. Muir (Member – effectively minister –

---

[27] Webb to Strachey, 17 May 1950, Strachey Papers, Box 11.
[28] Coates to OFC Board, 8 Mar 1950, T 223/86.
[29] Lee to Dodd (OFC), 4 Apr 1950, T 223/86.

for Agriculture) and Bruce Hutt (Member for Development), both with long experience of the country and a wider understanding of what the government were doing there; the Colonial Office was represented by Geoffrey Clay, its Agricultural Adviser, and academic expertise was provided by Dr H.H. Storey, the Deputy Director of the East African Agricultural Research Organisation, and S.H. Frankel, Professor of Colonial Economic Affairs at Nuffield College, Oxford. The majority of the members had devoted their lives to tropical agriculture and economic development, knew Africa and Tanganyika well and had not hitherto been involved with the scheme. Clay, who had visited the scheme in January 1949 and advised them to reduce the dependence on mechanisation and integrate the scheme with local African production, had grumbled only three months before that, 'I have never been consulted by Mr Wakefield or the OFC'.[30] There was not a newspaper man, Labour Party stalwart or spin doctor among them. They were to become Coates's instrument for putting the scheme out of its misery.[31]

Covering up?

There was no let-up in the public scrutiny. Following the public furore of 1949, the public eye was firmly focussed on the scheme. Every move was scrutinised and dissected. British daily papers began to publish weather reports from Kongwa, discussing the rainfall patterns and groundnut yields. It was an irresistible subject: 'It has sunk to the level of a music hall joke', muttered Dr Bunting – unfortunately overheard by a *Times* journalist and quoted in its gossip column.[32]

The Conservatives continued to demand an inquiry and the transfer of the scheme to the Colonial Office. Denied either, they used all the Parliamentary instruments at their disposal to make sure the scheme stayed on the political agenda. The Public Accounts Committee was their principal tool. It provided the first real opportunity for MPs to quiz the officials and others directly involved. During March, April and May 1950 they took many hours of evidence from the principal actors, publishing their conclusions on the first Annual Report on 12 June – by a strange coincidence the same day the Government announced the establishment of the Kongwa Working Party.[33]

[30] Clay minute, 5 Jan 1950, CO 691/210/3.
[31] Papers on the Kongwa Working Party in TNA 41265 and TNA 35781.
[32] *The Times*, 11 Mar 1950; cuttings in Fabian Colonial Bureau papers, FCB 52/6, Bodleian Libraries, Oxford.
[33] *Second Report of the Public Accounts Committee into the Groundnut Scheme*, May 1950; see also *PAC Evidence*, 23 Mar–9 May 1950, passim; and the report in *The Times*, 13 Jun 1950.

The picture of muddle, mayhem and misuse of funds presented in the PAC Report was overwhelming. The Committee concluded that to undertake such a scheme in conditions of post-war shortages was simply impossible, and the priority given to clearing and production as a result of the urgency of the food situation meant that administration and accounting had been wholly neglected – with disastrous results. The Report was also a clear demonstration that the instruments of Parliamentary accountability were sufficiently robust to hold even an arms-length quango such as the OFC to account for the use of taxpayers' money. They could run, but they could not hide.

Critics of the scheme were provided with another gift in Alan Wood's attempts to publish a book with his own account of the scandal, *The Groundnut Affair*. Wood had already made clear in the press his views on the scheme at the time of his resignation. Working flat out, he had completed a manuscript of the book by January 1950 and submitted it to the left-wing publisher, Victor Gollancz. Gollancz decided it was wise to consult his old friend, John Strachey, who asked him to hang on to the book in the hope of making it less objectionable. But once he had read it, Strachey admitted to Gollancz that he didn't know how to deal with it. He had many comments of detail, but ultimately,

> the whole tone of the latter part of the book is thoroughly objectionable and reveals that it is motivated by spite ... I fear his desire to write an independent book combined with his hostility to Plummer has led him to adopt smear tactics which are more suitable for the *Daily Express* than for a serious book to be published by you.

Ultimately, if Gollancz went ahead and published 'this frankly vile book', Strachey said he would have to denounce it.[34]

Gollancz withdrew the offer of publication to Wood. Wood promptly went public, accusing Strachey of trying to block publication, and the Opposition equally promptly denounced the attempted 'cover-up'. Gollancz was forced to write to *The Times*, claiming that while he had had contact with Strachey, who had sent him a letter with 'astonishing' information, the decision not to publish was his own. Embarrassed by another bout of bad publicity, Attlee once more summoned Strachey, and required him to make a formal statement in the House on 22 March denying that he had made any attempt to prevent the publication of the book.[35]

Still the affair rumbled on. In Parliamentary Questions to the Minister of Food on 27 March, Stanley asked Webb to publish Strachey's letter to Gollancz, saying that as it had been written by Strachey while he was Minister of Food, it must be part of the public record. Webb refused, adding that in any case they couldn't find it in the Ministry

---

[34] Strachey to Gollancz, 13 Mar 1950, Strachey Papers, Box 10.
[35] Draft of Parliamentary statement, Mar 1950, Strachey Papers, Box 10.

records.³⁶ But the mud stuck. It looked inevitably as though the Government were doing all in its power to prevent the true story of the Groundnut Scheme becoming public. Unfortunately for them, as a semi-autonomous agency, employees of the OFC were not covered by the Official Secrets Act, so Wood could publish what he liked. Unless there was something strictly libellous, there was nothing they could do.

Fortunately for Wood there was no lack of publishers in London and, assured of an even greater market for the book, it was swiftly published by The Bodley Head, a staunchly independent imprint. It sold out in weeks.

The Beaverbrook press, however, was clearly out to get Strachey, the Labour Party or both. Apparently on instructions from their proprietor, it chose this moment to run a story that Strachey had himself never left the Communist Party. In the prevailing atmosphere of Cold War paranoia, and following the arrest in January of the spy Klaus Fuchs, an atomic scientist working for the Government nuclear research programme who had been leaking nuclear secrets to the Russians, this was explosive. The public, said the *Evening Standard*, could scarcely sleep safe in its bed when its own Minister for War might be at the least a fellow traveller. Strachey's denials were vehement and honest. Determined at first to sue for libel, he was eventually dissuaded. His reputation for honesty was, just at this moment, a little weakened. Retrospectively, Attlee commented that Strachey, 'while unjustly hunted by the Press, chose to drop a very full-sized brick.'³⁷

With depressingly unavoidable regularity, the Parliamentary timetable brought round the annual Ministry of Food Supply debate on 18 July. This turned into another six-and-a-half hours devoted solely to the Groundnut Scheme. The PAC Report gave the Opposition ample ammunition. Led by Lennox-Boyd, the Conservatives launched their most remorseless attack on Strachey: 'It is not at all the mistakes that we condemn, but the fact that the Minister glossed over the mistakes, misled the House and, in the words of Mr Wood, brought needless discredit on the Government.'³⁸ To others he was 'impervious to reason' on the scheme. Mr Hurd again put his finger on Strachey's problem: 'the real trouble with the former Minister of Food was that to him the groundnut scheme was like a mistress: she was always looking at her best and he would never hear any criticism of any kind about her or her behaviour.'³⁹

---

³⁶ *Hansard*, vol. 473, col. 23, 27 Mar 1950; also *The Times*, 22–27 Mar 1950; *Daily Mail*, 3 Mar 1950.
³⁷ See the draft autobiography in Attlee Papers, Box 1/17, p. 17. Also items in Strachey Papers, Boxes 11 and 12, and Thomas, *Strachey*, pp. 259–60.
³⁸ Lennox Boyd in *Hansard*, vol. 477, col. 2047, 18 Jul 1950.
³⁹ Hurd, ibid., col. 2069.

Webb did his best in reply. He heaped praise on Sir Eric Coates for having mastered the accounts and sent out the Kongwa Working Party. He also signalled a tactical retreat which in reality marked a fundamental shift in the direction of the whole scheme:

> [I]t is clear to me that this groundnut plan must go forward. To abandon it now, or even to retreat in any fundamental way, would be wholly wrong. But I am equally satisfied that ultimately, if it is to prosper and flourish, and bring security and well-being both to the territory and to our own people, it must be fashioned and shaped as a broad project of colonial development with a wide and varied agriculturist content rather than the purely food producing ideas on which it was first established.[40]

For the first time, the British Government acknowledged explicitly that in reforming the scheme the development of Africa would predominate over the imperial requirement for sterling food supplies. The rationale for the scheme was turned on its head. On that basis the economic arguments would inevitably begin to weigh over and above the domestic political ones.

Other Labour speakers, including a young Ian Mikardo, were enrolled to accuse the Tories of playing party politics with colonial development. But it was apparent to most spectators that the government were on the ropes. It survived the division by only nine votes, 299 to 290.

On the spot

In East Africa, fate was no kinder to the scheme. The rains in 1950, though not failing, were poorly distributed and led to another disappointing crop. At Kongwa a drought was followed by torrential rains, and the crop was so poor that what little of it could be saved had to be lifted by hand. The yield per acre fell to 184 lbs, and the cost of production per acre rose to £9 18s 6d. In Urambo, the crop was fine, but harvesting was problematic, with about a quarter of the harvest left in the sun-baked ground. In the Southern Province clearing was still taking far longer than expected, and there was virtually no crop at all. The technique of chain-clearing had now been perfected, dragging a heavy anchor chain between two Shervicks that effectively flattened every tree or bush in their path. But it was still hard keeping the vehicles going: the Shervicks were unreliable and the cost of purely mechanised clearing was now recognised as unbearably high.

The level of desperation the government was feeling is illustrated by a Ministry of Food file from this period in The National Archives in Kew

---

[40] Webb, ibid., col. 2054.

Photo 8.1 Chain-clearing of bush by bulldozers and Shervicks in Southern Province, near Nachingwea (CO 691/213, The National Archives, Kew)

entitled 'Artificial production of rain'.[41] It contains scientific articles on the seeding of clouds and other rational techniques for creating miracles. The only thing they did not try, it seems, was to employ the local Wagogo rainmaker. But alas, neither scientific skill nor political will could change the weather at Kongwa.

On the spot, morale sank lower. The lack of married quarters in Urambo led to a steady exodus of married staff, and the end of cost-plus contracts brought the departure of most of the Mowlems as well as Taylor Woodrow staff from the south. The turnover of management there was also unsettling for staff. Prof. Phillips was moved out of a management role to become Chief Agricultural Adviser to the Scheme, while George Raby became sole Managing Director. Troughton, having wielded his axe, resigned and departed the field. Governor Twining paid another visit, but even his pomp and circumstance could do little to restore faith in the project. Only the scientists continued undeterred, certain that at least some useful information could be gleaned for the future from the scheme.[42]

The Parliamentary Secretary to the Ministry of Food, F.T. Willey, visited Kongwa in September and reported back personally to Webb. Though morale seemed buoyed by the belief that the Government would continue to support the scheme through thick and thin, he

---

[41] See MAF 83/1988. Some of this work found its way into articles in *Nature*, e.g. 167 (1951), 169 (1952), 171 (1953) and 174 (1954), cited in Esselborn, 'Environment, Memory and the Groundnut Scheme', p. 74.

[42] Papers in TNA 35113; Deputy Governor to Colonial Secretary, 25 Mar 1950, CO 691/211/5; *Manchester Guardian*, 26 May 1950.

was unimpressed by the unwieldy administrative organisation, and confirmed that the Scheme still focussed primarily on the UK: 'a scheme organised by the British for the British, which only happens to operate in East Africa', not on the development needs of Tanganyika. As a result, local people and officials remained sceptical of its value. He concluded that only transferring responsibility to the Colonial Office would remedy this.[43]

Meantime, the Kongwa Working Party had been accumulating evidence, and on 18 August it presented its recommendations to the OFC Board. Its conclusion was brutal, succinct and clear: so far as Kongwa was concerned, 'the Working Party were left in no doubt that large-scale agriculture on the lines so far practised should be discontinued'. Immediately. It would never succeed. It recommended putting the bulk of the 100,000 acres cleared under grass and using it for cattle ranching. Only 24,000 acres showed any future arable potential, and that should be divided into four farms experimenting with various rotations of groundnuts and sorghum on 12,000 acres each year. Sunflower was hopeless and should be dropped.[44] There was no escape from the fact that large-scale mechanised farming of groundnuts at Kongwa never had worked, and never would.

On 15 September, the report was put to Cabinet. Both the OFC and the Minister of Food accepted its conclusions that 'it would be folly to press on with large-scale agriculture for another season'. Once again the OFC was asked to present a revised plan taking account of this. Of course, given the public interest, the Working Party Report would be published.[45] The Cabinet made no comment. It was preoccupied, as was Strachey himself, with the Korean War, which had broken out in June when North Korean troops had crossed the 38th Parallel into the south, and was now entering a critical phase. Groundnuts were something they could now well do without.[46]

After reading the Cabinet paper, Max Nicholson told Morrison ruefully: 'At least this scheme will live as a monument to the importance of looking at the scientific problems before we leap with the big investments'.[47]

---

[43] Willey, quoted in Morgan, *Colonial Development*, Vol. II, p. 293. Willey also visited Nachingwea, where he had a public row with Tom Unwin over Strachey and Plummer's dishonesty. Unwin asked for redundancy. Letters of 15 Oct and 6 Nov 1950, Unwin Papers.
[44] 'Recommendations on Future Agricultural Policy at Kongwa', Report of the Kongwa Working Party, 18 Aug 1950, in TNA 41265 and MAF 83/1978.
[45] Memorandum by the Minister of Food, 15 Sep 1950, CP(50)208, CAB 124/123.
[46] Harris, *Attlee*, pp. 454–8.
[47] Nicholson minute, 26 Sep 1950, CAB 124/123.

9

A Sudden Death

On 23 October 1950, Sir Eric Coates presented the OFC's eagerly awaited Revised Long Term Plan for the scheme. But even this could not satisfy the new Chancellor, Hugh Gaitskill, and by January 1951 the Cabinet had decided effectively to close the scheme and write off the loss. A fig leaf remained, but withered swiftly in the tropical sun.

The Long Term Plan

The Plan aimed, over a seven-year period, to create a viable Corporation within the financial limits set by the ORD Act. It admitted that this could only be done through a further drastic reduction in the scheme's scope and objectives, and without meeting the ORD's obligation to repay the money so far advanced by the Government. Almost as a revelation, it noted that 'the groundnut is not a plant which lends itself readily to mass methods over vast acreages', and that purely 'mechanical clearing can be done, but it cannot be done at an economic cost'. It therefore adopted the Kongwa Working Party's conclusions, stopping production on the bulk of the area, to be turned over to ranching, and focussing on experimental farming in the small fertile area. There would be no further expansion at Urambo, though the existing cleared area would continue to be cultivated with a variety of crops to see which were most suitable. But, in the south, they proposed to continue clearing, by hand as well as machine, and to expand production. They admitted that the scale of production proposed a year before was no longer capable of fulfilment within the budget limits, but proposed clearing 105,000 acres by 1957, with the possibility of 45,000 more thereafter.[1]

One reason for this continued optimism about the prospects for the Southern Province was the engagement – at last – of both the Tanga-

---

[1] Coates to Lee, 23 Oct 1950, CO 691/210/3. The Plan is reprinted in OFC, *The Future of the Overseas Food Corporation*, Cmd 8125, 9 Jan 1951 (London, HMSO).

nyika Administration and the Colonial Office. The colonial authorities had finally begun to focus on the territory's Cinderella province and drawn up an ambitious development plan for the south, predicated on a central role for the scheme at Nachingwea, the railway line and the deep-water harbour at Mtwara. The last was still under construction, but forecasts of potential crop exports by peasant producers in the Southern Province Development Plan suggested that there would be enough trade to justify completing it, even with a smaller output from the scheme itself. The Administration also supported a proposed 70-mile extension inland of the railway which would open up new areas to commercial farming.

In the Colonial Office, the Under-Secretary for Africa, Andrew Cohen, took an increasingly firm grip on policy-making – on the scheme as on everything else. Conscious that the Long Term Plan gave rise to serious, and politically sensitive, policy issues concerning who should run the scheme, which minister would be responsible, and whether the southern railway and port were economically viable, he decided to visit Tanganyika himself to examine these issues on the spot. At the end of October, Cohen flew to Nairobi to talk to Twining and Mitchell together, then on to Dar es Salaam and from there to Lindi, Nachingwea and Mtwara. His conclusion was emphatic, that 'it would be absolutely wrong to abandon the great enterprise which has been established at Nachingwea', and equally wrong to abandon Mtwara. 'I was astonished at the magnitude of the installations necessary for constructing the deep water port; to dissipate this now would, I believe, be most ill-judged ... in the long run from the financial point of view its completion will pay.' The fact that construction had been bedevilled for months by subsidence did not worry him. Though earlier the quay wall had been dropping at a rate of 4 inches a week, 'it had only dropped ¾" in the three weeks preceding our visit'. He also identified with the wishes of Twining and his colleagues that the scheme should become the responsibility of the Colonial Office, that the OFC Board should be based in Tanganyika, and that, once the scheme was economically viable (but not before), it should be transferred to the Tanganyika Government.[2]

On his return, Cohen met with the Colonial Secretary Jim Griffiths, his Permanent Secretary Sir T.I.K. Lloyd, and other senior CO officials. They decided to support the OFC's proposals and to propose that the Colonial Secretary assume responsibility for the scheme and the OFC, *provided* the losses to date were written off by the Treasury. The ultimate aim would be to transfer the scheme to Tanganyika, but this would not yet be declared for fear of a collapse in morale among the scheme's staff. There was a long debate over whether the scheme

---

[2] Cohen, 'Notes on points affecting OFC arising from Mr Cohen's visit to East Africa' (Secret), 3 Nov 1950, and other papers in CO 691/210/3.

should be transferred to the CDC. It would be financially and organisationally neater, but the arguments that it would damage the CDC's (also rather precarious) reputation, and could not be done without legislation allowing the CDC not to balance its books, won out. It would remain separate. But in future, both the Tanganyika Government and the CDC should be represented on its Board.[3]

In short, the development interests of Tanganyika were beginning to have a predominant influence on the future planning of the scheme, and the Colonial Office had become its principal champion. They were beginning to conceive it as a genuine development scheme with the primary objective of developing the territory's resources for the benefit of its inhabitants. But the OFC and Colonial Office still had to face the domestic interests of the rest of the British Government. The Ministry of Food and the Treasury were both considerably less sanguine about the scheme's future.

While welcoming the OFC's honesty, the Ministry of Food's economic analysis of the plan identified that it would result in Tanganyika delivering *less* oil to the UK even than it had before the war, on the basis of purely African peasant production. It also concluded that 'there can be no assurance that the revenue from the agricultural land will be able to cover the costs of cultivation', and therefore 'the Ministry of Food could not justify the risks of this enterprise on commercial grounds'. Given that it was proposed to become in effect 'an experiment in mixed tropical agriculture', the Ministry believed the Colonial Office should have it, and pay for it. But the plan sounded to them more like the efforts of a receiver to glean what he could from a bankrupt company.[4] The Treasury too continued to press – as they always had – for a minimal scheme smaller even than that proposed by the OFC – just enough to save face without the risk of incurring any further loss. But the Colonial Office was determined, and persuaded the MoF at least to support a joint paper to Cabinet recommending the OFC proposals.

Once more Max Nicholson counselled Morrison to question their assumptions. In his view there was no justification for spending another penny on the scheme. With the Korean War dominating the political scene, resources were going to be very tight, including for tropical development:

> [E]very £ put into groundnuts in East Africa is a £ denied to, say, expanding dollar-earning crops in South East Asia, or developments of strategic importance in the Middle East ... The testimony of the Groundnut Scheme merely confirm[s] previous experience that

---

[3] Rogers, 'Note of a meeting with the Secretary of State', 8 Nov 1950, and other papers, CO 691/210/3.
[4] 'A note of some economic aspects of the Plan' (Secret), Ministry of Food, 13 Nov 1950, CO 691/210/3.

bringing in new marginal lands is normally far less profitable and productive of increased supplies than improving the productivity of the existing cultivable land, and this is particularly true in Asia where large acreages of suitable land could multiply their yields if they were given a small fraction of the resources which have been lavished on the Tanganyika wilderness.[5]

He proposed winding up the scheme 'and leaving this intractable and infertile area to the lions.' For once Morrison listened, writing to Attlee in support of complete abandonment.[6]

Again, Maurice Webb took the unusual step of sending Strachey a personal copy of the paper before it was discussed in Cabinet. 'After your original efforts the present development must be deeply disappointing to you', he wrote. 'But, alas, we can do no other, given the Board's intimation that they can no longer meet their obligations.'[7]

Not only times, but tactics had changed. Webb and Griffiths had not taken the trouble to talk it through with Hugh Gaitskell, now Chancellor of the Exchequer in his own right, in advance of Cabinet.

Gaitskell's views on the scheme had not been tested before. His views of John Strachey had undergone a change during his time in Government. In December 1947 he had confided to his diary:, 'He is still I think too much inclined to abstract theory ... He is a very able negotiator and influential at Cabinet – states his case forcibly though with exaggeration. Is he to be trusted? Probably not.' But two years later, in February 1950, Gaitskell had succumbed to Strachey's charm, describing him as a colleague 'with whom one can have that emotional and intellectual intercourse which is really the stuff of friendship'.[8]

Gaitskell's views on the Groundnut Scheme, however, had moved in the opposite direction. In Cabinet on 7 December, Webb acknowledged that the original project had proven 'a costly failure', but he and Griffiths argued that something needed to be salvaged from the investment already made, that pressure on food supplies would continue to increase, and that finding out how best to develop large-scale tropical agriculture for the benefit of its subjects was an obligation of a great colonial power. Gaitskell was unmoved: 'the original scheme had clearly failed and the Government must expect political criticism on that account ... From his point of view [the proposal] had the great disadvantage that it contained no assurance that substantial further losses would not be incurred.' While agricultural experimental work was justified, it need not be on so large a scale. He blocked a decision. After an unusually robust discussion,

---

[5] Nicholson to Morrison, 6 Dec 1950, CAB 124/123.
[6] Morrison to Attlee, 31 Dec 1950, ibid.
[7] Webb to Strachey (Personal), 30 Nov 1950, Strachey Papers, Box 13.
[8] Gaitskell's diary, 4 Dec 1947 and 1 Feb 1950, quoted in Philip Williams, *Hugh Gaitskell* (Oxford, OUP, 1982), pp. 129, 150.

in which Morrison blamed Webb for not making more progress in sorting out the scheme, the Cabinet concluded that it would be best for the Chancellor, Colonial Secretary and Minister of Food to discuss it among themselves and come back to Cabinet with an agreed proposal.[9]

Immediately after Cabinet, Webb wrote to Morrison to justify his actions, adding a plaintive P.S. 'Please, when you tick me off again, make quite sure that I have in fact been at fault. The truth is I've been holding this baby for all of you with some skill, I may say, for some months.'[10] He, like everyone else, just wanted to be shot of the scheme as swiftly as possible.

A period of intense discussion followed, with the ministers meeting twice, on 15 and 18 December. The Colonial Office was particularly concerned that complete abandonment would send a signal to Africa and the world that the whole scheme had indeed been an example of imperial exploitation. It would be perceived that as soon as the scheme failed to deliver a useful supply of oil to the UK, it was being abandoned. Hence the importance of keeping something running, and publicising that the benefits would fall to Africa in terms of improved farming techniques. Governor Twining, who had flown over to join the meetings, added that abandonment would have repercussions on the political equilibrium of the territory and 'would probably shatter local feeling in favour of public ownership in East Africa.' Abandoning the scheme in seven years' time would have far less impact. The figures also showed that, while immediate abandonment would cost a further £4.5 million, continuing with the OFC's plan would cost £6.75m, but a 60,000 acre scheme only £4.4m.[11]

Gaitskell quizzed them about the potential for ultimate profitability. Coates, for the OFC, could give no assurances. Gaitskell therefore concluded that, while he was willing to allow the scheme to continue on a very limited basis, it should be on no more than 60,000 acres in the south, and should be reviewed again in 1954. The Colonial Office would take it over, and the accumulated losses to date be written off. The southern railway and port could continue, as long as the Tanganyika Government paid its share.[12]

When the Cabinet re-convened on 2 January 1951, Gaitskell presented his deal.

> There was general agreement that the balance of advantage lay in continuing the scheme on the lines proposed in C.P.(50)324 [Gaitskell's paper]. Complete abandonment would have serious consequences in

---

[9] Cabinet Conclusions, 7 Dec 1950, CM 83(50)4, CAB 128/18 (also in Hyam, *BDEE*, vol. A.2.II, doc. 136)
[10] Webb to Morrison, 7 Dec 1950, CAB 124/123.
[11] 'Record of meetings in the Chancellor's Room', 15 and 18 Dec 1950, CO 691/210/3.
[12] Ibid.

Tanganyika and would harm the prestige of this country in all African Colonies.[13]

But everyone knew that in practice the Groundnut Scheme was dead. The Labour Government had finally decided they had no option but to come clean, write off the loss and take the flak.

So it was that a Government that in November 1949 had signed up to a 600,000-acre scheme, by December 1950 had resigned itself to a 60,000-acre one. Looking further back, it is telling that, whereas in 1947 the Cabinet would risk tens of millions of taxpayers' pounds in order to increase the domestic fats ration, in 1950 they would *not* risk further millions merely to develop a colonial territory. Certainly, the scheme had failed, and it made perfect sense to cut the losses. But it also illustrates a growing awareness in London that if the colonial empire was going to end up costing the imperial government too much, British political opinion would turn against it. Within 10 years, this logic was being applied across the whole colonial empire, and the costs and benefits of imperialism were being more rigorously examined than ever before.[14]

Taking the flak

But that was the long term. In the short term, the Cabinet's decision required legislation to amend the ORD Act to allow the write-off of the debts and the transfer of responsibility, and hence a full Parliamentary process. The Tories rubbed their hands with glee. On anything to do with the Groundnut Scheme, the Labour Government was not merely on the ropes – it was on the floor with the referee counting down.

The Long Term Plan, adapted to reflect the Cabinet's further cuts, was published as a White Paper on 9 January 1951. At last the public were told plainly that:

> The original aims of the scheme have proved incapable of fulfilment ... The scheme must now be regarded as a scheme of large-scale experimental development to establish the economics of clearing and mechanised or partially mechanised agriculture under tropical conditions.[15]

---

[13] Cabinet Conclusions, 2 Jan 1951, CM 1(51)7, CAB 128/19 (also in Hyam, *BDEE*, vol. A.2.II, doc. 137), Memorandum by the Chancellor, CP(50)324, CAB 129/42.

[14] See Morgan, *Colonial Development, Vol. V*, pp. 88–115 on Macmillan's cost-benefit analysis of the colonial empire; also Hyam, *Britain's Declining Empire*, ch. 4. The Groundnut Scheme was the first and most glaring case of this fundamental imperial reality, though it took a few more years for the conclusion to be generalised in Africa.

[15] *The Future of the Overseas Food Corporation*, Cmd 8125 (London, HMSO, Jan 1951), pp. 1–5.

The total expenditure to date on the scheme, £36.5 million, would be written off before the transfer to the Colonial Office, and a maximum of £6 million was made available for the next seven years. This compared to the maximum original cost of £25 million for the whole scheme, including railway. In today's money, the sum written off was equivalent to around £1.1 billion[16] – a vast sum then, as now, and all the more painful as much of it had been spent in hard US dollars. As Alan Wood pointed out, after all this expense, the Groundnut Scheme ended up importing more groundnuts as seed than it ever exported, to the UK or anywhere else. By 1951, when Wakefield had projected *annual* exports of 600,000 tons of nuts, the scheme's *total* production to date had been 9,120 tons of shelled nuts, mostly used for seed. None had been exported.[17]

This alone gave the Conservatives more than enough ammunition for their assault on the Government. During the debate on the ORD Act amendment bill on 20 February 1951, Captain Crookshank delivered a peroration of sustained entertainment ('a jolly knock-about speech' according to the Liberal spokesman) that not only pilloried John Strachey (who 'never quite acted on the old principle of "the truth, the whole truth and nothing but the truth"'), but declared the OFC to be exactly what it was, effectively bankrupt. He said what the Government knew but would not say: 'In fact the new scheme at any rate – let us be quite frank – finishes groundnuts for good and all. The Groundnut Scheme is dead, dead, dead ... There will never be any question any more of gathering nuts in May.'[18] Anthony Hurd pointed out that £36.5 million was a lot to spend to find out why Africans had left this area alone, and Alan Lennox-Boyd noted that the amount written off was more than Tanganyika's total revenue for the previous four years put together. He quoted an (anonymous) colonial administrator from the territory who complained that 'if only a third of the money frittered away on this pipe-dream had been applied to building roads and improving transport facilities in Tanganyika, it would have moved our country 50 years ahead.'[19]

Griffiths responded, as governments always do, that the decision to go ahead had been taken on the basis of the best available evidence at the time and with the support of all the experts who had been consulted – and was no more convincing than his many successors who have used the same argument, with the same amnesia of what people actually

---

[16] Current equivalent calculated using the Bank of England price deflator: www.bankofengland.co.uk/monetary-policy/inflation/inflation-calculator (accessed 19 Jun 2019).
[17] Wood, *Groundnut Affair*, p. 231; Hogendorn and Scott, 'Very large-scale agricultural projects', p. 191.
[18] *Hansard*, vol. 484, col. 1100, 20 Feb 1951.
[19] Ibid., col. 1179.

said at the time.[20] Under the blanket of official secrecy, Max Nicholson reminded them that he and all the experts *he* had consulted had advised unanimously against it from the start.[21] The Government scraped by with a vote of 302 to 295, and the revised ORD Bill became law. But this victory was as Pyrrhic as the last.

Closing down

Breaking the news to the scheme's own staff was not much easier. Following the decision to move the headquarters to Tanganyika, the OFC's 170 staff in London were to be reduced not just to the 70 proposed in the Long Term Plan, but to none. Not surprisingly, Coates reported that they were suffering from acute and increasing depression. At Kongwa, the number of Europeans would fall from 150 to 11, and the total employed by the scheme in Tanganyika be reduced from 1,700 to 600 by 1953.[22] The Governor reported that OFC staff on the spot were at least relieved that something would continue and that the efforts of the last three years would not be entirely thrown away. There was no doubt relief among others that the pretence was over. That stalwart of the scheme, Tom Unwin, who had been with it since early 1947, was offered a job by the colonial administration, and left to become a District Officer in March 1951.[23] In the Tanganyikan press, the overwhelming sentiment was, 'we told you so'.[24]

Twining also reported that there was almost no discernable reaction to the announcement among Africans. The African workers, 14,700 of whom were laid off in 1951, seemed phlegmatic, took their pay-off and went to find work and use their newly acquired skills elsewhere.[25] An undertone of opposition in some quarters that it remained a surreptitious way of alienating land remained muted. But significantly, the main nationalist organisation, the African Association, did not even discuss it. The Groundnut Scheme had not really impinged on their political concerns at all, though Twining attributed the silence to their 'lack of appreciation of the benefits which the scheme can bring'.[26] Nevertheless, politically the scheme's failure may have been a good thing from the Africans' perspective. As John Iliffe has pointed out, had it succeeded, it could have complicated the decolonisation process by

---

[20] Ibid., col. 1188.
[21] Nicholson to Lord President, 6 Dec 1950, CAB 124/123.
[22] Coates to Cohen, 9 Jan 1951, CO 691/211/1.
[23] Letters of 5 and 12 Mar 1951, Unwin Papers.
[24] Twining to Cohen, 1 Feb 1951, CO 691/211/1.
[25] Hogendorn and Scott, 'Lessons of the East African Groundnut Scheme', p. 185.
[26] Ibid.

giving Britain a more direct imperial interest to defend. In the event, the British Government felt it could cut loose from Tanganyika with little compunction and little loss.[27]

In May a further round of changes were made to the Board. Coates had agreed to stay on and see through the transition until June, when he handed over to J.C. Muir, now the Tanganyika Administration's Member for Agriculture and Natural Resources, who handed over soon after to the former Kenyan Director of Agriculture, Dr Stuart Gillett. Professor Phillips, increasingly unhappy, was not reappointed to the new Board and left soon after to join the staff of the University of the Gold Coast at Achimota, where he wrote a book on African agriculture that drew heavily on his experience of the scheme.[28] McFadyen, judged by Cohen to make no material contribution to the policy of the OFC whatsoever, was also not reappointed, though Webb gave him a warm send-off in Parliament. Raby, 'a man of character and decision' who had 'served the scheme magnificently' was also retained until the following year to help clear up the mess. Perrott, from the MoF, was no longer needed and the Colonial Office decided not to put its Agricultural Adviser, Geoffrey Clay, on the Board as the Tanganyika Administration was already well represented. The one survivor from the original Board who was retained was Sir Charles Lockhart, given his intellectual and organisational skills, and despite his 'acid tongue ... which makes him unpopular with the middle and lower staff of the Corporation in the field.'[29]

Among the casualties was Hugh Bunting, finally sacked in June 1951. The management said they wanted an agriculturalist not a scientist in charge. Very few others had been with the scheme from start to finish, or played as critical a role in its history, and he was to carry the lessons with him for the rest of his life. For the moment, though, he fought hard for his staff to be allowed to continue and become integrated into the Tanganyika Agricultural Research Service (which most of them were), where their knowledge would be a lasting benefit to the territory.[30]

Through all this, the farming went on. Ironically, the crop at Kongwa in 1951 was a good one, though patchy rain meant that it was still not up to the level originally forecast. In Urambo, the crops grew well, but harvesting was prevented by incessant rain, which resulted in a large part of the crop rotting in the ground. In the south, there were still only

[27] Iliffe, *Tanganyika*, p. 442.
[28] Phillips to Twining, 6 Jan 1953, TNA 35147/III. On Gillet, see Throup, *Mau Mau*, p. 268; J. Phillips, *Agriculture and Ecology in Africa: A study of actual and potential development south of the Sahara* (London, Faber and Faber, 1959), discussed in more detail in Chapter 10 below.
[29] Cohen minute, 9 Dec, and Cohen to Twining, 21 Dec 1950, CO 537/5876; 'Notes on personalities', 22 May 1951, CO 691/211/III.
[30] Bunting to Hutt, 12 Jun, and Bunting to Chief Secretary, 24 Aug 1951, TNA 39096.

experimental plots, which did well enough to encourage hopes that the 60,000 acres would be productive and profitable. Visiting the scheme in April 1951, Clay commented that 'to see vast areas of good crops, well cultivated and clean, was indeed a stirring sight', and a South African groundnut expert went so far as to write to Winston Churchill after his own visit pleading for the scheme to be continued.[31] The construction of the port and railway in the south also continued, though some extra line put down beyond Kongwa at the request of Plummer in 1948 was lifted and re-deployed. The sinking quay stopped sinking, and occasional wash-outs on the line to Nachingwea were repaired. As is the way with these things, in 1952 the survivors of the scheme's Scientific Department moved into its long-awaited, purpose-built, brand new laboratory building in Kongwa. And two years later, the first ship sailed into the impressive new port of Mtwara and moored at the rock-solid, un-sinking quayside.[32]

Nevertheless, as Captain Crookshank had said, to all intents and purposes, the Groundnut Scheme was dead. It was to be followed to the grave only a few months later by the Labour Government itself.

In September 1951 Attlee announced a general election for the 25th October, barely 18 months since the last. The Labour Government was exhausted and divided. They had been surviving in Parliament for months on wafer thin majorities. Bevan's impetuous resignation earlier in the year over Gaitskell's efforts to contain the costs of the NHS, followed by Harold Wilson's a day later, had split the party. Morrison, an ineffective and unfortunate choice to replace Bevin at the Foreign Office after the latter's death, was hopelessly entangled in the intractable problems of the Middle East, from Egypt to Iran. Even King George himself urged Attlee to call an early election.[33]

There was no shortage of targets for the Conservative Opposition to attack. But the Groundnut Scheme still had its modest part to play. Looking back from 30 years later, Manny Shinwell could not deny that 'the ridicule to which we were subjected at the time was a factor in our defeat'.[34]

In the event, the Conservative victory was smaller than might have been expected, with 321 seats to Labour's 295, though Labour still won a higher percentage of the vote (48.8% to 48.0%). Strachey once more survived in Dundee, though with a majority shaved down to only just

---

[31] 'Meeting in CO', 7 May 1951, CO 691/211/III; Morgan, *Colonial Development*, Vol. IV, p. 54.
[32] Peter Le Mare interview, 12 Oct 2007; Moffett, *Handbook of Tanganyika*, p. 142.
[33] Harris, *Attlee*, pp. 484–94.
[34] Shinwell quoted in BBC Radio 4, 'The Great Groundnut Scandal', 28 Jul 1982.

over 3,000. Attlee and Vi packed their bags and quietly vacated No. 10. Winston Churchill returned, his Government taking over responsibility for – among other things – the remains of the scheme it had so vociferously lambasted in Opposition. Labour was to be consigned to the Opposition benches for the next 14 years. By the time it returned to Government in 1964, under Harold Wilson, not only was the Groundnut Scheme history, so too was the British Empire in East Africa.

The end

Once in power, the Conservatives effectively ignored the scheme, choosing not to waste time and resources on post-mortems or inquiries. The Long Term Plan, in its reduced form, was implemented without fuss by the colonial authorities. This last phase has been diligently chronicled by D.J. Morgan in his *Official History of Colonial Development*.[35] In brief, the OFC moved as planned to Tanganyika, limited work continued, though even the research budget needed to be cut more than originally planned. Hopes were high when 1952 proved to be a good season with excellent crops everywhere. The scheme – for the first time ever – actually turned a profit on its agricultural operations. But hopes were once more dashed when 1953 brought a drought as severe as any yet at Kongwa, and the crop was a total failure.

The promised review in 1954, therefore concluded that all farming operations should cease at Kongwa except cattle ranching – which, as the locals pointed out, is exactly what they had used the area for before the Groundnut Scheme in all its glory ploughed up the plains.[36] At Urambo, it was clear that groundnuts and cereals did not do well, the former because of persistent problems with rosette disease, exactly as Mr Roddan had predicted in 1946. But more recent experiments had shown that tobacco grew rather well. The cleared land was divided into smaller plots, given to local out-growers, and 12,000 acres of the 17,000 cleared at Urambo became the centre of a reasonably prosperous flue-cured tobacco industry which survives to the present day. In the south, the cost of clearing, at over £15 per acre, continued to exceed estimates, and only 20,000 of the 60,000 acres planned were ever cleared. On that, again, groundnuts proved a poor crop. Soya beans did better, but after many trials, success was finally achieved with cashew trees. Once more it was on the basis of production by local tenant farmers that southern Tanzania has become a

[35] Morgan, *Colonial Development, Vol. IV*, pp. 54–91.
[36] *The Future of the Overseas Food Corporation*, Cmd 9158 (London, HMSO, May 1954); N.R. Fuggles-Couchman, *Agricultural Change in Tanganyika, 1945–1960* (Stanford, Food Research Institute, 1964), pp. 83–4.

major source of cashew nut production, exported through Mtwara for processing in India.[37]

The cost of the railway and the port at Mtwara also escalated, from £4.5 million to over £6 million. To avoid it bankrupting the recently established East African Railways and Harbours (EARH), the British Government agreed to write off an additional £3.6 million and the rest of the debts were divided between Tanganyika and the EARH. Even so, the railway never paid its way, and in the 1960s the whole track was lifted. The route can still be followed on foot, through the countryside from Mtwara to Nachingwea, though heavily overgrown. Instead, it was the Chinese who finally linked Tanzania to the countries to its south, through the Tanzania–Zambia Railway (TAZARA), a flagship project of cooperation between the People's Republic of China and Julius Nyerere's Tanzanian government. It finally opened in 1975, 29 years after Wakefield's fateful report.[38]

The OFC was transformed into the Tanganyika Agriculture Corporation (TAC), and even Sir Charles Lockhart was finally pensioned off. The new Board, chaired by Stuart Gillet, was made up entirely of Tanganyika Government or local representatives, including Mr A.M.A. Karimjee and Chief Humbi Ziots, unofficial members of the Tanganyika Legislative Council. Another unofficial member, now retired from public service, also spoke in the debate approving the creation of the TAC: R.W.R. Miller, one of the original godfathers of the scheme, gave the new Corporation his blessing.[39]

It was this Corporation that was transferred to the new Government of Tanganyika on its independence in 1961, and which was finally incorporated into the wider National Development Corporation of Tanzania in 1964. Even then, only the ranch at Kongwa was a self-supporting commercial proposition with 80,000 acres given over to a herd of 8,000 cattle, though the farm at Nachingwea had finally turned a profit for the first time in 1960.[40]

Julius Nyerere's new nationalist government was interested not only in achieving a revolution in agriculture, but also achieving the liberation of countries still under colonial or white minority rule further south. In the late 1960s, the facilities built for the Groundnut Scheme proved ideal housing, and the wide open spaces ideal training grounds for Africa's liberation movements. Nachingwea became the main training base in exile for FRELIMO, the Mozambican liberation move-

---

[37] See ch.11 below.
[38] N.R. Fuggles-Couchman, 'Report of the Southern Province Railway Working Party', 1956, Fuggles-Couchman Papers, Bodleian Libraries, Oxford; Richard Hall and Hugh Peyman, *The Great Uhuru Railway* (London, Gollancz, 1976).
[39] Morgan, *Colonial Development*, Vol. IV, pp. 71–2.
[40] Ibid., pp. 82–4.

ment; and – as I found – Kongwa provided a safe haven for the training of ANC cadres before they returned to the struggle in South Africa. The scheme thus played an indirect part in a rather different transformation of Africa to that envisaged by its originators.[41]

There was one last, strange twist of fate.

It is told that when, in 1947, John Wakefield had the ingenious idea of converting Sherman tanks into tractors, an enterprising arms merchant bought up the gun turrets and armour plating which were no longer needed. Finding them still on his hands five years later, he bought the remaining Shervicks back from the OFC for a song, and proceeded to put the two back together. The resulting reconstituted Sherman tanks were sold cheap to the new state of Israel, desperate to put together an armoured capability to defend itself from its neighbours. During the Six Day War in 1967 these Shermans played a key role in the rapid Israeli advance, but were clearly outclassed by the more modern Russian tanks of their Arab opponents. They were swiftly replaced and sold off to Israel's newest friend in Africa, President Idi Amin of Uganda. When Tanzanian forces invaded Uganda in 1979 to topple Amin, it was these tanks that they faced, and demolished, on the road to Kampala. When I visited Kampala in 1982, their burnt out wrecks could still be seen along the road out of the city. The Tanzanian troops were no doubt unaware that the tanks they destroyed had once ploughed their own soil.[42]

Aftermath

Like the scheme's machines, the human actors in this drama also came to diverse ends. It is worth looking briefly at what became of them. In his book *The Groundnut Affair*, Alan Wood wondered: 'Was there something about the groundnut scheme, like any other inspiring vision, which made all who touched it a little mad?'[43]

It was John Strachey's vision, more than anyone else's, that drove the scheme forward. With his enquiring intellect and characteristic flexibility, when moved from the Ministry of Food, Strachey threw himself with gusto into his new job as Secretary for War, becoming thoroughly engrossed in the challenges posed by the Korean War, the Malayan Emergency and the risks of a nuclear holocaust. Following Labour's election defeat in 1951 he remained the Opposition front bench spokesman

---

[41] Personal information. See also Gregory F. Houston, 'Report on Military Bases and Camps of the Liberation Movement, 1961–1990' (2013), www.hsrc.ac.za/en/research-outputs/ktree-doc/13802 (accessed 3 Mar 2020).
[42] Information from the late Michael Cohen, a scrupulous and much missed historian, shortly before he died. Sadly I have found no documentary proof of this, yet.
[43] Wood, *Groundnut Affair*, p. 151.

on defence – a difficult position with the Bevanites and Gaitskellites as divided on that as on everything else. With sympathy for both sides, Strachey committed himself to neither, becoming a rather lonely figure in the centre of the party, respected for his intellect and eloquence but reviled by both factions for his lack of commitment.[44] As a result, he had little power within the party, and his hopes of reaching the top of the political tree began to fade. He nevertheless continued to make a serious intellectual contribution, and remained a visionary to the end. During the years in Opposition he published three significant books, *Contemporary Capitalism* (1956), *The End of Empire* (1959) and *The Prevention of War* (1962). The first continued his struggle to marry Marx and Keynes, but with an incisive brilliance and economic comprehension that made it a joy to read. His thoughts on empire were more discursive, arguing (implausibly) that Britain made no real profit from the empire until oil was discovered in the Middle East. The fundamental ambiguity of his view, illustrated so well by the Groundnut Scheme itself, was still apparent: 'the author is rather too inclined to have it both ways where England is concerned' observed one reviewer.[45] He could see the Empire was vanishing, but believed Britain could still lead the developing world as a model of socialism and pioneer of global change – an approach with a strangely contemporary ring to it.

On defence, however, he moved firmly into the Gaitskellite camp, building alliances and friendships with both George Brown and Jim Callaghan. Following the unexpected deaths of both Bevan in 1960 and Gaitskell in January 1963, Strachey rallied behind Harold Wilson as Labour leader. He was retained on the front bench as shadow Commonwealth Secretary, and as a centrist within the party. He was looking forward a further spell in Government following the impending general election when, after an operation on his back, he died suddenly in July 1963, aged only 62.

The folder of condolence letters in his private papers illustrates how widely he was respected, and how much he was missed. Clement Attlee, with whom he had remained on good terms until the end, wrote to his widow Celia: 'John was a very good and able colleague. He had a rough time at the Food Ministry, being quite unjustly criticised.' His old friend Bill Mallalieu was less equivocal: 'I think he was the best Food Minister this country ever had.'[46] This story has, of its nature, illustrated only one side of that job. His skilful negotiations with the Americans, Argentines and Indians to secure the best food supplies at an affordable price have passed unremarked. But the story of the Groundnut Scheme

---

[44] Thomas, *Strachey*, chs18–19.
[45] Andrew Shonfield, quoted in Thomas, *Strachey*, p. 282.
[46] Letters from Attlee and Mallalieu to Celia Strachey, Jul 1963, Strachey Papers, Box 10.

has illustrated the man as he was – brilliant of intellect, passionate in his vision, eloquent in his advocacy, determined in his pursuit and, just sometimes, blind to the political and financial consequences of his actions. Without him, the scheme would never have been the same – might never even have happened at all.

It is one of those coincidences that less than a month before Strachey, his old comrade in arms, Dick Plummer had also died. Sir Leslie Plummer as he had become (with Strachey's help) had – unlike his mentor – disappeared from public life after his dismissal from the OFC. He had taken the money and the knighthood and lain low. Strachey had supported his search for a job with the UN's Food and Agriculture Organization, but for some reason they did not take him on.[47]

Both had outlasted poor old Maurice Webb who died, aged 51, in 1956. Creech Jones left political life when he lost his seat, but his successor Jim Griffiths proved the political survivor, serving with honour as Secretary of State for Wales under Wilson in the 1960s and dying in 1975.[48]

Wakefield, Rosa and Samuel all disappear from view, living out their days in quiet retirement. But Samuel at least had the insight to deliver what was almost a *mea culpa*, writing in the journal *Tropical Agriculture* in 1951:

> There has been a great deal of wishful thinking on the part of many writers and speakers who have, since the war, created an impression that Tropical Africa is an El Dorado of wealth sorely neglected in the past and capable of being developed rapidly on a grand scale. I take a more sober view of the situation.[49]

But some of the civil servants involved found their engagement with the scheme no bar to advancement. Sir Frank Lee became successively Secretary to the Board of Trade, then second Permanent Secretary to the Treasury, retiring in 1962 to become the Master of Corpus Christi College, Cambridge. Sir George Bishop, in many ways the official closest to Strachey, remained at what became the Ministry of Agriculture, Fisheries and Food, negotiating international agreements on wheat and sugar, and becoming its youngest ever Deputy Secretary in 1959 at the age of 46. It was said that his experience of the Groundnut Scheme left him with an abiding scepticism of grandiose agricultural projects promoted with untested assumptions of yield, production and profit. In 1961 he left public service to become first a director and eventually Chairman of Booker McConnell, the sugar company with exten-

[47] Strachey to Norris Dodd, Director General of the UN FAO, 19 May 1950, Strachey Papers, Box 11.
[48] Information from obituaries in *The Times*.
[49] Frank Samuel, 'Economic Potential of Colonial Africa', *Tropical Agriculture* 28, 7–12 (1951), p. 205, quoted in Hodge, Hodl and Kopf, *Developing Africa*, p. 2.

sive interests in Africa, and after retirement President of the Royal Geographical Society (1983–86) and a keen mountaineer.[50]

Sir Andrew Cohen became Governor of Uganda, where he found shepherding a country towards independence harder than it had seemed from the Colonial Office. But, returning in 1961 to London, he took charge of what became in 1965 the new Ministry of Overseas Development under Barbara Castle, and was its first Permanent Secretary until his sudden death from a heart attack in 1968. He is remembered as the key figure in planning British decolonisation in Africa and establishing Britain's overseas aid policy.[51]

As for the groundnutters, some stayed in Tanganyika and made their lives there. Some, like Vivienne Bell, began a love affair with Africa and worked their way southward, in her case as a secretary in the colonial administration, and the rest scattered across the colonial empire, or returned to a homeland that, with the Festival of Britain in full swing, was beginning to pull itself out of that era of post-war austerity that gave birth to the ill-fated scheme. But for all who had worked on it, the scheme left an indelible impression, reflected now in the many family photos that have found their way onto the internet.[52]

Of the African workers, little is recorded. The West Africans, like Mr Danquah, returned whence they came; Mzee Mbogo, the one-time accounts clerk I met on my visit in 1982, used his income to become a farmer and the respected headman of the village of Kongwa, while Julius Mtenda, in the Southern Province, used his experience with the scheme to become a very successful trader as the region developed during the 1950s.[53]

If this story has any heroes, they are Max Nicholson – the man who was always right – and Hugh Bunting. Both were fundamentally honest men who understood what was happening, had the courage to say so, and who learnt the lessons of the fiasco and applied them afterwards.

Max Nicholson left the civil service in 1952 after Labour's defeat (having played a key part in organising the Festival of Britain) and began a new career as one of the earliest and most effective environmental campaigners in Britain. Born in 1904, he had all his adult life been an enthusiastic naturalist and bird-watcher, and in 1952 was

---

[50] Entries for Lee and Bishop in the *Dictionary of National Biography*; Obituary of Sir George Bishop, *The Independent*, 17 Apr 1999.
[51] Ronald Robinson, 'Sir Andrew Cohen: Proconsul of African nationalism', in L.H. Gann and p. Duignan, *African Proconsuls* (New York, The Free Press, 1978), pp. 353–64. As Cohen was a substantial man, the Department was unkindly dubbed 'The Elephant and Castle'.
[52] Bell, *Wind of Change*, passim; search for the Groundnut Scheme on Flickr and you will find them.
[53] Rizzo, 'Becoming Wealthy', pp. 228–30. Interview with Mzee Mbogo, 12 Jul 1982.

appointed the first Director-General of the Nature Conservancy (now English Nature), a job he filled until 1966. He was at one stage or another involved with virtually every environmental and birding NGO in the country, including as President of the Royal Society for the Protection of Birds from 1980–85, and the first Chairman of Earthwatch Europe from 1985–90. He was, in 1961, one of the founders of the World Wildlife Fund and sat on its international council for many years. He remained active well into his eighties, publishing his ninth volume of *The Birds of the Western Palearctic* in 1994, and in 1996 setting up the New Renaissance Group which supported a College of the Environment as an international training centre for biodiversity. He is a man to whom the whole environmental movement in the UK is deeply indebted. His death in 2003 at the age of 98 is commemorated by a modest monument at the Wetlands Centre in Barnes that he helped to found with Peter Scott. He was in many ways a man before his time, and only now is his environmental message being heeded – but more effectively, we must hope, than his advice on the Groundnut Scheme was in the 1940s.[54]

Dr, later Professor, Hugh Bunting became the doyen of tropical agriculturalists. Still a young man when sacked from the scheme, he published the results of the research work at Kongwa[55], and was recruited by the British Administration in Sudan to work on the Gezira Scheme for five years before returning to the UK. There, he founded the Department of Tropical Agriculture at Reading University, becoming its first and longest-serving professor. For African agricultural scientists, Reading became the place to go, and Bunting had a profound influence on generations of them until he finally retired in 1982. His students remembered vividly the lecture he would invariably give about the Groundnut Scheme to each new generation, explaining why it failed:

> One might as well ask why a baby who can't even crawl can't succeed in the 200m hurdles. No-one knew how to do the job, and those of us who knew how to find out did not have the time to do it. I went to Kongwa on the same train as the first bulldozers. Had there been less pressure, more time, and a proper sequence of investigation, pilot scale trials, training and practical planning, the job could probably have been done (though not in the agricultural pattern intended at the start) in the Southern Province; Kongwa was too dry: it is cattle country; Urambo was too wet for groundnuts but we did well enough with tobacco.[56]

If it was his mistake in 1947 to have advised that Kongwa would be a suitable place to begin cultivation, he more than anyone learnt from the

---

[54] Obituary in *The Independent*, 29 Apr 2003.
[55] Bunting, 'Agricultural Research in the Groundnut Scheme'.
[56] A.H. Bunting, Letter on 'The Groundnut Scheme', *Tanzanian Affairs*, 25, 1 Sep 1986 (www.tzaffairs.org/1986/09/the-groundnut-scheme, accessed 18 Jan 2020).

Photo 9.1 Groundnut field at Kongwa with baobab, 1949 (Sheila Unwin, courtesy of Vicky Unwin)

mistakes, made amends, and did his utmost to avoid others falling into the same trap by ensuring that governments would look at the scientific problems before they leapt with the big investments, as Nicholson had advised. He died, aged 84, in 2002, and with him died the greatest knowledge of the scheme anywhere.[57]

---

[57] A.H. Bunting, 'A Personal Note', Faculty of Agriculture and Food, Reading University, 1989 (lent me by Edward Bunting, to whom I am most grateful).

10

Legacy and Lessons

At the end of the film *Passport to Pimlico*, the summer heat wave ends, the temperature drops, the vision vanishes, the temporary madness ceases, and life returns to dull normality. The independent patch of ancient Burgundy vanished from post-war London's bomb-sites, leaving only vague memories and tall tales.

The film is almost a metaphor for the Groundnut Scheme. But the scheme's legacy and its lessons have had a lasting influence – and where they have not, perhaps they should have done. In 1950, one MP predicted: 'It will really baffle the historian in the future. Many will write a thesis about it, but they will all end in question marks.'[1] He was wrong about the theses – there is only one that I know of – but it is still worth trying to answer those questions.[2]

This story has been told as a narrative, as only thus can the interaction of the various forces that affected the scheme's destiny be understood. It has focussed on the political and policy dynamic, as much as on the obstacles to implementation on the ground, as in many ways it was the former that dictated the outcome. This chapter is thematic, pulling together conclusions on the issues raised in the Introduction and examining the implications for both the study of development and the experience of managing megaprojects. It examines, firstly, why the scheme failed. It then looks at four wider issues which have been neglected by previous studies. Firstly, where did the money go? Secondly, what was the impact on Tanganyika, on Britain's imperial project in Africa, and on post-colonial Tanzania? Thirdly, it examines the impact of the scheme on the policy, planning and practice of development schemes in general and agricultural schemes in particular. Finally, it assesses the

---

[1] Godfrey Nicholson, MP for Farnham, *Hansard*, vol. 477, col. 2107, 18 Jul 1950.
[2] Matteo Rizzo's PhD thesis (SOAS, 2004) is the only one I know, though the questions have attracted some attention. See in particular Phillips, *Agriculture and Ecology*, pp. 330–82, and Hogendorn and Scott, 'Very large-scale agricultural projects'.

impact on the management of large-scale schemes, or megaprojects, particularly by governments both in Britain and more widely, and tries to draw some lessons we should learn if we are to avoid falling into the same old traps over and over again.

Why did it fail?

In retrospect, like a Greek tragedy, the failure of the Groundnut Scheme was fore-doomed and foretold. Its fate was inevitable. So the first question must be: why was it ever launched in the first place?

As set out in Chapters 2 and 3, there were two fundamental reasons: firstly, it appeared as an answer to the prayers of the post-war Labour Government. It was what they needed, just when they needed it, so they willingly suspended judgement and went ahead. Secondly, their willingness to do this was profoundly influenced by the war itself, which led many to believe that determination, ingenuity and technology were sufficient to solve any problem and overcome any challenge, without paying too much attention to cost. It was very much a product of its time: it appeared as a modern solution to an ancient problem, and something that Britain could bring to Africa, to Africa's benefit and Britain's own.

It was this logic which led to the first underlying cause of failure: *the gross under-estimation of cost and risk*. The proponents of the Groundnut Scheme were trying something that in Africa was new, innovative and ambitious. Though some attempts at mechanisation had been tried before, for example by the *Office du Niger* or on the Northern Province Wheat Scheme, mass production by mechanised means on this scale was unprecedented. One cannot help feeling that those who had tried it, specifically Ralph Miller, should have known better than to encourage another hasty attempt. The result of this innovative approach, with so little previous experience to base it on, was that the assumptions set out in the original Plan proved wildly over-optimistic in terms of the speed of development and of its cost. Costs in all areas – transport, accommodation, labour, infrastructure of all kinds, but above all the cost of mechanical clearing in the face of poor equipment and a harsh environment – were all vastly under-estimated. It was revealing that, having assumed all the problems of mechanisation had been solved in the US, they were surprised to find they had not, but pressed on regardless, while failing to make any objective assessment of the scale of the risks they were running. Both Strachey and Wakefield admitted that this was a risky venture, and we must recognise that risk analysis for commercial or government projects was still in its infancy in the 1940s; but their response was simply to assert that risks must be taken to make progress, not to assess how to mitigate those risks and minimise the chances of failure.

It did not help that the Government were led up the garden path by the United Africa Company. With decades of experience of operating in Africa, the UAC was better placed than most to realise the risks involved in the scheme. They recognised well enough that they did not wish to (and could not afford to) run those risks themselves. So they were more than happy to hand the whole risk of the enterprise over to the government knowing that if it worked they would reap profit and if it did not, they would lose nothing.[3] But it has to be admitted that John Strachey was willingly led. While the Treasury, the Colonial Office and even parts of his own Ministry of Food questioned the UAC's motivation and the scale of the risks to be run, Strachey was not only seduced by the vision unfolded before him, but proceeded to sell it to his Cabinet colleagues with all the wit, conviction and persuasion at his disposal. It was in practice a classic case of what one colonial official in Tanganyika described as 'the "Pilgrim Fathers Complex", an attitude of boundless optimism founded on faith, courage and lack of knowledge.'[4]

The second fundamental cause of failure was the reason these estimates proved so far adrift from reality: *the intractable nature of the African environment*. No effort was made to learn the most important lesson of its ill-fated predecessor, the Northern Province Wheat Scheme: that the African bush cannot be treated like the Canadian prairie. Nature, they found, proved a far more resilient enemy than the Nazis. All the men, machines, manure and will-power in the world could not transform dry bush into lush farmland overnight. The assumptions in the Wakefield report were so wide of the mark that Strachey's subsequent disillusion with the author is understandable. To take just one example, Wakefield had predicted that drought might affect the scheme one year in five. In fact, in three years out of six the crop was destroyed by drought. The long-suffering General Manager of the scheme, Professor Phillips, noted later that 'the fundamental ecological setting ... was never adequately studied before commencing its development', and concluded that: 'with its original aims and time schedule and its ecological setting no power on earth could have led the undertaking to success.'[5]

One of the wisest commentators on the scheme at the time was Professor Herbert Frankel. As the first (and only) Professor of Colonial Economics at Oxford University and a member of the Kongwa Working Party in 1950, he identified the futility of embarking on a scheme of

---

[3] Fieldhouse, *Merchant Capital*, p. 218, remarks that the Scheme 'constitutes one of the most surprising events in the history of the company, mainly because it was so untypical of its normal mode of operations', which was to proceed cautiously, examine carefully and undertake extensive pilot schemes first.
[4] C. Gillman, *Tanganyika Standard*, 30 Apr 1944, quoted in Koponen, 'Development in south-east Tanganyika', p. 50.
[5] Phillips, *Agriculture and Ecology*, p. 34.

capital-intensive mechanised agriculture in an environment where its likelihood of success had not even been tested, let alone proven, as the critical reason for failure. This appears to have had a profound impact on Frankel's own thinking, as he became a deep sceptic of large-scale, state-run development schemes, as illustrated by his later questioning of the emerging World Bank orthodoxy that this should be the preferred means of developing poor countries.[6] The lack of time to experiment and build up the scheme slowly in such a difficult environment also reflected some of Hugh Bunting's own retrospective thoughts. Bunting underlined that they had seriously under-estimated the extent to which it was an engineering as much as agricultural project, and that the whole thing depended heavily on good communications, which were utterly lacking in most of the areas to be developed.[7] For these misjudgements, Wakefield must carry a good deal of the responsibility.

Some of these problems could certainly have been overcome with time and patience. But the third fundamental cause of failure was *haste*. There is an old Swahili saying that the newcomers ignored; *Haraka haraka haina baraka* ('Haste brings no blessings'), or as Professor Phillips put it in a central chapter of his book: 'Haste is Waste'.[8] Because the whole scheme was politically driven by a political timetable – to deliver an increased margarine ration before the next election in 1950 – it was accepted that everything should be sacrificed to speed. As people identified almost from the outset, the 'headlong' manner in which it was pursued, the overriding imperative to meet the political deadlines, ensured that difficulty turned to disaster. The need for speed overrode all technical advice and caution. The impetuous purchasing of anything and everything; the determination to begin production without a pilot phase and simply learn lessons as they went along (very expensive lessons as they proved to be); the deal struck with the managing agents and contractors; and the lack of maintenance facilities and basic infrastructure that massively increased the cost and forced unforeseen delays – all compounded the problems the scheme faced. The managing agents' arrangements also inevitably condemned the scheme to a chaotic start. Basic management, storekeeping and

---

[6] S. Herbert Frankel, 'The Kongwa Experiment', *The Times*, 4 and 5 Oct 1950. An amended version was reproduced in S.H. Frankel, *The Economic Impact on Under-Developed Societies* (Oxford, OUP, 1953). The effect of the scheme on his thinking is reflected in his review of the World Bank's publication, 'United Nations Primer for Development', *The Quarterly Journal of Economics*, 66: 3 (Aug 1952), pp. 301–26. Frankel's views on development are discussed in detail in William Easterly, *Tyranny of Experts*, pp. 98–101.

[7] Hugh Bunting, 'Reflections on Three Years', *Our World*, Jan 1950 (copy in TNA 35147). See also Esselborn, 'Environment, Memory and the Groundnut Scheme', pp. 70–75.

[8] Phillips, *Agriculture and Ecology*, ch. 31.

accounts were neglected in a way that the company would never have accepted had they had responsibility for the enterprise themselves. But it was the government's money they were spending, and they were being told to 'just get on and do it', and this led to the chaos from which the scheme never recovered.

This haste underlines the fourth fundamental cause of failure, that it was not a true development scheme at all but a *political project, decided by politicians for political purposes*. This manifested itself repeatedly in the willingness of politicians – not just Strachey, but the whole Cabinet – to ignore and override the caution of officials. For the truth was that those who knew about tropical agriculture (with the notable exception of Wakefield), those who knew about previous attempts at mechanisation, who knew about the state of infrastructure in Tanganyika, all urged caution and a slower approach. But in this debate, the political repeatedly overrode the practical, and the proud exponents of a great socialist experiment in developing Africa walked gaily and obliviously down the primrose path to perdition.

This also explains why, even when it became apparent early on that things were not going according to plan, the government refused to face reality or cut its losses by re-organising the scheme earlier. Three things contributed to this outcome. Firstly, almost none of the decision-makers understood or had any first-hand experience of either Africa or agriculture. They relied on experts to guide them, but *only* on those experts who gave them the advice they wanted to hear. Plummer's fundamental failure to grasp what was happening on the ground, as probably the only person who could have told Strachey directly that it was all a disastrous mistake, meant that both took decisions that damned the scheme to a game of double or quits and kept the money pouring in and the debts mounting up. Putting the OFC headquarters in Mayfair rather than on the ground in Tanganyika also reflected the domestic political prioritisation of the scheme, and enabled the management board to remain insulated from the realities on the ground for too long. Secondly, the reasoning behind the launch of the scheme explicitly *excluded* its financial viability. It would still produce food, which was desperately needed, and it would still save dollars. So the fact that it was losing money was no reason not to continue. We see this logic played out again and again in the Cabinet discussions.

But come 1949, a third factor came to dominate. This was a flagship socialist enterprise for the Labour Government and it could not be allowed to fail, especially as the next general election loomed. There was a political imperative that the enterprise must succeed, so the scheme had to continue in one form or another until success could be declared. While failure was not an option, in this case neither was it avoidable. So the scheme became not only an economic failure but a political disaster, for which Labour duly paid a price. This is one aspect of Attlee's Government in the post-war years that has tended to be forgotten, but which should, in a balanced assessment of those crucial years, be put alongside its many and justifiably lauded achievements.

This political imperative for the scheme points to what is the most important underlying reason for its failure: that it was above all an exercise in *wish fulfilment*. The post-war world wanted and needed inspiring visions, and above all Britain needed hope. The Groundnut Scheme seemed to be exactly what was needed – for the 'housewife', the government and the colonial empire – and therefore people and politicians wanted to believe in it, and assured themselves that it *had* to be made to work. Faith and hope triumphed over charity – or at least over the desire to develop the poorest regions of the colonial empire for the benefit of its people. Blinded by what they wanted to see, British politicians fell into a trap entirely of their own making; and not, sadly, for the last time.[9]

Where did the money go?

Though it failed in all its objectives, the Groundnut Scheme was nevertheless the largest single transfer of resources from Britain to its colonial empire in the post-war period. At a time when, despite the platitudes of colonial development, Britain was milking its empire for hard currency to support its own reconstruction through the system of sterling balances (see Chapter 1) this was a huge flow of money, including hard currency dollars, in the opposite direction. The £36.5 million (equivalent to over £1.1 billion in 2019) written off amounted to £2 per head for every taxpayer in Britain, and was roughly equal to the *total* expenditure on colonial development and welfare for the *whole* colonial empire from 1945 to 1951.[10] So where, precisely did this money go?[11]

Much of it, of course, was simply ploughed into the dry, sandy soils of Kongwa, doing nobody any good at all. But some of it can be traced. As

---

[9] In recent years, the classic example of this tendency towards political wish fulfilment, in the face of all evidence, has been Brexit – but that is another book.
[10] Total Colonial Development and Welfare spending 1945–51 was £40 million, while money extracted from the sterling area to the benefit of Britain through the sterling balances amounted to £140 million in the same period: John Iliffe, *Africans: The history of a continent* (Cambridge, CUP, 3rd edition 2017), p. 238. For a fuller discussion of sterling balances, see Havinden and Meredith, *Colonialism and Development*, ch. 11. Income taxpayers in the UK in 1948–49 were 14,500,000: this and other figures in Tom Clark and Andrew Dilnot, *Long Term Trends in British Taxation and Spending* (Institute for Fiscal Studies, Briefing Note No. 25, 2002 – accessed on 30 Dec 2019 at www.ifs.org.uk/bns/bn25.pdf).
[11] Hogendorn and Scott are blunt in their conclusion: 'The money, in effect, was thrown away'. 'Lessons of the East African Groundnut Scheme', p. 192.

Strachey himself said, the British Exchequer made at least something out of the sale of army surplus stores to the scheme. It is hard to put a figure on it, but probably around £2–3 million went simply from one government account to another.

But the big winners were the Managing Agent and the other contractors. Almost £9 million was paid to the UAC during its one year as the Managing Agent, and that, with the cost-plus contracts for clearing and construction given to Paulings, Mowlems, Taylor Woodrow and Gladwell's company (later bought by the OFC) consumed around £20 million of the total, according to the press.[12] Cost-plus, of course meant that a 'fair' profit was assured, but the contracts also enabled them to build up a local presence from which they profitably bid for other work in post-war colonial development, in both public and private sectors. Mowlems and Taylor Woodrow remained firmly embedded in the local market long after independence, well into the 1980s and '90s.[13] The accountants, Cooper Bros (later Coopers and Lybrand), who were recruited to bring some order to the accounts books, also found the scheme a major boost to their profile and presence in East Africa. They too never looked back and continued as the auditor of choice for countless aid agencies and projects into the 1990s, especially in Tanzania. On the transport side, shippers made a killing transporting cargoes of army surplus goods from one side of the world to the other – from the Philippines via London to Dar es Salaam for example.[14] The number of flights to and from East Africa taken by the OFC as well as their chartering of an aircraft for their journeys around Tanganyika also gave a boost to the viability of the East African route for what became the British Overseas Airways Corporation (BOAC, eventually British Airways – BA). Land Rover built a model, a reputation and a whole company on the prototype and initial order from the Groundnut Scheme. The Defender model continued to be produced well into the next century (including after Land Rover transferred into Indian ownership).

So the bulk of the money went to expatriate British enterprises, illustrating again the way the imperial economy operated to the benefit of British capitalism.[15] A great deal of cash was nevertheless pumped into the Tanganyikan economy, as well as into the companies' bottom lines, which did have a significant impact (see below).

As noted, the scheme fits neatly into the pattern of late imperial British economic policy.[16] During the Depression, the hitherto satisfac-

---

[12] OFC, *First Annual Report*, p. 77; *Tanganyika Standard*, 26 Jan 1950 (copy in TNA 35147). Fieldhouse, *Merchant Capital*, doesn't dwell on this.
[13] See for example Jenkins, *On Site*, passim.
[14] Hogendorn and Scott, 'Lessons of the East African Groundnut Scheme', p. 175.
[15] Cain and Hopkins, *British Imperialism*, pp. 201–34.
[16] In addition to the literature cited in the Introduction, see the excellent summary in B.R. Tomlinson, 'Imperialism and after: the economy of the empire

tory imperial structure of a raw material producing periphery trading with a manufacture-exporting metropolis had come under growing strain as falling commodity prices and reduced manufacturing export made some colonies uneconomic. Starved of funds and suffering economically, the colonial periphery began to fall prey to unrest, most violently in the West Indies, but also in Africa. Imperial preference was tried, but did little good. During the war, the global economic situation was transformed, and the economic resources of the empire were mobilised as ruthlessly as those at home to achieve victory, but at a heavy price. Post-war economic policy used the instruments that had enabled Britain to mobilise those resources – sterling balances, bulk-purchase arrangements – to provide a crutch for Britain's domestic economic recovery. A key element of this was the increased expenditure on the development of colonial resources, through the Colonial Development and Welfare Act, the CDC and the OFC. Of these three, the OFC was the most explicitly geared to supporting British domestic economic needs, and the most generously provided with ready cash. The investment was made with the clear objective of providing a swift and substantial economic return to the UK in terms of food supplied and dollars saved.

As we have seen, this motive changed over time. As the scale of the disaster sank in, and the scale of ambition was reduced, the benefit to the colony became the predominant motive, and the resources made available were accordingly cut back. In the end it became what it should have been at the outset – a small-scale experimental agricultural project from which benefits to the local economy might spring, which could have been achieved at a fraction of the capital outlay.

In considering where the money went, it is important therefore to take a wider look at the profit and loss account of the scheme in its imperial economic context, and in particular at the *opportunity cost* of the project which forms a significant part of its legacy. In these terms, the costs were even greater than the headline loss might appear. We must look at what did *not* get done instead – where the money did *not* go – to understand the overall impact on Britain's imperial enterprise.

A thousand miles away, on the other side of the continent in northern Nigeria, peasant farmers had been growing groundnuts for years. Conditions there, as further west in Senegal and Gambia, were ideal for groundnut cultivation. All it needed was the means to get the crops to market. In 1911, the colonial government completed the extension of the railway from Lagos to Kano, the capital of northern Nigeria. Groundnut production exploded, without any formal encouragement from colonial authorities other than imposing the obligation to pay tax. In 1913, 19,300 tons were exported; in 1920, shipments were 45,000 tons and in

---

on the periphery', in Judith Brown and Wm Roger Louis (eds), *The Oxford History of the British Empire, Vol. IV: The twentieth century* (Oxford, OUP, 1999), ch. 15.

1937 reached a maximum of 350,000 tons. By 1946, the region was still producing around 300,000 tons a year for export despite the constraints of war. This expansion was achieved through the individual enterprise of peasant producers and local merchants, the colonial administration's efforts to get them to grow cotton having no impact (cotton required more work for less return, and couldn't even in a bad year be eaten). By 1937, roughly a million acres in the Kano region were under groundnut cultivation, producing consistently high yields.[17]

The problem in the 1940s was not production, but transport. During the war, the railway network in Nigeria, as everywhere else in Africa, had been worked flat out. Loads had been increased, maintenance skimped, engines made to run until they were worn out. The great post-war quest for oils and fats had identified that there was surplus production of groundnuts in northern Nigeria with inadequate means of transporting it to the coast for export. What they desperately needed were new engines and new rolling stock. This could only be provided with priority allocation of scarce steel and with explicit government instructions to British engineering companies to deliver to the colonies first. This did not happen, not least because the only colonial market to be given such priority was Tanganyika, for the Groundnut Scheme.[18]

In April 1948, the Colonial Office's Economic Policy Committee discussed the issue and noted that:

> At Kano in Northern Nigeria, there were at the end of October 1947 immense tarpaulin-covered pyramids containing 92,000 tons of groundnuts. These would be available to help maintain our fats ration if they could be moved to port, but for lack of railway materials the pyramids are likely to grow to at least 145,000 tons by the end of October 1948. Had part of the effort devoted to starting the East African groundnut scheme been put into obtaining supplies for the existing Nigerian railway, we believe they would have yielded far larger short-term results.[19]

In October 1949, there were 155,000 tons awaiting shipment, and it was only in the early 1950s that Nigeria finally received the locomotives and rolling stock it needed to shift the groundnuts for export.

Had the same effort, priority and resources been put into solving the West African transport problems as went into the Groundnut Scheme, both the British consumer and colonial producer would have been significantly better off in those days of post-war austerity. Even Unilever's crushing plants in the UK would have benefited. In particular, Nigerian

---

[17] A.G. Hopkins, *An Economic History of West Africa* (London, Longman, 1973), pp. 219–20; Hogendorn and Scott, 'Lessons of the East African Groundnut Scheme', pp. 187–91.
[18] Morgan, *Colonial Development, Vol. II*, ch.4.
[19] EPC (48) 35, 27 Apr 1948, quoted in Morgan, *Colonial Development, Vol. II*, p. 196.

peasant producers would have responded far more rapidly to price and market incentives than any mechanised mass production could do on the other side of the continent. But it did not happen. Worse than that, the CDC compounded the problem by seeking to imitate the Groundnut Scheme by investing in a fully mechanised Niger Agricultural Project in northern Nigeria, which failed as miserably as its East African counterpart, though at lower cost.[20]

Strachey's vision had swept all before it and dictated an irrational use of resources through the government planning arrangements that still gripped the British economy. All the effort went into Tanganyika.

The impact on Tanganyika

The impact of the scheme on Tanganyika was in some ways negligible, in other ways profound.

The scheme of course failed and Kongwa was gradually abandoned. 'Half London' became a ghost town, echoing with the departed voices of Cockneys, Mancunians, Yorkshiremen, South Africans, West Africans and ex-servicemen of every stripe. The southern railway was eventually pulled up, leaving no more than a long, straight clearing through the trees. Dar es Salaam port never had to cope with those 600,000 tons of groundnut exports that had been planned, nor did the administration benefit from the additional export revenue and income tax it had anticipated. The development benefits never materialised, and by independence in 1961, Tanganyika remained one of the poorest of Britain's colonies, with annual GDP per capita estimated at anywhere between £6 (World Bank) and £21 (Government statistics) – either way one of the lowest in the world.[21]

But there were still impacts, both negative and positive. After all, much of the money spent – probably well over £10m – ended up, as cash, in Tanganyika itself. Most, however, went into consumption rather than productive investment. The old Tanganyika hands grumbled into their whisky and soda because the free-spending Groundnut Scheme had driven up the price of drink, and the price of African labour too. Africans were equally hit by the rapid post-war inflation, even if this was caused as much by import restrictions that were a consequence of the UK's sterling policies as by money splashed about by the scheme. But they benefited from the rise in wages. Sisal workers received a step-change in pay and conditions because of the competition from the

---

[20] Havinden and Meredith, *Colonialism and Development*, p. 291.
[21] Cranford Pratt, *The Critical Phase in Tanzania, 1945–1968* (Cambridge, CUP, 1976), p. 21; C. Ehrlich, 'The poor country: Tanganyika', in Low and Smith (eds), *History of East Africa, Vol. III*, p. 330.

more lavish scheme; and any artisan with a skill – mechanics, carpenters, drivers, builders – could command higher rates than ever before as demand for their services so far exceeded supply. The model employment conditions that the scheme sought to apply to its workforce, even if imperfectly implemented, set a new standard that other local employers had to pay heed to if, in a condition of labour shortage, they wanted to attract good workers.[22]

At its peak, the scheme employed nearly 27,000 Africans, making it the second largest employer of African labour in the territory after the sisal industry (which had 150,000 by 1950, though spread among many different estates and companies). Of these, roughly half were classified as skilled, and many were trained in those skills by the OFC itself. A training school was set up in a former Polish refugee camp at Ifunda in the Southern Highlands to teach basic civil and mechanical engineering and secretarial skills to 1,000 employees a year. Interestingly, Tanganyika could not furnish enough school leavers capable of taking the courses, so more were brought in from Kenya to make up the numbers – an indication of just how poor the existing educational facilities in Tanganyika were. Those lucky enough to get the training had no difficulty picking up jobs elsewhere, and when the OFC wound down, the training centre was transferred to the Education Department and further expanded.[23]

The other Africans who benefited most directly were those who chose to exploit the market that the scheme created. Tom Bain, the man who brought the scheme to Kongwa in the first place, had done very nicely from supplying the Europeans' need for beef and bacon by the time the scheme closed. But he was emulated by many local African farmers who became accustomed to producing for the OFC market and continued afterwards to hunt down other local markets for their products. This too injected more cash into the local economy which the Wagogo, of course, soon converted into cattle. As a result, the bride price for marriageable Wagogo girls went up.[24]

In the Southern Province, the scheme had brought an abrupt intrusion of the outside world into an isolated and backward area. The missionaries may have lamented, but Africans made the most of the opportunities it offered, and the colonial officials welcomed it: 'All of us in the Tanganyika Administration serving in the Southern Province were 100% 'groundnutters'', recalled one District Officer.[25] The Provincial Commissioner, A.H. Pike, used it to help speed up recognition of the

[22] Westcott, 'Impact of the Second World War' (PhD), ch. 8.
[23] OFC, *Second Annual Report*, pp. 46–52; Moffett, *Handbook of Tanganyika*, p. 366.
[24] Dodoma District Annual Reports, 1948–51, TNA.
[25] P. Johnston, 'The Groundnut Scheme: A personal memoir, *Habitat International*, 7 Jan 1983, quoted in Esselborn, 'Environment, Memory and the Groundnut Scheme', p. 70.

need for a development plan for the whole region. His 'Southern Province Development Plan' was the first time anyone had given serious forward thinking to how to develop what had previously been seen as a national backwater. Matteo Rizzo's detailed analysis of the scheme's impact in the south shows clearly how it created 'these days of great prosperity' (in the phrase of an African Field Assistant at Farm No. 2, Mr Makwinja), and some of the first serious African entrepreneurs in the territory.[26] The demand for labour and food as well as retail supplies did more to boost the local economy than any development plans, and the local people took full advantage of it.

The aftermath of the scheme also saw a dramatic increase in the production of cashew nuts in the Southern Province. Trees had been introduced from Mozambique in the 1930s and in 1939 Tanganyika exported 928 tons of nuts for processing in India. By 1952 this had risen dramatically to 11,700 tons, and by 1961 Tanzania was exporting over 40,000 tons or 25% of total global production of cashew nuts. This transformed the local economy, provided a product to export from the brand new port at Mtwara, and had nothing whatsoever to do with the Groundnut Scheme, except that some of the cleared land was converted to cashew trees. Though Provincial Commissioner Pike encouraged cultivation of cashews from 1950 on, the growth was almost entirely self-generated by peasant farmers owning small numbers of trees (anything from 10 to 100), stimulated by the market incentive of a cash crop that was relatively easy work and lucrative.[27] Though Mtwara port itself has hardly grown since it was first built, it remains the transport hub for the south and a focus for its development plans ever since, though its potential remains to be fully tapped.

The scheme also impacted on social and gender relations. In 1948, Provincial Commissioner Pike reported:

> The position of African women in Masasi District is a matter of considerable concern to the tribal elders, the Provincial Administration and the Missions. In this area, where the Wamakua follow matriarchal [matrilineal] principles, the impact of modern civilisation seems to have encouraged the women to throw off many of the old restraints. As there is no dowry paid the woman apparently considers herself entitled to leave her husband and children at any time for some other man. Parents and others constantly bemoan the lack of control over

---

[26] Rizzo, 'Groundnut Scheme', pp. 212–36, and 'Becoming Wealthy', pp. 221–31. Interview with A.H. Pike, 3 Nov 1978.
[27] Johani Koponen, 'From dead end to new lease of life: development in south-east Tanganyika from the late 1930s to the 1950s', in Hodge, Hodl and Kopf (eds), *Developing Africa*, pp. 37–62; Donald Mitchell, 'Tanzania's Cashew Sector: Constraints and challenges in a global environment', World Bank, Africa Region Working Paper Series No. 70, Jun 2004.

their girls, who are frequently attracted away to development areas where money is plentiful and life more exciting. The question of instituting a small dowry payment is now being considered by the tribal elders, but the weight of feminine opinion is against such an innovation, which makes any change difficult.[28]

The nearest 'development areas' were of course Nachingwea and Mtwara. The contrast with the patrilineal Wagogo, where a rising bride price profited the menfolk not the women, is striking, and illustrates the difficulty of generalising about social impacts. In that other great generator of accelerated social change, the capital Dar es Salaam, the impact of the scheme was largely subsumed within the overall post-war period of rapid growth, rising wages, loosening morals and political awakening.[29]

In September 1950, the *Tanganyika Standard* reviewed what the scheme had brought to the territory. From its firmly paternalist colonial perspective, it recognised that, despite its many failures, it had brought

> a great deal of prosperity to Dar es Salaam and other parts of Tanganyika and has given the Africans a splendid opportunity to carry out various trades for which they have been prepared while serving with the army or learnt at post-war training centres. It has also provided the native inhabitants ... with an opportunity to work for a living and appreciate a higher standard of life and better health than ever before. From this angle, Kongwa has not been a failure.

So too it acknowledged that, 'the millions spent at Kongwa did one thing: they put Tanganyika on the map, and kept it there'.[30]

Looking back on the scheme in 1964, the Chairman of the OFC's successor, the Tanganyika Agricultural Corporation, Chief Harun Lugusha, tried to enumerate the benefits. The port, he thought was the largest, then the training of artisans and the setting up of tenant farmer schemes on the residual cleared areas. But all this, he felt could have been done for a fraction of the sum invested: 'I would find it impossible to account for more than about £7 million worth of assets, including the training of Africans, at 1950 prices. Under Tanganyika conditions, with our desperate need for capital, what a waste.'[31] As we have shown, many colonial officials at the time felt the same. Writing in 1976, Cyril Ehrlich made an even more pessimistic judgement that the scheme's impact on Tanganyika was 'almost wholly negative'. It distorted communications, diverted energy from more productive uses and, he believes, left a negative impression of the country in the mind of potential investors. Some local Africans even regarded it as 'like a

[28] Southern Province Annual Report, 1948 (A.H. Pike), p. 87, TNA.
[29] Westcott, 'Impact of the Second World War' (PhD), pp. 277–318.
[30] *Tanganyika Standard*, 29 Sep 1950, copy in TNA 41265.
[31] Listowel, *Making of Tanganyika*, p. 155.

war' – rushing through, leaving waste, chaos and disorientation in its wake.[32]

One thing it did reveal was how little the colonial administration really knew about the country it governed. The environmental conditions, the natural resources and the developmental potential of the different regions were scarcely known, or understood only in the most sketchy way. The colonial administrators realised that if they were to steer investment productively, they needed to know a great deal more about the country. This was reflected in two heavyweight studies undertaken during the 1950s by J.F.R Hill and J.P. Moffett, *Tanganyika: A study of its resources and their development*, published in 1955, and Moffett's *Handbook of Tanganyika,* published in 1958.[33] These remain a goldmine of information about Tanganyika in the last years of colonial rule, but were effectively shelved and forgotten on independence.

The Administration also realised a far more collective and coordinated effort was needed if development was to be achieved. The stand-offishness they had shown towards the abrupt intrusion of the scheme was recognised as counterproductive, simply exacerbating the terrible waste of resources by outsiders who knew even less than they did. Relations between the Administration and the OFC in the 1950s became much smoother and more harmonious, and the absorption of the scheme's remnants into the wider plans for development of the territory presaged the approach that would be taken after independence.[34]

Some of the lessons learnt were immediately applied in the largest of the regional development schemes in the 1950s, that in Sukumaland. Rohland Schuknecht's study shows how the Sukumaland Development Plan was far more in line with the overall post-war policy of colonial development than the Groundnut Scheme, particularly in its emphasis on the development of peasant production and its wariness of mechanisation, even if the emphasis on soil conservation methods was to prove as contentious here as in other colonial territories. While this development scheme focussed closer to the ground, it was still some way from the 'bottom-up development' that is now favoured.[35]

---

[32] Ehrlich, 'The poor country', pp. 311–12.
[33] Both published by the Government Printer, Dar es Salaam. At the same time the economist Phyllis Deane undertook the first attempt to produce national income statistics for Britain's African economies, including Tanganyika: P. Deane, *Colonial Social Accounting* (Cambridge, CUP, 1953).
[34] Andrew Coulson, *Tanzania: A political economy* (Oxford, OUP, 1982), esp. pp. 60–69, 135–44.
[35] Rohland Schuknecht, *British Colonial Development Policy after the Second World War: The case of Sukumaland* (Berlin, LIT Verlag, 2010), and still worth reading G. Andrew Maguire, *Towards 'Uhuru' in Tanzania: The politics of participation* (Cambridge, CUP, 1969), pp. 1–41.

In stark contrast to its political impact in Britain, the scheme had almost no impact on politics in Tanganyika. Far from being controversial, the nationalist politicians paid it virtually no attention at all. As John Iliffe concluded, the failure of this European attempt to restructure Tanganyika's economy meant that there was no significant imperial interest to complicate the decolonisation process, which moved much faster than in neighbouring Kenya.[36] While British imperial prestige was undoubtedly harmed, the dire predictions of a devastating loss of credibility proved exaggerated. There were far more serious things undermining Britain's imperial credibility in the 1950s, from Mau Mau in Kenya, the Malaysian Emergency and the Suez crisis, to the imprisonment or exile of nationalist politicians in colonies across the continent.

But the lack of impact also meant that very few of the scheme's crucial lessons were carried over across the political divide created by independence or were ever embedded in the mindset of nationalist politicians who sought above all a decisive break with the colonial past.

Julius Nyerere, the founding President of independent Tanzania (as it was re-named after the union with Zanzibar in 1964), refers to the scheme in his collected speeches only twice: as an example of the superior wisdom of local farmers over foreign experts, and for the distortion of the country's transport network that it caused.[37] The risks of large-scale, state-run enterprises and politically driven development schemes pursued with haste and without adequate preparation never registered. Like many post-independence states, Tanzania was a country in a hurry, and its political leaders felt it was their duty to deliver as swiftly as possible the development, along with freedom, that they believed had been denied them by the colonial powers. Nyerere was in many ways the embodiment of this approach, and brought a wide range of reference, from India and China as much as from Britain and the World Bank, to bear on Tanzania's challenges. But he also remained deeply influenced by the Fabian socialism of the British Labour tradition that he encountered when he studied in Scotland in the 1940s, the tradition that had underpinned the Groundnut Scheme itself. Already in 1946, he was rejecting foreign investment, and lobbied Creech Jones: 'We want all the chief natural resources of this country such as gold, coal, diamond and tin mines to be developed by the Government and the money obtained to be used for our education and general development.'[38]

Impatient with more traditional development approaches, in January 1967 he issued the Arusha Declaration which proclaimed a fast-track

---

[36] Iliffe, *Modern History of Tanganyika*, p. 442.
[37] Julius K. Nyerere, *Freedom and Development* (Oxford, OUP, 1965), pp. 27, 233.
[38] J.K. Nyerere to Creech Jones, 1 Aug 1946, TNA 34905/50. See also Thomas Molony, *Nyerere: The early years* (Oxford, James Currey, 2016).

route to achieve 'African Socialism'.³⁹ In two particular areas the implementation that followed replicated a number of mistakes the Groundnut Scheme had pioneered: industrial development and rural transformation. Anxious to develop a manufacturing base, the state moved swiftly to establish a state-run textile industry, through the setting up of the Chinese-built Urafiki Textile Mill in Dar es Salaam, and the French-backed Mwatex mills in Mwanza. Not unsuccessful to start with, they fell foul of the deteriorating economic climate and power supply to become uneconomic and a serious drain on state resources. On the agricultural side, Nyerere saw the strategy of encouraging successful peasant farmers as resulting only in increased inequality in rural areas, and therefore proposed a radical programme of enforced villagisation – into *ujamaa* villages to be run on socialist lines – which, bluntly implemented by local party cadres, had a profoundly disruptive effect on food production and social relations in many areas of Tanzania. Mechanised agriculture on state farms was explicitly seen, once more, as a short-cut to overcome perceived peasant conservatism and obstruction to his plans for economic transformation. That it ended badly would have been no surprise to the long-departed agriculturalists in Kongwa. While a politician of consummate skill, Nyerere's economic policies repeated some of the critical mistakes of the Groundnut Scheme, barely 20 years after its spectacular failure.⁴⁰ The most recent study of agricultural development in Tanzania, sadly concludes that, after nearly 60 years of independence,

> [t]he failure of so many agricultural interventions and projects by government and donors cannot be ascribed to an inherent resistance of small farmers to change. It is not small farmers who have failed to identify and exploit potential development opportunities, but rather the 'experts' who have designed and implemented flawed rural programmes ... Part of the explanation lies in politically motivated choices that led to negative results.⁴¹

Sadly, it has not been just in agriculture. The planning bug is deeply embedded in Tanzania, and the waste of state resources on uneconomic or misdirected schemes has continued – amidst, it must be said, some other perfectly successful projects. The building of a new capital in Dodoma, the geographic centre of the country but, like Kongwa, hand-

---

³⁹ 'The Arusha Declaration', 29 Jan 1967, Julius K. Nyerere, *Freedom and Socialism* (Oxford, OUP, 1968), pp. 231–50.
⁴⁰ Among various accounts, I have used: Pratt, *Critical Phase in Tanzania*, pp. 227–61; Coulson, *Tanzania*, pp. 235–89; Scott, *Seeing Like a State*, pp. 223–62; Esselborn, 'Environment, Memory and the Groundnut Scheme', pp. 85–6.
⁴¹ Brian van Arkadie, 'Agricultural development in Tanzania', in D. Potts (ed.), *Tanzanian Development: A comparative perspective* (Oxford, James Currey, 2019), p. 59.

icapped by poor communications and a lack of water, has been plagued by problems, delays, escalating costs, waste and inefficiency. The Dar es Salaam Area Rapid Transport project to bring faster public bus transport to the city has been plagued by delays and cost overruns as the government sought to balance its financial, political and workers' interests.[42] Major infrastructure projects, like the long-promised dam at Stiegler's Gorge (the opposite of the Groundnut Scheme, in that it has been planned on and off since 1938, but never been built), the high-speed rail link to Morogoro, and the ambitious agricultural development scheme known as the Southern Agricultural Growth Corridor of Tanzania (SAGCOT), have all reflected some of the problems that bedevilled the Groundnut Scheme and might have benefited from the experience it provided of 'How Not To Do It'.[43]

The impact on agricultural development policy

The implications and consequences of the scheme, however, went far wider than just Tanzania. It had a profound influence on development policy more widely – at least for a while. This section examines the scheme's impact during the last decade of colonial rule and how that weakened in the transition to post-colonial development planning. The following section looks at the wider implications for the role of the state, and how failing to learn the real reasons for failure has condemned us to repeat the scheme's mistakes over and over again.

The Groundnut Scheme took place in the context of a debate about how to stimulate economic growth in some of the poorest countries in the world, whatever the motives underlying that push for growth – whether to help the imperial power or improve the living standard of the local people. Obviously the objective makes a difference to the proposed solution, as we have seen with the scheme itself. But the common challenge was how difficult environments can be made to yield a better living for those that use them or live there. That debate has continued to the present.

Development economics is still a relatively young discipline. The question of economic change and growth has been at the heart of economic

---

[42] Matteo Rizzo, *Taken for a Ride: Grounding neoliberalism, precarious labour and public transport in an African metropolis* (Oxford, OUP, 2017), pp. 142–70.
[43] These more recent schemes have been less studied in the academic literature, but on SAGCOT see Serena Stein and Marc Kalina, 'Becoming an Agricultural Growth Corridor', *Environment and Society*, 10:1, 2019; on Stiegler's Gorge see e.g. https://en.wikipedia.org/wiki/Stiegler%27s_Gorge_Hydroelectric_Power_Station (accessed 19 Dec 2019). Wood's phrase in *News Chronicle*, 21 Oct 1949.

thinking since Adam Smith, but the more specific question of how to stimulate that growth in poor, peripheral regions of the world economy was only just beginning to be asked in the 1940s. As mentioned, most colonial officials drew their model of economic development directly from Britain's own experience. But a few economists were starting to look in more detail at the challenges that faced African economies in the mid-20th century. Herbert Frankel at Oxford and W. Arthur Lewis at the London School of Economics were two of the pioneers of the discipline, and both followed the fate of the scheme closely.[44]

In terms of the development of tropical agriculture, the Groundnut Scheme has been held up to generations of students as the prime example of what not to do. The scheme was from the outset an ambitious attempt to make a one-off transformation in the productivity of African agriculture through wholesale mechanisation. Miller, Wakefield, Mitchell and others were obsessed with the inefficiency of traditional peasant production and its inability to respond to the growing economic and food needs of the colonies. Something transformational was needed, and from their point of view this could only be the introduction of capital-intensive cultivation with 'modern' farming methods. Frankel was the first to spot that this was an assumption based on no evidence whatsoever. The scheme, on the contrary, provided all the evidence that was needed to show that the assumption was wrong. Tanganyika's existing plantation industry, sisal, demonstrated that in a low wage economy with poor soils, little infrastructure and a shortage of water, labour-intensive farming was likely to be more sustainable and more economic – though the inherent limit on labour supply in an under-populated territory did mean that nothing on the scale proposed by Wakefield would have been possible without massive wage inflation. The conclusion reached in Tanganyika, that small-holder peasant production was the best way forward in the circumstances, was then applied across most of the African colonial empire.

The disillusion with mechanised farming was already setting in during the late 1940s. The West African oilseeds mission did indeed recommend a mechanised groundnut scheme for the Gold Coast, but the CDC wisely refused to back it, and the idea was dropped. The attempt to mechanise in Nigeria led to the question, why mechanise when peasants were producing more than could be shipped by themselves? The lesson was clear, that nature could not be 'bustled a bit'.[45] The ignominious failure of the CDC's Gambia Poultry Scheme showed that it was

---

[44] Robert Tignor, *W. Arthur Lewis and the Birth of Development Economics* (Princeton University Press, 2005).

[45] M.V. Backhouse, Resident at Niger, Nigeria, commenting in 1953 on CDC's Niger Agricultural Project, quoted in Morgan, *Colonial Development, Vol. II*, pp. 210–15, 307–8.

not just mechanised but mass production of all kinds that needed more careful consideration and planning than the enthusiasts for agricultural transformation in Africa were doing. By 1953, the East African Royal Commission recognised that the term 'Development Corporation' should be avoided as it conjured up in the public's mind 'an impression of grandiose projects embarked upon in the highest hopes and financed from a bottomless purse, with eventual disillusionment and a heavy loss to the taxpayer'.[46]

Even so, the Groundnut Scheme was by no means the only attempt to bring European know-how and husbandry techniques to Africa only to find them fail in the face of the relentless environmental challenges. In Northern Rhodesia (now Zambia) around the same time, Stewart Gore-Browne ploughed his considerable energies and not inconsiderable fortune into efforts to make his estate at Shiwa Nganda into a profitable model farm on modern lines. But nature was against him too. Apart from a few years in the 1940s when he was able to make a profit on essential oils, the estate lost money year in year out until the fortune was exhausted.[47] Here, as in central Tanzania, the environment was one of dry bushland from which a living could be wrung only with great effort, risk and experience. The local inhabitants knew this, and continued to pursue a life that was tough, poor and very risk averse. For a while the white man's madness brought them jobs and money, but that too passed away and life resumed its normal course.

The more cautious approach to agricultural development was represented in British Africa by the Gezira Scheme, which though large, ambitious and dependent on substantial irrigation works, evolved more slowly and adapted to lessons as it went. The question whether it constituted real development, or simply a static scheme for export production, has been debated, but relative to the Groundnut Scheme, it certainly counts as a success.[48]

Professor Phillips drew on 30 years of experience in African agriculture, including the Groundnut Scheme and eight years in Ghana before and after independence, in writing his 1959 book *Agriculture and Ecology in Africa*. Drawing lessons from a wide range of large-scale mechanised schemes, including the CDC's various schemes in Nigeria, Gambia, Botswana, the Damongo (Volta River) scheme in the Gold Coast, and groundnut schemes in French West and Equatorial Africa, he concluded: 'In almost all these the success won from the original

---

[46] Acting Governor Tanganyika to CO, 9 Jun 1953, EAF 53/02/B, quoted in Morgan, *Colonial Development, Vol. IV*, p. 66. For the Gambian poultry scheme, which proved the downfall of CDC's first chairman, Lord Trefgarne, see Havinden and Meredith, *Colonialism and Development*, pp. 285–92.
[47] Christina Lamb, *The Africa House* (London, Penguin, 1999).
[48] Barnett, *Gezira Scheme*, pp. 6–15.

undertakings has been slight or the failure complete'.[49] The final chapters of the book reflect at length on the lessons of the Gezira, Groundnuts and Volta schemes, the dangers of making haste and the importance of studying ecology: 'May it be abundantly clear that failure to study and understand Nature inevitably leads to disaster', a message he hoped the newly independent governments would take to heart.[50]

As Phillips identified, the same issues arose in francophone and lusophone colonies on the continent. Joseph Hodge, who edited a wide-ranging study of colonial development across the whole of Africa, concluded:

> Of all the interventions of the colonial state in Africa, those designed for agricultural intensification and rural modernisation, such as the groundnut scheme, the Office du Niger, the Congolese *paysannats* or the Portuguese *colonatos*, were perhaps the greatest debacles of the age. They consumed massive amounts of investment funds and resources, including technical and administrative staff, while offering very little in return.[51]

The lessons were at least heeded by the CDC, the OFC's more successful twin. Though not exclusively agricultural, after suffering a number of early disasters its first Chairman, Lord Trefgarne, resigned and was replaced by the austere and resolute Lord Reith, under whom it evolved a successful model of long-term agricultural investment in wattle, tea, coffee and teak plantations, that provided a viable industry and reliable profits over many years. It transitioned on independence from the Colonial to the Commonwealth Development Corporation, but continued as a valuable source of development finance for agricultural schemes in much of independent Africa. More recently the CDC has been through a number of iterations, selling off many of its estates in the 1990s, and pursuing, as Actis, a more private equity model of investment. But agriculture is coming back into fashion and the CDC has lately returned to the field with growing investments in the sector.[52]

Nevertheless, the transition to independence produced a revival, in new form, of much of the thinking that underlay the Groundnut Scheme. Unlike Frankel, Arthur Lewis remained a proponent of state-led development, and volunteered to support Nkrumah in developing Ghana's post-independence planning, only to fall out with him swiftly when he realised that it was political factors, not economic, that dominated

---

[49] Phillips, *Agriculture and Ecology*, p. 34.
[50] Ibid., p. 358, and more generally pp. 330–96.
[51] Hodge's Introduction to Hodge, Hodl and Kopf, *Developing Africa*, p. 20.
[52] Brain and Cable, *CDC: Pioneering development*, passim, and Havinden and Meredith, *Colonialism and Development*, pp. 283–95; also CDC *Report and Accounts for 1948* (London, HMSO, 1949, No. 188), and *Annual Reports*, 2017–18.

his plans.⁵³ This has been a repeated theme of post-independence planning. John Iliffe has noted that throughout Africa, because economic development became a core legitimising project after independence in order to shore up frail states and fragile regimes, 'the development strategies pursued since independence had been largely political rather than economic in design'.⁵⁴

Agriculture has remained a favoured area for donor support. The transition from colonial development to international aid agencies and the continuities of thinking between the two has been well chronicled by others.⁵⁵ The evolution of development thinking and relative priorities can be followed in the annual Development Reports of the World Bank and periodic White Papers of the British Department for International Development (DFID). In 2008, the World Bank's report was devoted entirely to *Agriculture for Development*, in which many of the familiar themes can be found.⁵⁶ But the track record of agricultural development schemes has been at best patchy. In 1981, Robert Bates identified that the political impetus behind many post-independence agricultural projects was one of the principle causes of failure.⁵⁷ One of the wisest analysts of African agriculture, Sara Berry, concluded in 1993:

> From the well-known failures of the late colonial period – such as the Niger Agricultural Project, the Tanganyika Groundnut Scheme, or mechanised farming projects in the Gambia – to recent donor financed schemes in northern Ghana, Nigeria and Sudan, mechanization projects have contributed little to either agricultural output or rural living standards.⁵⁸

African cultivation practices, she argues, owe as much to the structure of social relations as to the economics of farming, and therefore, 'agricultural intensification is neither inevitable nor continuous in African farming systems'.⁵⁹ More important to African farmers is flexibility, and this is the reason, she argues, that there has not yet been a 'green revolution' in Africa.

---

⁵³ Easterly, *Tyranny of the Experts*, pp. 100–3.
⁵⁴ Iliffe, *Africans*, first edition (1995), p. 256.
⁵⁵ It is a repeated theme of Easterly's books, *White Man's Burden* and *Tyranny of Experts*, as of Cohen and Shenton. But see also Hodge, *Triumph of the Expert*, pp. 254–76, and Esselborn, 'Environment, Memory and the Groundnut Scheme', pp. 77–80.
⁵⁶ World Bank, *Agriculture for Development: Annual development report, 2008* (Washington DC, 2008). See also DFID, *Eliminating World Poverty: Building our common future*, Cmd 7656 (London, The Stationary Office, 2009).
⁵⁷ Robert Bates, *Markets and States in Tropical Africa: The political basis of agricultural policies* (Berkeley, University of California Press, 1981).
⁵⁸ Sara Berry, *No Condition is Permanent:* p. 182.
⁵⁹ Ibid., p. 189.

But this in no way inhibits people from trying to accelerate the process. The dreams of modernising African agriculture and transforming the wilderness into a productive asset live on. The miracle of making the desert bloom like the rose has been achieved in countries such as Israel and Saudi Arabia, but only, it must be said, with the input of huge resources, technology, much water, and great ingenuity. India is more commonly cited as the example Africa should follow. Kofi Annan, the former UN Secretary General, believed that an agricultural transformation was essential if Africa was ever to accelerate its development. To this end he supported the formation of an Alliance for a Green Revolution in Africa (AGRA), which is seeking to achieve the same transformation in Africa that enabled India to feed itself in the 1980s.[60]

Some foreign countries, however, still believed they could transform African agriculture if they were given free access to suitably uninhabited areas. In 2009, attention was drawn to the purchase by China, Korea, India and a number of Middle Eastern sovereign wealth funds, of large tracts of uninhabited African bush which were to be transformed into productive land to feed these overcrowded countries that could no longer feed themselves. These were big deals, covering 1–2 million acres each, and Africa was spoken of as a potential future bread-basket for the world.[61] One of these schemes illustrates that the challenges have not changed so much. A joint Brazilian-Japanese organisation, Prosavana, proposed to transform agriculture on over 100,000 square kilometres of northern Mozambique through a mixture of small-holder farming and giant plantations using modern farming techniques and $2 billion raised through a private equity fund. A decade later, 'there is nothing to show for it, except a small research lab and a few model farms.'[62]. Why? It seems the land was less uninhabited than expected, the local farmers more attached to their traditional ways which worked in their environment, and were more willing to mobilise politically against the scheme.

A recent report by one African economic think tank, the African Centre for Economic Transformation (ACET), noted the lack of success of mechanisation to date, for uncannily familiar reasons:

> In the past, several African governments tried to address the mechanization challenge by importing agricultural machinery to use on state farms or to rent to farmers. These approaches failed because of inefficiencies and poor governance in the state-run agencies and because of

[60] See the AGRA website: https://agra.org (accessed 10 Jul 2019).
[61] *The Economist*, 'Outsourcing's Third Wave', 23 May 2009, pp. 65–8; *Reuters*, 'China Asks to Grow 2 Million ha of Jatropha in Zambia', 31 Mar 2009; Muchena Zigomo, 'China Asks to Plant Jatropha in Zambia', *Manitoba Co-operator*, 9 Apr 2009.
[62] *The Economist*, 16 Nov 2019, p. 44.

the failure to adequately address other fundamental challenges that affect the profitability of farming and consequently farmers' willingness and ability to pay for mechanization services.[63]

They propose instead that 'preference should be given to bringing in a large number of small tractors rather than a small number of large tractors', and ensuring that there are adequate mechanics and repair facilities to minimise tractor downtime. In an earlier report it also noted:

> Improvements in agricultural technology have come slowly to Africa, and not much is known about the diffusion of better technologies. In many ways, Africa is late in developing research capacity, and many crops and commodities have had very little research effort until the past 10–20 years.[64]

The study cites as obstacles continued poor communications, the lack of power and irrigation, weak competition and insecure or obscure property rights. Experience continues to suggest that many parts of Africa do indeed have a harsh and unforgiving environment, and that technology and markets have yet to find a way of making these areas more agriculturally productive. Meanwhile, the small fertile patches of highland Africa have become areas of intense political and economic competition, as in Ethiopia, Kenya and Zimbabwe – the last being a classic case of economic efficiency being sacrificed to political expediency and a country being turned from one of food surplus to food deficit through deliberate political choices (albeit aided and abetted by drought).[65]

This is an issue not just in Africa, and not just of government-run projects. In an important study, 'Why Are Farms So Small?', Johnson and Ruttan, examined four private-sector-led large-scale agricultural schemes in Venezuela, Brazil, Iran and the Philippines, and concluded that they 'had in common ... the belief that large-scale production had inherent technical advantages over small-scale production [But] the fact that none of the projects examined here proved successful suggests that that superiority is an illusion.'[66]

---

[63] African Centre for Economic Transformation (ACET) *Agriculture Powering Africa's Economic Transformation* (Accra, ACET, 2017), p. 9.

[64] ACET *Growth with Depth: 2014 African Transformation Report* (Accra, ACET, 2014), p. 108.

[65] *The Economist*, 'The Underground Revolution: Better seeds could help African farmers grow more', 28 Sep 2019, www.economist.com/middle-east-and-africa/2019/09/28/better-seeds-could-help-african-farmers-grow-far-more (accessed 3 Mar 2020)'.. On Zimbabwe, see the useful survey of literature in Grasian Mkodzongi and Peter Lawrence, 'The Fast-Track Land Reform and Agrarian Change in Zimbabwe', *Review of African Political Economy*, 46:159, 2019; and Privilege Musvanhiri, 'Zimbabwe: Between land ownership and food security, *Deutsche Welle*, 4 Jun 2019, www.dw.com/en/zimbabwe-between-land-ownership-and-food-security/a-49056618 (accessed 6 Jan 2020).

[66] Johnson and Ruttan, 'Why Are Farms So Small?' pp. 691–2.

James C. Scott sees wider reasons 'why a model of modern scientific agriculture that has apparently been successful in the temperate, industrialising West has so often foundered in the Third World'. The schemes, he argues, often represent bureaucratic rather than productive exercises in which those implementing them apply unexamined assumptions and take no account of the local context or 'externalities'; and, fundamentally, farmers are pragmatists and agricultural planners are not.[67]

At least for a while, the Groundnut Scheme led to a victory of the pragmatists over the planners. If nothing else, the scheme produced a body of scientific research and a group of tropical agricultural experts whose experience was invaluable in efforts across the continent to transform its agriculture.[68] The team that Bunting brought together eventually dispersed across Africa to other research establishments, carrying the lessons with them. Colonial governments were, at least, assiduous in establishing agricultural research stations. These continued to flourish during the 1960s, but many fell on hard times during the economic ruin that afflicted much of Africa during the 1970s and '80s. They are only now being revived to take forward the work that had flourished, albeit briefly, during the late colonial and early independence period. Without environmentally appropriate agricultural research, all the efforts to transform African agriculture are likely to come to nought.

Beyond agriculture, the debate continues over the appropriate role of the state in African economic development. The balance between the state and the market in promoting African development has been an issue since the cocoa hold-ups of the 1930s and the introduction of commodity marketing boards – long excoriated by P.T. Bauer.[69] It is heavily influenced by both the state of the global economy and ideological fashion. The post-independence enthusiasm for state-led development has left the African landscape littered with the industrial skeletons of failed parastatals and state-run enterprises – effectively Africa's first, and failed, industrial revolution. Like Strachey, and Nyerere, many African leaders thought the state should step in where private enterprise was reluctant, or indeed where they believed good profits could be made, but to benefit the state. Not just textile factories but airlines, steel industries (like Nigeria's notorious Abeokuta steel mill), aluminium industries (in Ghana's case) and even Zaire's ill-fated nuclear programme bear testament to the triumph of political will over economic or commercial rationality. David Landes, an economic histo-

---

[67] Scott, *Seeing Like a State*, p. 263.
[68] Bunting, 'Agricultural Research in the Groundnut Scheme', p. 804; OFC, *Annual Reports*, 1949–51 and 1954–55.
[69] Bauer, *West African Trade* and *Dissent on Development*.

rian, explicitly refers to the Groundnut Scheme as the mother of all such projects. Far from reflecting either the triumph or the tyranny of experts, the scheme illustrated the triumph, and tragedy, of the politician.[70]

In time, these failures were exposed and the policy undermined by the crippling economic crises that afflicted many African countries in the 1970s and '80s, bankrupting many of the parastatals that had drained, not supported, their national economies. This era led to a fundamental re-think and the controversial introduction of structural adjustment policies, championed by the IMF, the World Bank and Western donors, fed up with seeing their aid money effectively wasted, and under pressure from their shareholders, taxpayers and voters to stop the waste.[71]

This reflects an important point. Donor governments are by and large accountable to their taxpayers for the money spent. African governments are accountable to those who control political power in their country – sometimes the people, sometimes the military, sometimes businesses, but rarely taxpayers. Often, government is seen as something you get money *from*, not something you give money *to*. The money flows into government accounts from donors, customs, or natural resource revenues, but rarely from the people. Politics therefore revolves around who gets what from the bounty the government receives. This fundamentally changes the political dynamic of accountability; accountability, as the Groundnut Scheme illustrated, is at the heart of effective development.[72]

The last decade has seen the pendulum swing back towards support for greater state involvement in development. The financial crisis of 2008–09 led to disillusion with the free-market ethos of globalisation,

---

[70] David Landes, *The Wealth and Poverty of Nations: Why some are so rich and some so poor* (New York, W.W. Norton, 1999), pp. 499–507 (in the chapter titled 'Losers'). This is not to refute either Hodge's or Easterly's theses, but to recognise the powerful political reasoning and impetus behind the critical decisions.
[71] Robert Bates' book, *Markets and States* marked a turning point in the debate. For a layman's summary see Martin Meredith, *The State of Africa* (London, The Free Press, 2005), chs 16 and 22, and for a practitioner's view, Greg Mills, *Why Africa is poor, and What Africans Can Do About It* (London, Penguin, 2010). The widespread criticism of the neo-liberal 'Washington consensus' and the inequality of growth it created too often overlooks the abject failure of earlier post-independence economic policies and the need to find an alternative that worked. Any critique also needs to recognise that states take decisions for political reasons and that, without adequate accountability (through solid democratic institutions, for example), these decisions will reflect the interests of the rulers, not the ruled. South Africa under Zuma illustrates this just as well as the Groundnut Scheme under Strachey.
[72] See Mick Moore, Odd-Helge Fjeldstad and Wilson Prichard, *Taxing Africa: Coercion, reform and development* (London, Zed Books, 2018); Nicholas Westcott, 'Trust the People', *The World Today*, 65:3, Mar 2009, pp. 24–6.

and has increased the profile and popularity in Africa of what is often considered the 'Chinese model' of directed (or authoritarian) development. Ethiopia and Rwanda are seen as the leading, and most successful, representatives of this trend.[73] Economists point out the crucial role of the state in the rapid growth of countries like South Korea. But while such an approach can accelerate growth, as in Ethiopia it can also create political challenges that make this growth potentially fragile. Few African countries have been able to match the scale of Chinese economic growth, not least because independent African governments have struggled to overcome the fragmented national economic structures left by colonialism. But that is an altogether wider debate which needs a separate study to do it justice. Suffice it to say that one lesson of the Groundnut Scheme is that such 'directed development' should be treated with caution and rigorous scrutiny, as its long-term success will still depend on the effective level of accountability to those it is trying to help.

Megaprojects and mega-disasters

Why do so many megaprojects fail?

In Britain, the Groundnut Scheme became directly a byword for government incompetence and extravagance. As we have seen, it was used as a shibboleth by the Conservatives to beat the Labour Government in 1950 and 1951. Most politically damaging, however, it made the Government the object of ridicule and the scheme itself (as Bunting said) a music hall joke. Manny Shinwell admitted many years later that 'the worst thing for a Government is to be laughed at'.[74]

The Groundnut Scheme became a point of reference whenever British governments committed similar *folies de grandeur*, great projects launched with fanfare to meet a noble need, driven politically to ever greater cost or to ultimate disaster. As seen above (p. xi), there is a Spike Milligan cartoon of a boy and his father gazing up into the sky as Concorde flies by: 'What is that Dad?' 'That is a flying Groundnut Scheme, son'.[75]

It was not just Concorde (which at least got off the ground). In Britain alone, the roll-call is long – Blue Streak, De Lorean cars, the Millennium Dome, the NHS integrated IT project, HS2 (the high-speed rail link to

---

[73] One example of this shift is Tim Kelsall, *Business, Politics and the State in Africa: Challenging the orthodoxies on growth and transformation* (London, Zed Books, 2013).
[74] Shinwell, quoted in the BBC documentary, 'The Great Groundnut Scandal', 28 Jul 1982. Prime Ministers Macmillan, Major and May might all ruefully agree with that judgement.
[75] Spike Milligan, *The Milligan Book of Records* (London, Star Books, 1977), p. 67.

the north of England), Crossrail in London. Many of these failures from the last 40 years have been analysed by King and Crewe in *The Blunders of Our Governments* (2013). They reached strikingly similar conclusions to those of this study. In IT for example, the modern equivalent of mechanisation, they conclude: 'One of the most striking features of successive governments' ventures into the field of IT is that they have gone on and on making the same mistakes. They never seem to learn.'[76] And of the Metronet London Underground renovation project: 'Almost everything that the critics predicted ahead of time would go wrong did go wrong'.[77]

One of the clearest examples of the failure to learn the lessons of the Groundnut Scheme was the notorious scandal surrounding Mrs Thatcher's agreement in 1993 to finance the Pergau Dam in Malaysia with British aid money in return for Malaysia signing a major arms contract with the UK. The World Development Movement went so far as to take the British Government to court over the improper use of British aid, and won. A detailed study by Tim Lankester, who was Permanent Secretary at the Overseas Development Administration (then still under the Foreign and Commonwealth Office) at the time illustrates how officials advised firmly against funding the dam because the economics of the project were so 'unambiguously bad', but were overruled by both the Foreign Secretary and the Prime Minister, and directed to proceed. Lankester rightfully concluded:

> The decision to back the project was taken primarily to boost Britain's trade and political relations with Malaysia. Most controversially of all, there was an indirect linkage to an agreement between Britain and Malaysia on the sale of defence equipment to the tune of £1 billion.[78]

The British courts eventually judged it an 'unlawful' use of the aid budget. The Government lost the case, its face, and the money.

The political complexion of the government appears to play no part in success or failure. The Groundnut Scheme itself was an explicitly socialist enterprise, launched at a time when socialism was an aspiration for many. The Pergau Dam scandal was perpetrated by a Conservative Government in pursuit of jobs in the British arms industry. Authoritarian, democratic, liberal, revolutionary, populist, communist or conservative governments, all are subject to the factors inherent in the political process that can drive governments to repeat such disasters, given the determination of political leaders to satisfy their political base – wherever that may be and whether it derives from a ballot box, a media outlet, the party or the barrel of a gun.

[76] King and Crewe, *Blunders of Our Governments*, p. 184.
[77] Ibid., p. 215
[78] Tim Lankester, *The Politics and Economics of Britain's Foreign Aid: The Pergau Dam affair* (London, Routledge, 2012), pp. 2–3.

Working in government for 35 years has left an indelible impression of the irresistible temptation for politicians to launch initiatives, pursue signature policies, and have something (often literally) concrete to demonstrate that they made a difference. Sadly, all too often the announcement seems more important than the delivery, or the project is aimed primarily at the aggrandisement of the originator. But in other cases, as James Scott argues, the whole objective is to force a change in society or in the environment to bring them under the state's control.[79]

What are now called 'megaprojects' are proliferating globally, far beyond Britain and Africa and far beyond the realm of development. Recent research on megaprojects has illustrated that they all too often demonstrate many of the failings pioneered by the Groundnut Scheme. Bent Flyvbjerg, the doyen of such research, has proposed an 'iron law of megaprojects [which are] overbudget, over time, over and over again'. He describes the process as the 'survival of the unfittest' because invariably their cost-benefit analyses are the most misleadingly over-optimistic and the risks most grossly under-estimated. Infrastructure schemes are the most common cases, but megaproject syndrome can strike any area of government where social, aesthetic or patriotic motives can distort a proper analysis.[80]

A classic case in the United States was the 'Desertron', the Superconducting Super Collider, to be built in Texas and designed to outclass the Large Hadron Collider at the European Organization for Nuclear Research (CERN) in Switzerland as the world's largest particle accelerator. Begun in 1983, the project proved over-ambitious, over budget, badly planned and badly managed. Politically contentious and its value scientifically disputed, Congress finally pulled the plug in 1993 to prevent losses mounting further, with a total loss to the US taxpayer of well over $1 billion. Again, over-optimism, under-budgeting and political pressures all played their part.[81]

In Europe, the long-running saga of the new Berlin Brandenburg Airport, originally due to open in 2011, but now postponed to 2020 at the earliest, is another classic example of a megaproject that spun out of control. This one, however, could not be dropped, as a new airport in Berlin was essential given the inadequacy of the existing ones. A private-sector option was requested but rejected in 2003 and the project proceeded as a public sector one. In 2009, with work well under way,

---

[79] Scott, *Seeing Like a State*, pp. 1–6.
[80] Bent Flyvbjerg, 'What you should know about megaprojects and why: An overview', *Project Management Journal*, 2014, among other articles. See the accessible summary by Jacques Leslie, 'The Trouble with Megaprojects', *The New Yorker*, 11 Apr 2015.
[81] Michael Riordan, Lillian Hoddeson, and Adrienne W. Kolb, *Tunnel Visions: The Rise and Fall of the Superconducting Super Collider* (Chicago, University of Chicago Press, 2015).

the total cost was estimated as €2.8 billion (£2.4 billion) but by 2018 this had more than tripled to over €10 billion (£8.5 billion). Many of the original cost and financing estimates turned out to be way off the mark, with the civil engineering work and the environmental constraints far more complex than envisaged.[82]

Besides airports (Spain's Ciudad Real Central Airport, now closed, is another example, though it cost only €1.1 billion), nuclear power plants (Chernobyl, most infamously), massive tunnels (such as Boston's notorious 'Big Dig'), major bridges (the San Francisco-Oakland Bay Bridge replacement) and many a massive IT project (including the US Air Force's Expeditionary Combat Support System, written off in 2012 with another loss of over $1 billion) have all suffered from megaproject syndrome, going way over budget and suffering loose fiscal and management control.[83]

More recent research has also shown that such projects are by no means the exclusive preserve of states, let alone 'authoritarian high modernist' ones. Schindler and Fadaee's collection of articles (2019), shows that agriculture remains a favoured area for such projects. But whereas private-sector-led mega-plantations in Southeast Asia have delivered commercial success, though at a high environmental cost, agricultural growth corridor projects in Africa (like SACGOT in Tanzania) have repeatedly encountered opposition from existing residents and farmers and suffered unforeseen complications.[84]

Above all, the story of the Groundnut Scheme underlines the absolute importance of effective accountability as the main way to minimise the risks of such megaprojects recurring. Every country and every government has its own way of providing such accountability, some more effective than others. In Britain it rested on Parliament and the civil service.

This study has devoted a good deal of space to the Parliamentary debates, Cabinet discussions, and to the minuting of one civil servant to another because all are central to understanding precisely why decisions were taken and how people were held accountable for them (or not). They illustrate how easily, even in a long-established democracy such as Britain, that process can be distorted and Parliament misled by unscrupulous, or even well-intentioned, politicians on a mission. The story has shown too how the press had its role to play in exposing the

---

[82] Information from https://en.wikipedia.org/wiki/Berlin_Brandenburg_Airport (accessed 7 Dec 2019).
[83] A useful compendium of these disastrous megaprojects (and there are many) can be found at www.lovemoney.com/gallerylist/88014/expensive-megaprojects-that-went-wrong (accessed 7 Dec 2019).
[84] Schindler and Fadaee, *Megaproject*; Miles Kenney-Lazar and Noburu Ishikawa, 'Mega-Plantations in Southeast Asia'; Stein and Kalina, 'Becoming an Agricultural Growth Corridor'.

scandal, though that role can equally become double-edged if elements of the media choose to take a partisan position and ignore rather than expose inconvenient facts, or even – in this age of post-factual politics – themselves promote 'fake news'.[85] The ability of the British Parliament to call government to account, on the floor of the House and through the structure of Parliamentary committees, is vital for ensuring that answers to tough questions must be given and can be heard. This accountability will not always stop the folly. But it can force governments to pause for thought and help expose the folly if they go ahead.

Behind the scenes, the expert and impartial advice of civil servants may often seem to ministers inconvenient, even obstructive. But the Groundnut Scheme provides reason enough for them to be listened to and engaged with, not subverted or side-lined. There are certainly examples where political vision and leadership have enabled changes that bring benefit to humankind, sometimes in the teeth of excessive bureaucratic caution. But in almost every case of disaster, you will find some that saw it coming, and said so. It is vital to the health of the governmental system that the freedom to express dissent *within* government is maintained, and that sceptical views are heard and not dismissed or suppressed. This may not altogether avoid disaster, but it will reduce the risk of it. Once fantasists take control, and those who are not 'one of us' (in Mrs Thatcher's ominous phrase) are exiled or ignored, disaster inevitably follows.[86]

Lasting lessons

The sections above have illustrated how the legacy of the Groundnut Scheme has, and in many cases has not, impacted on projects agricultural, developmental, governmental, or just mega. By way of a final conclusion, it is worth summarising the lessons that can be learnt from the scheme, for the benefit of those engaged in future development projects.[87]

The path to success or failure is often set at the very outset of a project. So, first and foremost, it is essential that those who embark on such schemes – governments, NGOs or businesses – understand the true

---

[85] The habit of some contemporary politicians to call any inconvenient fact they dislike 'fake news', while promoting genuinely false information as 'fact', is positively Orwellian.

[86] King and Crewe, *The Blunders of Our Governments*, make similar points in relation to Prime Minister Thatcher's Poll Tax. That mother of all megaprojects, Brexit, is proving this once again to be true.

[87] For a more conventional list of agricultural lessons, see Hogendorn and Scott, 'Lessons of the East African Groundnut Scheme' in Rotberg, *Imperialism, Colonialism and Hunger*, pp. 167–98.

motives of those promoting them. Is it profit, the people's development, political advantage, or personal vanity and ambition? Often it may be a mixture of all these. But understanding which one is likely to predominate if they come into conflict is crucial to assessing the likelihood of success or failure. In the Groundnut Scheme it was the political imperative and the election timetable that drove the decisions, not scientific, ecological or commercial interest.

Secondly, when expert advice is sought, it is wise to heed it, even if it challenges the policy or the project. If the experts disagree among themselves (as happens with experts), the argument itself can help clarify what still needs to be determined in order to take a sensible decision. But the risks must always be assessed, including an honest look at the worst-case scenario, to enable some mitigation to be prepared before the worst case arises. We have seen how the proponents of the Groundnut Scheme threw caution to the wind, ignored the scale of the risks, remained remorselessly optimistic, and paid the price. Turning a blind eye to problems does not help deal with them; and for all the value of being a risk taker, a calculated risk will have a better chance of success than a cavalier one. Over-optimism or boosterism, can be popular, but can equally be fatal if it turns into blind faith. Dodgy assumptions and dubious facts should always be challenged. This can be difficult, especially where group-think has taken over, or a project is deemed 'politically essential' whatever the cost. It can be personally costly, as many whistle-blowers and officials who challenged their political masters have found. But to fail to do so can be financially – and politically – disastrous for everyone.

Thirdly, as Professor Phillips underlined, in implementation haste is waste. Adequate time to test, pilot and re-assess the risks and opportunities in the light of experience is essential. In some cases – emergency, disaster – there is not time for this. But in development projects and most megaprojects there is no excuse for setting political deadlines to 'get things moving' if they end up moving in the wrong direction, to everyone's cost and detriment. The maxim should be 'if at first you don't succeed, ask why before you try again'. More effort, more will and more money will never remedy a scheme that is fundamentally flawed, so a proper diagnosis of the problems is the essential first step to finding a solution. If the problem is management, change it. Loyalty is a virtue in most walks of life, but not if it imposes unbearable costs on others.

Finally, it is crucial to be absolutely clear where accountability lies. It helps to identify where the money is coming from, and why it is being provided. To whom ultimately will the project have to answer for its spending? How tight is the control, and who is exercising it? To whose parliament, to which agency, to what leader, what donor or what banker is the project responsible? Who will decide, and who will defend the decision? The answers to these questions will be critical to success or failure. As the Groundnut Scheme so graphically illustrated, where there was no clear accountability, costs rocketed out of control and could never be put back in their box.

If not all governments have learnt these lessons, and if millions of pounds, dollars, euros, shillings, yen or yuan have continued to be wasted on over-ambitious and ill-thought through development schemes and projects, it is not for want of experience or warning. This book has sought to uncover the full and real reasons for the spectacular failure of the Groundnut Scheme so that we can avoid such failures in the future. But human nature is slow to change, and unpopular lessons are hard to learn. If this tale of The Scheme That Went Wrong at least makes those involved with similar major projects in the future think twice and proceed with a little caution, even when the vision is glorious and the need overwhelming, it has been a story worth the telling.

In the end, as Euripedes put it in *Medea*:

> Many matters the gods bring to surprising ends.
> The things we thought would happen do not happen;
> The unexpected God makes possible;
> And such is the conclusion of this story.

Bibliography

Primary sources

Privately held archives
Bunting Papers
Strachey papers
Unwin papers

Libraries and public archives
Bodleian Libraries (papers formerly in Rhodes House Library), Oxford
    Battershill Papers, MSS Brit. Emp. s. 467
    Creech Jones Papers, MSS Brit. Emp. s. 332
    Fabian Colonial Bureau Papers, MSS Brit. Emp. s. 365
    Fuggles-Couchman Papers, MSS Afr. s. 886
    Pearson, Norman, 'Trade Unionist on Safari'
    Surridge Interview, MSS Afr. s. 1813
    UMCA Papers, SF 134
    Wakefield Papers, MSS Afr. s. 349–53
    Walter Papers, MSS Afr. s. 1864

Churchill College Archives, University of Cambridge
    Attlee papers
    Gorell Barnes papers

Liddell Hart Archives, King's College, London
    Woods Papers (Maj-Gen. T.F.M. Woods)

London School of Economics
    Dalton Diaries

The National Archives (formerly Public Record Office), Kew, UK
    Cabinet Office papers (CAB)
    Colonial Office papers (CO)

HM Treasury papers (T)
Ministry of Food papers (MAF)
Prime Minister's papers (PREM)

Tanzania National Archives (TNA), Dar es Salaam

University of Reading Archives
  Bunting Interview, recorded 2002

BBC Radio 4 documentary, 'The Great Groundnut Scandal', broadcast 28 July 1982

Personal interviews
Edward Bunting
Sir Sydney Caine
M.J. Davies
P.H. Le Mare
A.H. Pike
Mzee Ally Sykes
Mzee Mbogo

Official publications

A Plan for the Mechanised Production of Groundnuts in East and Central Africa, Cmd 7030 (HMSO February 1947)
African Population of Tanganyika (Nairobi, East African Statistical Office, 1950)
British Documents on the End of Empire – see Hyam below
Colonial Development Corporation, *Report and Accounts for 1948* (London, HMSO, No. 188, 21 June 1949)
DFID, *Eliminating World Poverty: Building our common future*, Cmd 7656 (London, The Stationary Office, 2009)
East African Groundnut Scheme: Review of progress to the end of November 1947, Cmd 7314 (London, HMSO, January 1948)
Overseas Food Corporation, *First Annual Report and Statement of Accounts* (London, HMSO No. 252, 27 September 1949)
Overseas Food Corporation, *[Second] Annual Report and Statement of Accounts to 31 March 1950* (London, HMSO, No. 147, 28 July 1950)
Overseas Food Corporation, *The Future of the Overseas Food Corporation*, Cmd 8125 (London, HMSO, 9 January 1951).
Parliamentary Debates (Hansard)
Report by Sir S. Armitage-Smith on a Financial Mission to Tanganyika, Cmd 1428 (London, HMSO, 1932)
Tanganyika Territory, *A Ten Year Development and Welfare Plan for*

Tanganyika Territory (Dar es Salaam, Government Printer, 1946)
Tanganyika Territory, *An Outline of Post-War Development Proposals* (Dar es Salaam, Government Printer, 1944)
Tanganyika Territory, *Estimates* and *Blue Books*, 1946–51 (Dar es Salaam, Government Printer)
Tanganyika Territory, *Report of the Central Development Committee* (Dar es Salaam, Government Printer, 1940)
The Future of the Overseas Food Corporation, Cmd 8125 (London, HMSO, January 1951)
The Future of the Overseas Food Corporation, Cmd 9158 (London, HMSO, May 1954)
The World Food Shortage, Cmd 6785 (London, HMSO, April 1946)

Secondary works

African Centre for Economic Transformation (ACET), *Agriculture Powering Africa's Economic Transformation* (Accra, ACET, 2017)
African Centre for Economic Transformation (ACET), *Growth with Depth: 2014 African Transformation Report* (Accra, ACET, 2014)
Anderson, David M., 'Depression, Dust bowl, Demography and Drought: The colonial state and soil conservation in East Africa during the 1930s', *African Affairs*, 83:332 (July 1984)
Barnett, Tony, *The Gezira Scheme: The illusion of development* (London, Cass, 1977)
Bates, Robert, *Markets and States in Tropical Africa: The political basis of agricultural policies* (Berkeley, University of California Press, 1981)
Bauer, P.T., *West African Trade* (Cambridge, Cambridge University Press, 1954)
Bauer, P.T., *Dissent on Development: Studies and debates on development economics* (Cambridge, MA, Harvard University Press, 1972)
Bell, Vivienne, *Blown by the Wind of Change* (Lewes, The Book Guild, 1986),
Berman, Bruce and John Lonsdale, *Unhappy Valley: Conflict in Kenya & Africa* (London, James Currey, 1992)
Berry, Sara, *No Condition is Permanent: The social dynamics of agrarian change in sub-Saharan Africa* (Madison, University of Wisconsin Press, 1993)
Bew, John, *Citizen Clem: A biography* (London, Quercus, 2016)
Bourbonniere, Michelle, 'Ripple Effects: The groundnut scheme failure and railway planning for colonial development in Tanganyika, 1947–1952', *Canadian Journal of African Studies*, 47:3, 2013
Brain, Christopher and Michael Cable, *CDC: Pioneering development* (CDC, London, 2008)
Brett, E.A., *Colonialism and Underdevelopment in East Africa: The poli-

tics of economic change, 1919–39 (London, Heinemann, 1973)
Brown, Judith and Wm Roger Louis (eds), *The Oxford History of the British Empire, Vol. IV: The twentieth century* (Oxford, Oxford University Press, 1999)
Bryant, Chris, *Stafford Cripps: The first modern chancellor* (London, Hodder & Stoughton, 1997)
Bullock, Alan, *Ernest Bevin: Foreign Secretary 1945–1951* (London, W.W. Norton, 1983)
Bunting, A.H., 'Agricultural Research in the Groundnut Scheme, 1947–51', *Nature*, 168, 10 November 1951, pp. 804–9
Bunting, A.H., 'The Groundnut Scheme', *Tanzanian Affairs*, 25, 1 September 1986
Burgess, Simon, *Stafford Cripps: A political life* (London, Gollancz, 1999)
Cain P.J. and A.G. Hopkins, *British Imperialism: Crisis and deconstruction, 1914–1990, Vols I, II* (Harlow, Longman, 1993)
Cairncross, Alec and Barry Eichengreen, *Sterling in Decline: The devaluations of 1931, 1949 and 1967* (Oxford, Oxford University Press, 1983)
Cairncross, Alec, *The Years of Recovery: British economic policy, 1945–51* (London, Methuen, 1985)
Clark, Tom and Andrew Dilnot, *Long Term Trends in British Taxation and Spending* (Institute for Fiscal Studies, Briefing Note No. 25, 2002)
Clarke, Peter, *The Cripps Version: The Life of Sir Stafford Cripps* (London, Allen Lane, 2002).
Clarke, Peter, *Hope and Glory: Britain 1900–2000* (London, Penguin, 2004)
Constantine, Stephen, *The Making of British Colonial Development Policy, 1914–1940* (London, Cass, 1984)
Cooper, Frederick, *Decolonization and African Society: The labour question in French and British Africa* (Cambridge, Cambridge University Press, 1996)
Coulson, Andrew, *Tanzania: A political economy* (Oxford, Oxford University Press, 1982)
Cowen, M.P., 'The Early Years of the CDC: British state enterprise overseas during late colonialism', *African Affairs*, 83: 330 (January 1984)
Cowen, Michael and Nicholas Westcott, 'British imperial economic policy during the war', in David Killingray and Richard Rathbone (eds), *Africa and the Second World War* (London, Macmillan, 1986), chapter 1
Darwin, John, *Unfinished Empire: The global expansion of Britain* (London, Penguin, 2013)
Deane, Phyllis, *Colonial Social Accounting* (Cambridge, Cambridge University Press, 1953).
Dictionary of National Biography, 1961–1970 (Oxford, Oxford University Press, 2004)
Dimier, Veronique and Sarah Stockwell (eds), *The Business of Devel-*

opment in Postcolonial Africa (London, Palgrave Macmillan, forthcoming 2020)

Drew, Allison, *Between Empire and Revolution: The life of Sidney Bunting* (London, Pickering and Chatto, 2007)

Easterly, William, *The Tyranny of Experts: Economists, dictators and the forgotten rights of the poor* (New York, Basic Books, 2013)

Easterly, William, *The White Man's Burden: Why the West's efforts to aid the rest have done so much ill and so little good* (London, Penguin, 2006)

Eatwell, John, *The 1945–1952 Labour Governments* (London, Batsford Academic, 1979)

Ehrlich, C., 'The poor country: Tanganyika', in D.A. Low and A. Smith (eds), *History of East Africa, Vol. III* (Oxford, OUP, 1976)

Esselborn, Stefan, 'Environment, Memory, and the Groundnut Scheme: Britain's largest colonial agricultural development project and its global legacy', *Global Environment 11* (2013) (available at: www.environmentandsociety.org/mml/environment-memory-and-groundnut-scheme-britains-largest-colonial-agricultural-development)

Field, Frank (ed.) *Attlee's Great Contemporaries* (London, Continuum, 2009)

Fieldhouse, D.K., *Unilever Overseas: The anatomy of a multinational* (London, Croom Helm, 1978)

Fieldhouse, D.K., *Merchant Capital and Economic Decolonization: The United Africa Company, 1929–1987* (Oxford, Oxford University Press, 1994)

Forbes Munro, J. *Africa and the International Economy, 1800–1960* (London, Dent, 1976)

Frankel, S. Herbert, 'United Nations Primer for Development', *The Quarterly Journal of Economics*, 66: 3 (August 1952), pp. 301–26

Frankel, S. Herbert, *The Economic Impact on Underdeveloped Societies: Essays on international development and social change* (Oxford, Oxford University Press, 1953)

Fuggles-Couchman, N.R. *Agricultural Change in Tanganyika, 1945–1960* (Stanford, Food Research Institute, 1964)

Gann, P.H. and P. Duignan, *African Proconsuls* (New York, The Free Press, 1978)

Gupta, P.S., *Imperialism and the British Labour Movement* (London, Palgrave Macmillan, 1975)

Hailey, Lord, *An African Survey* (Oxford, OUP, 1938)

Hall, Richard and Hugh Peyman, *The Great Uhuru Railway* (London, Gollancz, 1976)

Hammond, R.J., *Official History of the Second World War: Food, Vol. III* (London, HMSO, 1962)

Hancock, W.K. and M.M. Gowing, *British War Economy* (London, HMSO, 1949)

Harris, Kenneth, *Attlee* (London, Weidenfeld & Nicolson, 1982)

Harrison, D., 'Civil Engineering Problems of the East African Groundnuts Scheme', *The Engineer*, 30 July 1948

Havinden, Michael and David Meredith, *Colonialism and Development: Britain and its tropical colonies, 1850–1960* (London, Routledge, 1993)

Hennessy, Peter, *Never Again: Britain 1945–1951* (London, Cape 1992)

Hill, J.F.R. and J.P. Moffett (eds), *Tanganyika: A study of its resources and their development* (Dar es Salaam, Government Printer, 1955)

Hodge, Joseph Morgan, *Triumph of the Expert: Agrarian doctrines of development and the legacies of British colonialism* (Athens, Ohio University Press, 2007)

Hodge, Joseph M, Gerald Hodl and Martina Kopf (eds), *Developing Africa: Concepts and practices in 20th century colonialism* (Manchester, Manchester University Press, 2014)

Hogendorn, Jan S. and K.M. Scott, 'Very large-scale agricultural projects: The lessons of the East African Groundnut Scheme', in Robert I. Rotberg (ed.) *Imperialism, Colonialism and Hunger: East and Central Africa* (Lexington, the Lexington Press, 1983)

Hopkins, A.G., *An Economic History of West Africa* (London, Longman, 1973)

Houston, Gregory F. 'Report on Military Bases and Camps of the Liberation Movement, 1961–1990' (2013), www.hsrc.ac.za/en/research-outputs/ktree-doc/13802 (accessed 3 Mar 2020)

Hyam, Ronald, *Britain's Declining Empire: The road to decolonisation 1918–1968* (Cambridge, Cambridge University Press, 2006)

Hyam, Ronald (ed.), *The Labour Government and the End of Empire, 1945–1951, Part II, British Documents on the End of Empire, Series A Vol.2* (London, Institute of Commonwealth Studies, 1992)

Iliffe, John, 'A History of the Dockworkers of Dar es Salaam', *Tanzania Notes and Records*, 71 (1970)

Iliffe, John, *A Modern History of Tanganyika* (Cambridge, Cambridge University Press, 1979)

Iliffe, John, *Africans: The history of a continent* (Cambridge, Cambridge University Press, 3rd edition 2017)

Ittmann, Karl, 'The Colonial Office and the Population Question in the British Empire 1918–1962', *Journal of Imperial and Commonwealth Affairs*, 27:3 (1999)

Jay, Douglas, *Change and Fortune* (London, Hutchinson, 1980)

Jenkins, Alan, *On Site, 1921–71: First 50 years of Taylor Woodrow* (London, Heinemann, 1971)

Johnson, Nancy L. and Vernon W. Ruttan, 'Why are Farms So Small?' *World Development*, 22:5, 1994, pp. 691–706.

Kelsall, Tim, *Business, Politics and the State in Africa: Challenging the orthodoxies on growth and transformation* (London, Zed Books, 2013)

Killingray, David and Richard Rathbone (eds), *Africa and the Second World War* (London, Macmillan, 1986)
King, Anthony and Ivor Crewe, *The Blunders of Our Governments* (London, Oneworld, 2013)
King, Robert D. and Robin W. Kilson, *The Statecraft of British Imperialism: Essays in honour of Wm Roger Louis*, special issue, *Journal of Imperial and Commonwealth History*, 27:2, May 1999
Koponen, Johani, 'From dead end to new lease of life: development in south-east Tanganyika from the late 1930s to the 1950s', in J. Hodge, G. Hodl and M. Kopf (eds), *Developing Africa*, pp. 37–62
Kynaston, David, *Austerity Britain, 1945–51* (London, Bloomsbury, 2007)
Lamb, Christina, *The Africa House* (London, Penguin, 1999)
Landes, David, *The Wealth and Poverty of Nations: Why some are so rich and some so poor* (New York, W.W. Norton, 1999)
Tim Lankester, *The Politics and Economics of Britain's Foreign Aid: The Pergau Dam affair* (London, Routledge, 2012)
Lee, J.M. and Martin Petter, *The Colonial Office, War and Development Policy* (London, Institute of Commonwealth Studies, 1982)
Leys, Colin, *Underdevelopment in Kenya: The political economy of neo-colonialism* (London, Heinemann, 1975)
Listowel, Judith, *The Making of Tanganyika* (London, Chatto and Windus, 1965)
Low D.A. and A. Smith (eds), *History of East Africa, Vol. III* (Oxford, OUP, 1976).
Maguire, G. Andrew, *Towards 'Uhuru' in Tanzania: The politics of participation* (Cambridge, Cambridge University Press, 1969)
Meredith, Martin, *The State of Africa* (London, The Free Press, 2005)
Milligan, Spike, *The Milligan Book of Records* (London, 1977)
Mills, Greg, *Why Africa is Poor, and What Africans Can Do About It* (London, Penguin, 2010)
Milward, Alan S., *War Economy and Society, 1939–1945* (Harmondsworth, Allen Lane/Penguin, 1977)
Mitchell, Donald, 'Tanzania's Cashew Sector: Constraints and challenges in a global environment', World Bank, Africa Region Working Paper Series No. 70, June 2004
Mkodzongi, Grasian and Peter Lawrence, 'The Fast-Track Land Reform and Agrarian Change in Zimbabwe', *Review of African Political Economy*, 46:159, 2019
Moffett, J.P., *A Handbook of Tanganyika* (Dar es Salaam, Government Printer, 1958)
Moggridge, D. (ed.), *The Collected Writings of John Maynard Keynes, vol. XXIV* (London, Macmillan, 1979)
Moore, Mick, Odd-Helge Fjeldstad and Wilson Prichard, *Taxing Africa: Coercion, reform and development* (London, Zed Books, 2018)

Morgan, D.J., *The Official History of Colonial Development, Vol. I: The origins of British aid policy, 1924–1945; Vol. II: Developing British Colonial Resources, 1945–1951; Vol. IV: Changes in British Aid Policy, 1951–1970* (London, HMSO and Macmillan, 1980)

Moyo, Dambisa, *Dead Aid: Why aid is not working and how there is another way for Africa* (London, Allen Lane, 2009)

Musvanhiri, Privilege, 'Zimbabwe: Between land ownership and food security', *Deutsche Welle*, 4 Jun 2019, www.dw.com/en/zimbabwe-between-land-ownership-and-food-security/a-49056618 (accessed 6 Jan 2020)

Owen, Roger and Bob Sutcliffe (eds), *Studies in the Theory of Imperialism* (London, Longman, 1971)

Pearce, R.D., *The Turning Point in Africa: British colonial policy, 1938–1948* (London, Cass, 1982)

Penrose, Edith T., 'A Great African Project', *The Scientific Monthly*, LVI (1948)

Phillips, J., *Agriculture and Ecology in Africa: A study of actual and potential development south of the Sahara* (London, Faber and Faber, 1959)

Potts, D. (ed.), *Tanzanian Development: A comparative perspective* (Oxford, James Currey, 2019)

Pratt, Cranford, *The Critical Phase in Tanzania, 1945–1968* (Cambridge, Cambridge University Press, 1976)

Read, David, *Beating About the Bush* (London, David Read, 2000)

Reuters, 'China Asks to Grow 2 million ha of Jatropha in Zambia', 31 Mar 2009

Riordan, Michael, Lillian Hoddeson and Adrienne W. Kolb, *Tunnel Visions: The Rise and Fall of the Superconducting Super Collider* (Chicago, University of Chicago Press, 2015)

Rizzo, Matteo, 'What was left of the Groundnut Scheme? Development disaster and labour market in southern Tanganyika, 1946–1952', *Journal of Agrarian Change*, 6:2, April 2006

Rizzo, Matteo, 'Becoming Wealthy: The life history of a rural entrepreneur in Tanzania, 1922–1980s', *Journal of Eastern African Studies*, 3:2, 2009

Rizzo, Matteo, *Taken for a Ride: Grounding neoliberalism, precarious labour and public transport in an African metropolis* (Oxford, Oxford University Press, 2017)

Roberts, A.D. (ed.), *The Cambridge History of Africa, Vol. 7: 1905–1940* (Cambridge, Cambridge University Press, 1986)

Robinson, Ronald and John Gallagher, *Africa and the Victorians: The official mind of imperialism* (London, Macmillan, 1961)

Robinson, Ronald, 'Sir Andrew Cohen: Proconsul of African nationalism', in L.H. Gann and p. Duignan, *African Proconsuls* (New York, The Free Press, 1978)

Roll, Eric (Lord) *Crowded Hours* (London, Faber, 1985)

Rotberg, Robert I. (ed.), *Imperialism, Colonialism and Hunger: East and Central Africa* (Lexington, the Lexington Press, 1983)

Sayers, R.S., *Financial Policy, 1939–1945* (London HMSO, 1956)

Scott, James C., *Seeing Like a State: How certain schemes to improve the human condition have failed* (New Haven CT and London, Yale University Press, 1998)

Schindler, Seth and Simin Fadaee (eds), Megaprojects, special edition of *Environment and Society*, 10:1, 2019

Seabrook, A.T.P., 'The Groundnut Scheme in Retrospect', *Tanganyika Notes and Records*, 46 (Jan 1957)

Schuknecht, Rohland, *British Colonial Development Policy after the Second World War: The case of Sukumaland* (Berlin, LIT Verlag, 2010)

Skidelsky, Robert, *John Maynard Keynes, Vol. III: Fighting for Britain* (London, Macmillan, 2000)

Stein, Serena and Marc Kalina, 'Becoming an Agricultural Growth Corridor', *Environment and Society*, 10:1, 2019

Stirling, Leader, *Come Over and Help Us: A doctor in Africa* (Dar es Salaam, AMREF, 1995)

Strange, Susan, *Sterling and British Policy* (Oxford, Oxford University Press, 1971)

The Economist, 'Outsourcing's Third Wave', 23 May 2009, pp. 65–8

The Economist, 'The Underground Revolution: Better seeds could help African farmers grow more', 28 Sep 2019, www.economist.com/middle-east-and-africa/2019/09/28/better-seeds-could-help-african-farmers-grow-far-more (accessed 3 Mar 2020)'

Thomas, Hugh, *John Strachey* (London, Eyre Methuen, 1973)

Throup, David, *Economic & Social Origins of Mau Mau* (London, James Currey, 1987)

Tignor, Robert L., *W Arthur Lewis and the Birth of Development Economics* (Princeton, Princeton University Press, 2006)

Tomlinson, B.R., 'Imperialism and after: the economy of the empire on the periphery', in Judith Brown and Wm Roger Louis (eds), *The Oxford History of the British Empire, Vol. IV: The twentieth century* (Oxford, Oxford University Press, 1999)

Unwin, Vicky, *Love and War in the WRNS* (Stroud, The History Press, 2015)

Van Arkadie, Brian, 'Agricultural development in Tanzania', in D. Potts (ed.), *Tanzanian Development: A comparative perspective* (Oxford, James Currey, 2019)

Van Beusekom, Monica, *Negotiating Development: African farmers and colonial experts at the Office du Niger, 1920–1960* (Oxford, James Currey, 2002)

Waugh, Evelyn, *A Tourist in Africa* (London, Chapman and Hall, 1960)

Westcott, N.J., 'An East African Radical: The life of Erica Fiah', *Journal of African History*, 1981, 22:i, pp. 85–101

Westcott, Nicholas, 'Closer Union and the Future of East Africa, 1939–1948: A case study in the "Official Mind of Imperialism"', *Journal of Imperial and Commonwealth History*, 10:1, October 1981, pp. 67–88

Westcott, Nicholas, 'The Impact of the Second World War on Tanganyika 1939–51' (PhD thesis, Cambridge University, 1982)

Westcott, Nicholas, 'The impact of the Second World War on Tanganyika, 1939–49', in David Killingray and Richard Rathbone (eds), *Africa and the Second World War* (London, Macmillan, 1986), chapter 5

Westcott, Nicholas, 'The East African sisal industry, 1929–49: the marketing of a colonial commodity during depression and war', in B. Ingham and C. Simmons (eds) *Development Studies and Colonial Policy* (London, Cass, 1987)

Westcott, Nicholas, 'Trust the People', *The World Today*, 65:3, March 2009, pp. 24–6

Williams, Philip, *Hugh Gaitskell* (Oxford, Oxford University Press, 1982)

Wilson, Charles, *Unilever, 1945–65* (New York, Praeger, 1968)

World Bank, *Agriculture for Development: Annual development report, 2008* (Washington DC, 2008)

Wood, Alan, *The Groundnut Affair* (London, The Bodley Head, 1950)

Zigomo, Muchena, 'China Asks to Plant Jatropha in Zambia', *Manitoba Co-operator*, 9 Apr 2009

Index

A Plan for the Mechanised Production of Groundnuts (White Paper Cmd 7030), 53 n.50, 70, 76, 80, 139
Abeokuta steel mill, 2, 212
Accounts, 85, *see also* Overseas Food Corporation
Accountability, *passim*
Africa
  development in, 13–16, 82, 114–19, 162, 185
  British Empire in, 16–18, 35–6, 118, 190
African Centre for Economic Transformation (ACET), 210–11
African National Congress (ANC), 183
African Socialism, 204
Africans
  improvement for, 9–10 (and n.24), 55, 65, 76–7, 117–19, 201
  attitude to scheme, 18, 89, 91–2, 105, 111–13, 127, 178
  labour for scheme, 7, 91–7, 198–9, 201
  protest, 96–7
  'spiritual lives', 110
  women, 110–11, 200–1
Afrika Korps, 118
Agriculture
  Department (in Tanganyika), 37, 51
  development, 37–42, 205–12
  mechanisation, 39–40, 42, 47, 54, 126, 170, 176, 190, 204, 209, 210–11
  Plant More Crops campaign, 7
  productivity, 7, 76, 206, 211
  scientific farming, 10, 21–2, 53–5, 60, 77, 103, 176, 187, 204, 209, 211, 217
  soil conservation, 38, 40, 46–7, 54, 102, 202
  state vs private, 15, 21, 204, 210
  subsistence farming, 10, 37–9, 53, 89–90, 94, 107, 206–7
  food production for scheme, 93–4, 112, 199–200
  shifting cultivation, 89, 204
  see also Peasant production, groundnuts
Alice in Wonderland, 156
Alliance for a Green Revolution in Africa (AGRA), 210
Amery, Leo MP, 6
Army surplus equipment, *see* Procurement
Annan, Kofi, 210
Arusha, 39
Arusha Declaration, 203–4
Attlee, Clement, 1, 18–20, 25, 28, 31–2, 63–4, 70, 115–17, 133, 147–8, 150, 155, 157–9, 160–2, 166–7, 174, 180–1, 184

'Authoritarian high modernism', 21, 217

Bailey, Dr E.E. 58, 65–8, 71, 142–3
Bain, Tom, 52, 89, 199
Balfour Beatty, 107, 110
Bank of England, 35
Baobab trees, 99–101, photograph, 188
Barlow, Sir John MP, 139
Bates, Robert, 209, 213 n.71
Battershill, Sir William, 40, 47, 60–1, 88, 93, 97
Bauer, P.T. 15, 212
BBC World Service, 156
Beaverbrook, Lord, 119–20, 149, 167
Bedford trucks, 103, 105
Belgium, 85
Bell, Vivienne, 84, 103, 105, 111, 186
Berlin airport, 216–17
Berry, Sara, 209
Bevan, Nye MP, 20, 32, 125, 180
Bevin, Ernest MP, 20, 25, 29, 32, 35–6, 45 n.25, 117, 125, 140–1, 145, 147, 160, 180
Bew, John, 18 n.57
Bicycles, 112
Bishop, George, 56, 142, 155–6, 185–6
Blackman, Prof G.E. 148
Bostock, David, 79
Boston, 217
Brazil, 48, 76, 211
Bread, 29, 32
Brexit, 114 n.1, 194 n.9, 218 n.86
British Empire, 16–18, 35–6, 41, 59, 69, 72, 104–5, 117, 136, 142, 152–3, 175–6, 181, 194–8, 203, *see also* Imperialism
British Overseas Airways Corporation (BOAC), 50, 128–9, 195
Britten, Benjamin, 82

Broadley, Herbert, 45, 57
Brockway, Fenner MP, 29, 91
Brook, Sir Norman, 117–18, 146
Bugufi district, 7
Bulk purchase agreements, 27, 38
Bulldozers, 98–102, 139
  photographs, 86, 100
Bundu, 41, 154
Bunting, Dr Hugh, 78–80, 103, 104, 109, 112, 121, 154, 156–60, 165, 179, 186–8, 192, 212
Bunting, Sidney, 79
Bush, 37, 41, 77, 80, 88, 90, 99–102, 191, *and see* Clearing

Cabinet, 20, 33–4, 51, 61–5, 68–71, 116–18, 122–3, 133, 138, 145–7, 153, 170, 174–6, 193
Café Royale, 132
Caine, Sir Sydney, 9, 10 n.24, 12, 115
Callaghan, Jim, MP, 139, 184
Cameron, James, 88, 149
Canada, 32, 87–8, 99
Capper, Rev E.H. 110–11
Carstairs, C.Y. 11
Cash crops, 6, 38, 93
Cashew nuts, 182, 200
Castle, Barbara, 186
Cattle, 89, 170, 181, 182, 199
Central Development Committee (Tanganyika), 12
Central Line railway, 54, 61, 74, 78, 80
Central Province, 46, 47, 52–3, 57, 74, 94, 121
Ceylon (Sri Lanka), 87
Chagga, 93
Chamberlain, Joseph, 4–5
Chancellor of the Exchequer, *see* Cripps, Sir Stafford and Dalton, Hugh
Cheltenham, 88
Chevening, 32
China, 23, 72, 182, 203–4, 210, 214

Churchill, Sir Winston, 132, 180, 181
Civil service, 20, 67–8, 70, 217–18, 219
Civilisation, 5, 95, 118
Clarke, Peter, 17
Clarke, R.W.B. 'Otto', 62–3
Clauson, Gerard, 47
Clay, Geoffrey, 165, 179, 180
Clearing, 51–2, 99–102, 139, 145, 163, 168
  cost of, 51–2, 102, 122, 128–9, 168, 171, 181, 190
  photographs, 86, 169
  see also Bush
Coates, Sir Eric, 148, 164–5, 168, 171, 175, 179
Cohen, Sir Andrew, 13, 45–6, 57, 60, 74, 144, 172–3, 186
Cold War, 133
Colonial development, 1, 9–13, 66, 67, 74, 174, 176, 194
  origins, 5–7
  social impact, 10 n.24
  Scheme as part of, 59, 81, 113–18, 168, 173–4
  in Tanganyika, 7, 11–12, 88, 129, 172–3, 202
Colonial Development and Welfare (CD&W) Acts, 8–9, 13, 62–4, 114–15, 129, 196
Colonial Development Corporation (CDC), 13, 114–18, 145, 172–3, 196, 198, 206–8
Colonial Economic Development Council, 115, 120
Colonial Office, 20, 37, 95, 114–17, 128
  economic policy, 5, 8, 12–13, 73, 114–15, 196–8
  attitude towards the scheme, 45–8, 57–9, 62, 120, 143–4, 171–5, 191
  Treasury scepticism about, 58, 62–3, 144

white settlement policy, 90
  assumes responsibility for scheme, 144, 151, 170, 175
Commonwealth, 82
Communist Party, 23, 25, 31, 79, 156–60, 167
Conservative Party ('Tories'), 32–3, 34, 128, 139, 150–2, 154, 158, 159, 160–1, 165, 167–8, 176–8, 181, 214, 215, *see also* Parliament
Coopers Bros (later Coopers and Lybrand), 85, 124, 195
Cost-plus contracts, 138, *and see* UAC, as Managing Agent
Cotton, 7, 11, 38
Cowen, Michael, 13 n.37, 14, 183 n.42
Creech Jones, Arthur MP, 9, 13, 20, 36, 49, 91, 142, 148, 162, 185, 203
  supports scheme in Cabinet, 61–4, 144–6
  creation of CDC, 115–17
  concerns about scheme, 140, 143, 162
  defends in Parliament, 152
Crewe, Ivor, 22, 214
Crime, 94, 96
Cripps, Sir Stafford MP, 18–20, 25, 31, 36, 124–5, 132–3, 140–2, 144–5, 160–2
Crookshank, Captain MP, 24 n.68, 136–7, 177, 180
Crushing plants, *see* oils and fats

Daily Express, 88, 149, 166
Dalton, Hugh, 20, 25, 32, 35, 61–4, 69–70, 74, 115, 118–19, 125, 160–2
Danquah, Mr, 92, 186
Dar es Salaam, 8, 41, 50, 74, 78, 88, 89, 201, 205
  port (including congestion), 84–8, 96–7

Darwin, John, 16 n.47
David, Elizabeth, 26
Davies, Sir Herbert, 43
Decolonisation, 176, 178–9, 182, 203
Decortication, 66
Demography, *see* Population growth
Department for International Development (DFID), 209, 215
Depression, impact of, 6–7, 11, 13, 38, 69
Desertron, 2, 216
'Detribalised natives', 10, 96, 109–10
Devaluation of sterling, 34, 140–1
Development
 theory, 4–6, 13–16, 81, 205–6, 209, 212–14
 practice, 113–18, 189–90, 205–14
 'Chinese model', 203, 214
 see also Agriculture, Colonial development, Imperialism, Industrialisation
Dockworkers strike, 8, 86, 97–8
Dodoma, 94, 96, 204
Dollar policy, 17, 19, 33–6, 68, 115, 133, 173, 194, 196
Drought, 81, 134–5, 168, 181, 191
Dual Mandate, 4
Durham Miners' Gala, 32
Dyson, J.A. 66

Ealing comedies, 26
Earth Moving and Construction Ltd, *see* Gailey and Roberts Ltd
East Africa, 38–9, 51, 69
 federation, 90
East African Groundnut Scheme, *see* Groundnut Scheme
East African Railways and Harbours, 61, 88, 129, 182
Easterly, William, 14
Ecology and environment, 7, 37, 46, 98–100, 111, 191, 211

Education policy and plans, 12–13 (and n.35), 199
Egypt, 85
Ehrlich, Cyril, 201
Elections, *see* General Elections
Empire, *see* British Empire, Imperialism
Ethiopia, 214
Eton college, 29–30
Euripedes, 220
European settlers, *see* Settlers
Evening Standard, 167
Experts, 11, 21–2, 48, 66, 70, 76, 153, 177, 219, *see also* Agriculture
Exploitation, *see* Imperialism
Export crops, 6

Fabian Colonial Bureau, 9, 49, 55, 61, 77, 90, 203
Famine, 7, 27, 94–5
Farquharson, S. 61
Faure, William, 65, 85, 122, 128 n.45
Fertiliser, 60
Financial Times, 129
First World War, 6
Fisher, W.H. 140, 144–5, 153
Flyvbjerg, Bent, 216
Food
 post-war diet, 26–7
 shortage and supply, 8, 27–33, 63, 83, 161
 production in Tanganyika, 51, 89, 93
 price, 104, 141
Forbes, W.A. (District Commissioner), 94
Foreign Office, 91, 215
Forestry, 73, 108, 112
France, 76, *see also* Imperialism
Frankel, Prof S. Herbert, 165, 191–2, 206
FRELIMO, 182
French West Africa, 18, 70, 207

Index

Fuggles-Couchman, N.R.F. 40 n.8, 92

Gailey and Roberts Ltd (UAC subsidiary), 74, 81, 113
Gaitskell, Hugh MP, 25, 125, 161, 171, 174–6, 180, 184
Gallagher, Professor John, 17
Gater, Sir George, 45
Gavin, Sir William, 128 n.45
Gender issues, 3, 200–1, *and see* Women
General Election
  1945, 25
  1950, 146–7, 160–1
  1951, 180
German rule, 6, 90–1
Gezira Scheme, 10–11, 46, 117, 187, 207–8
Ghana, 207, 212
Gilbert, Sir Bernard, 140, 144
Gillett, Dr Stuart, 179, 182
Gin, price of, 88, 103
Gladwell, A.L. 51–2, 113
Gogo, *see* Wagogo
Gold Coast (Ghana), 92, 206, *see also*, Ghana
Gollancz, Victor, 31, 166
Gore Browne, Stewart, 207
Gorell Barnes, William, 63, 115
Griffiths, Jim MP, 162, 172, 174, 177, 185
Groundnut Scheme, *passim*
  summary, 23–4
  development thinking of, 15–16, 53–8, 168, 172–3, 190
  launched in Parliament, 65
  'Operation Groundnuts', 81, 118
  scientific department/research, 82, 103, 122, 169, 179–80
  military character, 55, 81, 83, 89, 98, 118, 121–2, 151, 190
  public reaction, 76–7, 82 n.15, 127, 161, 175, 201–2
  recruitment to, 81–4, 111
  criticism of, 46–7, 121, 133–4, 136–9, 145–6, 149–53, 160–1, 175
  cost of production, 53, 67, 68, 130–1, 168
  cost and financial problems, 66–7, 121–31, 136–7, 141–3, 149, 151, 163, 175, 177, 194
  scale of loss, 194
  benefits, 201
  speed, 55, 71, 81, 91, 122–4, 128, 130, 153, 192–3
  delay, 118, 121, 123, 130, 138
  acreage, *see* Clearing
  Enquiry, 150, 154, 165
  Revised Long Term Plan, 171–2, 176
  failure, causes of, xiii, 174–8, 187–8, 190–4, 214, 218–20
  lessons, 187, 206–20
  as political project, 193
  'put Tanganyika on the map', 201
  photographs, 104 n.15, 106, 126, 131, 149, 186
  see also Overseas Food Corporation
groundnuts
  crop, 41–3, 80, 102, 112, 138, 171
  world price, 53, 58, 122, 129
  yields, 43, 52–3, 63, 135, 143, 163, 168, 179
  in Nigeria, 196–8
'groundnutters', 3, 83, 88–9, 99, 101, 104–5, 186, 199
Gulwe, 78

Hailey, Lord, 14, 110
'Half London', *see* Kongwa
Hall, George MP, 48
Hall, Lord Robert, 155, 157
Harrison, Major-General Desmond, 100 n.2, 121–3, 127–9, 130–1, 133
  photograph, 126

236 Index

Health, *see* Medical facilities
Hinden, Rita, 9, 77
History, 3, 5
Hitchcock, Sir Eldred, 93
HM Treasury, *see* Treasury
Hodge, Joseph M, 3, 11, 66, 208
Hodgson, Vere, 26
Hoes, 84, 95
Hollins, Frank, 65–7
'Housewives', *see* Women
HS2, 2, 214
Hurd, Anthony MP, 151, 167, 177
Hutt, Bruce, 165

Iliffe, John, 203, 209
Imperialism
  British, 1–2, 16–18, 72, 117–19, 175–6, 194–8, 203
  and development, 4–16, 72–7, 95, 114, 152–3
  as exploitation, 59, 73–4, 114–19, 139, 175, 196
  law and order, 95
  French, 18, 207
  Portuguese, 18, 208
  See also British Empire
India, 23, 27, 76, 87, 210
Indirect rule, 5, 9, 95–6
Industrialisation, 74, 115, 204
Information technology, 214–15, 217
Irrigation, 11
Isherwood, Director of Education, 12 n.35
Israel, 183
Italians, 82, 92

Jay, Douglas, 45 n.25, 125
Johnston, Robin (District Commissioner), 96
Joke, 101
Jordan, Philip, 159

Kano, Nigeria, 196–7
Karimjee, A.M.A. 182

Kenya, 11, 14, 38, 39, 50, 53, 90, 93, 120, 155, 199, 203, 211
Kenya and Uganda Railways and Harbours, *see* East African Railways and Harbours
Keynes, John Maynard (Lord), 19, 33–5
Kidner, Archdeacon, 110–11
Kilimanjaro, Mount, 37, 38, 93
King, Ivor, 22, 215
King's African Rifles, 16, 91
Knight, Jasper, 41, 44–5, 48, 50, 57, 59
Kongwa, 78–83, 88–97, 102–6, 121–2, 125–7, 138, 154, 163, 170, 179, 181–2, 194, 198, 201, 204
  'Half London', xii, 103–6, 198
  site of scheme, 52, 54, 80–1, 148–9
  communications, 74, 86–7, 99
  accommodation, 83, 103–4, 122
  rations and food, 83, 94–5, 105–6
  population of, 88, 106
  Club, 91, 105
  airstrip, 92, 126 (photograph)
  District Office, 96
  school, 104
  social life, 103–4
  alcohol consumption, 103, 128, 198
  hospital, xii, 105
  weather reports, 165
Kongwa Working Party, 164–5, 168, 170, 171, 191
Korean War, 170, 173
Kynaston, David, 25

Labour Commissioner, 60–1
Labour Party
  Government, 1–2, 18–20, 23, 25, 34, 116, 180, 190, 194, 214
  Colonial development policies, 9, 90, 123, 193–4
  economic policy, 20, 33–5, 140–1

Conference, 140
See also, General Elections, Socialism
Labour policy, *see* Migrant labour
Labour supply, 61, 65, 66–7, 80, 102, 107, 112, 198–9, 206
   recruitment, 81–2, 91–7
   wages, 93 n.51, 94, 97, 112, 198–9
   protest, 97–8
   Italians, 82, 92
   Mauritians, 92
   Southern Province, 106, 112
   'unsuitable Europeans', 83, 111
Lake Province, 51
Lake Victoria, 37, 38
Land alienation, 65, 90–1, 96, 210
Land grabs, *see* Land alientation
Land Rover, 103, 195
Landes, David, 212–13
Lankester, Sir Tim, 215
Laski, Harold, 18
Le Mare, Peter, 102, 105, 109
League of Nations, *see* Mandate
Lee, Sir Frank, 138, 143, 156, 162, 163, 164, 185
Leechman, Barclay, 82–3
Lees-Milne, James, 26
Left Book Club, 31
Lend Lease, 17, 33, 35
Lennox-Boyd, Alan MP, 119 n.17, 123, 152, 167, 177
Leopard, *see* Wildlife
Lewis, W. Arthur, 206, 208–9
Liesching, Sir Percival, 56, 67, 71, 143
Lindi, 107–9, 109, 129
Liverpool, 28, 83
Livingstone, Dr David, 107
Liwale District, 91
Llewellyn Jones, Arwen, 110
Lloyd, Sir T.I.K. 172
Lockhart, Sir Charles, 120, 164, 179, 182

London, 25–6, 104, *see also* 'Half London'
Lonsdale, John, 13
Lugard, Lord, 4
Lugusha, Chief Harun, 201

Macdonald, Malcolm, 8
Machinery (*see also* Agriculture, Mechanisation)
   for coal mining, 63–4
   for agriculture, 65
   sourcing, 70
   import, 85–7
Mahenge, 107
Makonde, 107
Makwinja, Mr, 200
Malaysia, 215
Mallalieu, J.P.W. MP, 25, 32, 184
Malthus, Thomas, 8
Managing Agent, *see* United Africa Company
Manchester Guardian, 76, 139, 155
Mandate, League of Nations, 6, 90–1
Marchant, Colonel, 79, 154
Margarine, 40–1, 65, 68, 82, 121–2
Marshall Plan (and Aid), 34, 127, 133
Martin, David, 50, 66, 79, 83, 91, 102, 108, 134
   photograph, 126
Masasi, 51, 108, 110
Massey-Harris tractors, 98
McFadyen, James, 120, 147, 179
McGaw, Mac, 79
McLean, J.N. 156
Mechanisation, 39–40, 42, 54, 171, 176, 190–2, 204, 206–7, 209–11
   in the US, 66, 190
   in practice at Kongwa, 98–101, 126, 165, 170
Medical facilities, xii, 95, 104
Megaprojects, 2, 21–3, 77, 189–90, 214–18
Meteorology, 80, *see also* Rainfall

Middle East, 72, 99, 108, 173, 180, 210
Middle East Supply Centre, 39, 69
Migrant labour, 38, 42, 47, 60–1, 65, 91–7
Mikado, Ian MP, 168
Mikindani, 107
Miller, R.W.R. (Director of Agriculture), 37–43, 47, 51, 60, 69, 88, 182, 190, 206
Milward, A.S. 17
Ministers
　ignore official advice, 63, 67, 70–1, 193, 214–18
Ministry of Food, 28, 43–4, 56–7, 73–4, 107, 115–16, 141–3, 162, 167, 170, 191
　responsibility for the scheme, 58–9, 152, 170, 173
　Special Section, 62–8, 137
　Internal Audit, 123–5
Missionaries, 107, 110–11, *see also* UMCA
Mitchell, Sir Philip, 39, 142, 172, 206
Mobutu, President of Zaire, 2
Moffett, J.P. 202
Mombasa, 105
Montgomery of Alamein, Lord, 72, 100
Morality, 105, 111, *and see* Missionaries
Morgan, D.J. 2, 181
Morrison, Herbert MP, 20, 29, 32, 44 n.21, 58, 63, 69–70, 95, 115, 125, 128 n.45, 136, 148, 160, 173–5, 180
Mosley, Oswald, 30, 32
Mowlems, 81, 110, 142, 169, 195
Moyo, Dambisa, 14
Mozambique, 210
Mpanda lead mines, 61, 80
Mpwapwa, 52, 54, 60, 80, 89, 94
Mtenda, Julius, 94, 112, 186
Mtwara, port, 72, 107–8, 172, 175, 180, 182, 200
　photograph, 108
Muir, J.C. 164, 179
Mwanza, 204

Nachingwea, 109–11, 157, 172, 180, 182
Nairobi, 88, 125, 129, 139
National Health Service (NHS), 1, 2, 19, 160, 214–15
Nationalisation, *see* Public enterprise
Nationalism, 203
Native authorities, 90, 95–6
Nature, 76
Nestlé, George, 79
Newala, 112
News Chronicle, 149
Nicholson, Max, 69–70, 145–6, 150, 170, 173–4, 178, 186–7
Niger Agricultural Project, 198
Nigeria, 2, 41, 196–8, 212
Noble, Adam (UAC), photograph, 126
Noli sawmill, 109
North Africa, 81
Northern Province Wheat Scheme, 39–40, 69, 92, 190–1
Northern Rhodesia, 11, 37, 50, 53, 72, 207
Norton, Ian (District Officer), 96
Nyerere, Julius, 21, 182, 203, 212

Office du Niger, 10, 190, 208
Official Secrets Act, 167
oils and fats (*including* oilseeds), 27–9, 33, 40–1, 43, 45, 64, 67, 122, 126 n.45
　crushing plants, 41, 44, 75, 197
　price, *see* groundnuts
Olivier, Lawrence, 82
Orde-Browne, Major G. St J. 66
Ormsby-Gore, Sir William, 5, 10
Orwell, George, 26
Our World, 106 n.22, 129

Overseas Development
  Administration, *see* DFID
Overseas Food Corporation (OFC),
  114–31, 132–53, 181, 196, 199
  archives, 4
  creation, 13, 64–5, 114–19
  Board, 119–21, 132, 135, 140,
    146, 147–9, 151, 157, 163–4,
    170, 172–4
  handover from UAC, 81, 113,
    121–4, 127
  Accounts and budget, 122–3,
    130–1, 138, 141, 163–4, 166
  London HQ, 128, 152, 178, 193
  relations with Tanganyika
    Administration, 128–30, 170,
    202
  staff discontent, 121, 128, 130,
    133–4, 138–9, 151–2, 154–60,
    169, 178
  criticism, *see* Groundnut Scheme
  brought under Colonial Office,
    151–2, 165, 170, 172
  Revised Long Term Plan, 1950,
    171, 176, 178
  Transferred to Tanganyika
    Government, 172, 181–2
Overseas Resources Development
  Bill/Act, 114–19, 132, 171, 176–8
Oxford, 29, 80, 148, 165, 191, 206

Parliament, British, 24, 64–5, 114,
  217–18
  debates the scheme, 65, 123, 126,
    128, 136–8, 139, 150–2, 167–8,
    176–8
  ORD Bill debate, 118–19
Panter-Downes, Mollie, 160
Parastatals, 213
Passport to Pimlico, 26, 160, 189
Pastoralism, 38, *see also*
  Agriculture, Cattle
Pauling & Co, 79, 81, 92, 110, 142,
  195
Pearl Harbour, 17

Peasant production (and farmers),
  21–2, 38–9, 41, 55, 172–3, 181–2,
  196–8, 200, 202, 204
Pearson, Norman, 97–8
Pedler, F.J. 65
Penrose, Edith, 76
Pergau Dam, 215
Perrin Brown, Christopher, 110
Perrott, Sir Donald, 148, 155, 179
Philippines, 87, 99, 211
Phillips, Prof John, 134, 138, 139,
  155–8, 164, 169, 179, 191, 207–8,
  219
Picture Post, 106, 149–50
Pike, A.H. 52 n.48, 199–200
Plummer, Leslie 'Dick', 30, 119–20,
  122, 125, 132–4, 138, 148–9,
  151, 154–9, 163–4, 185, 193
  photograph, 126
Police, 96–7
Poll tax, 5
Ponsonby, Colonel MP, 136
Population growth, 7–8
Port, *see* Dar es Salaam, Mtwara
Portal, Lord, 115
Portuguese Empire, 18
Poynton, Sir Hilton, 144
Press, 76–7, 149, 158–9, 178, *and see
  individual newspaper titles*
Private sector, 71, 75
Procurement, 84
  Army surplus, 84–5, 108, 123,
    150, 194–5
  distraction from, 88
Prosavana, 210
Prostitution, 87, 95–6 (and n.62),
  110–11
Public Accounts Committee, 55, 66,
  67, 71, 138, 153, 165–6, 167
Public enterprise, 54–5, 58, 61–5,
  68, 70, 113–14, 123, 142, 145,
  203–4, 212–13

Raby, George, 134, 138, 153, 155–8,
  169, 179

Railways, 6, 61, 66, 72, 74, 87–8, 196–7
   Mtwara-Nachingwea, 61, 108–9, 111, 163, 175, 182, 198
Rainfall, 40, 46–7, 52, 54, 60, 80–1, 90, 95, 107, 111, 122 n.27, 134–5, 137, 165, 168, 179
   Artificial production of rain, 168–9
Rationing, 26, 27–8, 32, 65, 68
Reading University, 187
Reith, Lord, 208
Research, *see* Agriculture, Scientific research
Rhodesia, 11, *and see* Northern Rhodesia
Richards, Frank, 100
Rinderpest, 37
Risk, 219, *see also* Strachey, John
Rizzo, Matteo, 93–4, 200
Roads, *see* Transport
Roberts, Wilfred MP, 151
Robertson, Fyfe, 149–50, 154
Robins, R.E. 61
Roddan, C.M. 46, 181
Rodney, Walter, 15
Roll, Eric, 56–7
Rooters, 101
Rosa, John, 50–1, 55, 56, 58–9, 64, 66, 71, 81, 120, 124, 128, 130, 140, 147–8, 151, 156, 185
Rosette disease, 46, 113, 181
Rothamsted Experimental Station, 66, 79–80
Rothschild, Victor Lord, 120
Royal Air Force (RAF), 31, 78
Rufiji river, 109
Rush, Major Peter, 79
Russia, 30, 76
Ruvu river, 88
Rwanda, 214

Sahel, 10
Salisbury, Lord, 156
Samuel, Frank, 40–4, 47, 62, 65, 120, 147, 185
Schuknecht, Rohland, 202
Scientific research, 11, 82, 102, 169, 178, 211–12, *see also* Groundnut Scheme, Agriculture
Scott, James C. 21–2, 212, 216
Seabrook, A.T.P. 81 n.12, 88, 121
Second World War, 9, 13, 16, 33, 37, 43
Sen, Amartya, 15
Settlers (white), 7, 11–12, 38, 90–1, 92
Shenton, Robert, 14
Sherman tanks, 102–3, 183
'Shervicks', 102–3, 183
Shinwell, Emanuel MP, 20, 33, 152, 162, 180, 214
Sisal (crop and industry), 27, 38, 42, 61, 74–6, 92–3, 198, 206
Sisal Labour Bureau (SILABU), 42, 93
Smiles, Lt. Col. Sir Walter, 137
Smith, Adam, 69 n.42, 206
Smith, Sir Ben MP, 25, 28–9, 32, 43, 48
Smithers, Sir W. MP, 136
Smuts, General Jan, 134, 142
Socialism, 18–20, 68, 123, 142, 152, 193–4, 215
Soil erosion, 38, 40, 47, 101, *and see* Agriculture
South Africa, 2, 11, 79, 90, 107, 134
Southern Agricultural Growth Corridor (SAGCOT), 205, 217
Southern Highlands, 37
Southern Province, 50, 51, 53, 73, 74, 80, 81, 91–2, 93–4, 106–12, 144, 151, 154, 163, 168, 171–2, 181–2, 199–200
Soviet Union, 23, *see also* Russia
Spark, Muriel, 25–6
Special Section, *see* Ministry of Food
Stanley, Col. Oliver MP, 119, 136, 149, 151, 163, 166

Index 241

State-owned enterprises (SOEs), see Public enterprise
Sterling area, 17, 27, 35–6, 62, 115
Sterling balances, 17, 35, 194, 196
Sterling exchange rate, 19, 34, 129, 140–1
Stewart, Henderson MP, 137
Stiegler's Gorge, 205
Stirling, Dr Leader, 109, 112
Stockdale, Sir Frank, 39, 57
Storey, H.H. 165
Strachey, John
  as MP, 25, 30–1, 161–2, 180–1
  early life, 29–31
  later life, 183–5
  Minister of Food, 32–3, 56, 159, 161, 184
  photograph, 30, 126
  optimist, 84, 150, 167, 191
  pushes scheme through Cabinet, 61–4, 68–71, 115–17, 142–7
  in Parliament, 64–5, 91, 118–19, 126, 136–8, 150–2, 177
  misleading Parliament, 146–7, 152, 154–5, 166, 167, 177
  relations with Attlee, 31–2, 159, 166–7
  relations with Dalton, 32
  relations with Ministry, 67–8, 162
  relations with UAC, 65, 76, 122–4, 127, 191
  relations with OFC, 119–21, 154–60, 163–4, 167
  relations with Cripps, 125, 132–3
  relations with Bunting, 154–60
  relations with Gollancz, 30–1, 166
  relations with Gaitskell, 174
  relations with press, 161, 166–7
  relations with Plummer, see Plummer
  ORD Bill, 114–19
  attitude to development, 118, 193
  attitude to risk, 68, 146, 190
  as cuckoo, 119
  visits to Kongwa, 125–7, 138–9, 151, 155–7
  charm, 30, 127, 174
  and Communism, 30, 156–60, 167
  Minister for War, 162, 170
  continued interest in scheme, 163–4, 166–7, 174
  'influential in Cabinet', 174
  views on British Empire, 184
  Obituaries, 184–5
Strauss, George MP, 125
Subsistence farming, see Agriculture
Sudan, 10, 117, 187
Sukumaland, 202
Sunflower, 112, 135, 170
Superconducting Super Collider, 2, 216
Surridge, Rex, 60
Swinton, Lord, 156

Tabora, 112
Tanganyika, Lake, 37
Tanganyika Agricultural Corporation, 182, 202
Tanganyika Sisal Growers Association, 93
Tanganyika Standard, 89, 93, 101, 201
Tanganyika Territory, 3, 6–7, 16, 24, 37–9, 60–1, 198–205
  Administration, 82, 88, 90, 96–7, 127, 128–30, 164, 171–2, 199
  development plans, 7, 11–13, 88, 129, 200
  finances and budget, 6, 53, 128–9, 198
  forestry, 73
  German rule, 6, 89–90
  Labour Department, 7
  land rights, 73, 89–90
  white settlement policy, 11, 90

population, 37
site of scheme, 50–1, 53
attitude towards scheme, 50, 60–1, 96, 120, 128–30, 164–5, 171–3, 177, 199, 202
taxation, 73–4, 199
Tanzania, xiii, 195, 203–5
archives, 3, 52
Dodoma, 2
railways, 72, 182
development plans, 203–4, 217
villagization, 21, 204
war with Uganda, 183
Taxation, 73–4
Taylor Woodrow, 161, 169, 195
TAZARA railway, 182
Tempany, Sir Harold, 46–7, 57
Thatcher, Margaret, 22, 215, 218
The Economist, 76
The Spectator, 29
The Times, 76, 109, 139, 156, 165, 166
Timber, 73, 109, 113
Tizard, Sir Henry, 18
Tobacco, 181
'Traces', 100, 109
Tractors, 87–9, 99–102, 109, 122
photograph, 131
Trade unions, 97
Transport problems, 54, 61, 85–8, 102, 107–9
Treasury, HM, 5–6, 8–9, 35, 47–8, 58–9, 62–4, 69, 73–4, 107, 123–4, 132–3, 140–5, 153, 173–4, 191
Trefgarne, Lord, 208
Tribe, Sir Frank, 45, 56, 138
Troughton, Jack, 138, 155 n.2, 169
Truman, President Harry S. 33
Tsetse fly, 37, 39, 46, 112, 118
Twining, Sir Edward, 136, 142, 169, 172, 175, 178

Uganda, 70, 183
Ujamaa, 204
Underdevelopment, 15

Unilever, 4, 40–5, 56–7, 68, 74–5, 83, 102, 127, 197
United Africa Company (UAC), 4 n.3, 40–5, 50, 54, 72, 79, 85, 118, 152, 191 (and n.3)
as Managing Agent, 59, 62–5, 75–6, 81, 84–8, 102, 106, 110, 112–13, 120–4, 127, 147, 192–3, 195
accounts, 123–4
United Nations (including Trusteeship Council), 91, 117, 145
United States, 17, 19, 22, 29, 33–5, 40, 47, 54, 76, 102, 127, 145, 216–17
peanut farming, 54, 66
Universities Mission to Central Africa (UMCA), 51, 92 n.51, 110–11
Unwin, Sheila, 83, 87, 89, 94, 97, 103–6, 110, 121–2, 127, 134, 154, 157
Unwin, Tom, 83, 103, 157, 170 n.43, 178
Urambo, 112–13, 154, 157, 163, 168, 169, 171, 179, 181

Van den Berg, Clive (Unilever), 84, 88
Villagization, *see* Tanzania

Wages, 92–3 n.51, 198–9
Wagogo (tribe), 52, 89–90, 93, 94–6, 106, 199, 201
Wakefield, John, 7, 48–55 (photograph, 49), 78–80, 102, 140, 165, 177, 183, 185, 190–3, 206
Report, 53–5, 56–8, 62, 75, 99, 100, 130–1, 191
on OFC Board, 120
dismissal, 147–9, 151
Wall, Sir Roland, 43
Walter, Albert, 81

Waugh, Evelyn, 97
Wazungu, 92
Webb, Maurice, MP, 162–4, 166–7, 169, 174–5, 185
Welsh, Dr, 154
West Africa, 10, 39, 69, 87, 92, 206, *and see* Nigeria, French West Africa
West African Frontier Force, 16
West Indies, 8, 48
Western Province, 42, 51, 53, 61, 81, 112–13
Whalley, Tom, 79
Wheat, 32, *see also* Northern Province Wheat Scheme
White settlement, *see* Settlers *and* Agriculture
Wildlife, 79, 82, 99–100, 107
   baboon, 79, 107
   crocodiles, 109
   elephants, 100, 110
   leopard, 83, 110
   lion, 101, 107, 174
   rhinoceros, 83, 101

Willey, Frederick, MP, 161, 169–70
Wilson, Harold, 180–1, 184
Winchester School, 125
Winnifrith, A.J.D. 58 (and n.7)
Wish fulfilment, 194
Women, 3, 28, 41, 82, 83–4, 88, 95, 105, 110–11, 118, 136, 199, 200–1
Women's Royal Naval Service, 83
Wood, Alan, 2, 8, 87 n.34, 103, 128, 134, 149, 177
   life, 100 n.1
   The Groundnut Affair, 2, 8, 156, 166–7, 183
Woods, Maj-General Thomas, 79, 83, 84
World Bank, 192, 203, 209, 213

Yields, *see* Groundnuts

Zambia, 72, *see also* Northern Rhodesia
Zimbabwe, 211
Ziots, Chief Humbi, 182

Eastern Africa Series

Women's Land Rights & Privatization in Eastern Africa
BIRGIT ENGLERT
& ELIZABETH DALEY (EDS)

War & the Politics of Identity in Ethiopia
KJETIL TRONVOLL

Moving People in Ethiopia
ALULA PANKHURST
& FRANÇOIS PIGUET (EDS)

Living Terraces in Ethiopia
ELIZABETH E. WATSON

Eritrea
GAIM KIBREAB

Borders & Borderlands as Resources in the Horn of Africa
DEREJE FEYISSA
& MARKUS VIRGIL HOEHNE (EDS)

After the Comprehensive Peace Agreement in Sudan
ELKE GRAWERT (ED.)

Land, Governance, Conflict & the Nuba of Sudan
GUMA KUNDA KOMEY

Ethiopia
JOHN MARKAKIS

Resurrecting Cannibals
HEIKE BEHREND

Pastoralism & Politics in Northern Kenya & Southern Ethiopia
GÜNTHER SCHLEE
& ABDULLAHI A. SHONGOLO

Islam & Ethnicity in Northern Kenya & Southern Ethiopia
GÜNTHER SCHLEE
with ABDULLAHI A. SHONGOLO

Foundations of an African Civilisation
DAVID W. PHILLIPSON

Regional Integration, Identity & Citizenship in the Greater Horn of Africa
KIDANE MENGISTEAB
& REDIE BEREKETEAB (EDS)

Dealing with Government in South Sudan
CHERRY LEONARDI

The Quest for Socialist Utopia
BAHRU ZEWDE

Disrupting Territories
JÖRG GERTEL, RICHARD ROTTENBURG
& SANDRA CALKINS (EDS)

The African Garrison State
KJETIL TRONVOLL
& DANIEL R. MEKONNEN

The State of Post-conflict Reconstruction
NASEEM BADIEY

Gender, Home & Identity
KATARZYNA GRABSKA

Women, Land & Justice in Tanzania
HELEN DANCER

Remaking Mutirikwi
JOOST FONTEIN

The Oromo & the Christian Kingdom of Ethiopia
MOHAMMED HASSEN

Lost Nationalism
ELENA VEZZADINI

Darfur
CHRIS VAUGHAN

The Eritrean National Service
GAIM KIBREAB

Ploughing New Ground
GETNET BEKELE

Hawks & Doves in Sudan's Armed Conflict
SUAD M. E. MUSA

Ethiopian Warriorhood
TSEHAI BERHANE-SELASSIE

Land, Migration & Belonging
JOSEPH MUJERE

Land Tenure Security
SVEIN EGE (ED.)

Tanzanian Development
DAVID POTTS (ED.)

Nairobi in the Making
CONSTANCE SMITH

The Mission of Apolo Kivebulaya
EMMA WILD-WOOD

*The Crisis of Democratization
in the Greater Horn of Africa*
KIDANE MENGISTEAB (ED.)

The Struggle for Land & Justice in Kenya
AMBREENA MANJI

Imperialism & Development
NICHOLAS WESTCOTT

Kamba Proverbs from Eastern Kenya
JEREMIAH M. KITUNDA

*Sports & Modernity in Late Imperial
Ethiopia*
KATRIN BROMBER

Contested Sustainability
STEFANO PONTE, CHRISTINE NOE
& DAN BROCKINGTON (EDS)

*Decolonising State & Society in Uganda**
KATHERINE BRUCE-LOCKHART,
JONATHAN L. EARLE,
NAKANYIKE B. MUSISI
& EDGAR CHRIS TAYLOR (EDS)

*Reimagining the Gendered Nation**
CHRISTINA KENNY

*Kenya and Zambia's Relations with China
1949–2019**
JODIE YUZHOU SUN

* forthcoming

EASTERN AFRICAN STUDIES

These titles published in the United States and Canada by Ohio University Press

Revealing Prophets
Edited by DAVID M. ANDERSON &
DOUGLAS H. JOHNSON

*East African Expressions of
Christianity*
Edited by THOMAS SPEAR
& ISARIA N. KIMAMBO

The Poor Are Not Us
Edited by DAVID M. ANDERSON &
VIGDIS BROCH-DUE

Potent Brews
JUSTIN WILLIS

Swahili Origins
JAMES DE VERE ALLEN

Being Maasai
Edited by THOMAS SPEAR
& RICHARD WALLER

Jua Kali Kenya
KENNETH KING

Control & Crisis in Colonial Kenya
BRUCE BERMAN

Unhappy Valley
Book One: State & Class
Book Two: Violence & Ethnicity
BRUCE BERMAN
& JOHN LONSDALE

Mau Mau from Below
GREET KERSHAW

The Mau Mau War in Perspective
FRANK FUREDI

*Squatters & the Roots of Mau Mau
1905-63*
TABITHA KANOGO

*Economic & Social Origins of Mau
Mau 1945-53*
DAVID W. THROUP

Multi-Party Politics in Kenya
DAVID W. THROUP
& CHARLES HORNSBY

Empire State-Building
JOANNA LEWIS

*Decolonization & Independence in
Kenya 1940-93*
Edited by B.A. OGOT
& WILLIAM R. OCHIENG'

Eroding the Commons
DAVID ANDERSON

Penetration & Protest in Tanzania
ISARIA N. KIMAMBO

Custodians of the Land
Edited by GREGORY MADDOX,
JAMES L. GIBLIN & ISARIA N.
KIMAMBO

*Education in the Development of
Tanzania 1919-1990*
LENE BUCHERT

The Second Economy in Tanzania
T.L. MALIYAMKONO
& M.S.D. BAGACHWA

*Ecology Control & Economic
Development in East African History*
HELGE KJEKSHUS

Siaya
DAVID WILLIAM COHEN
& E.S. ATIENO ODHIAMBO

*Uganda Now • Changing Uganda
Developing Uganda • From Chaos
to Order • Religion & Politics in East
Africa*
Edited by HOLGER BERNT
HANSEN & MICHAEL TWADDLE

*Kakungulu & the Creation of Uganda
1868-1928*
MICHAEL TWADDLE

Controlling Anger
SUZETTE HEALD

Kampala Women Getting By
SANDRA WALLMAN

*Political Power in Pre-Colonial
Buganda*
RICHARD J. REID

Alice Lakwena & the Holy Spirits
HEIKE BEHREND

Slaves, Spices & Ivory in Zanzibar
ABDUL SHERIFF

Zanzibar Under Colonial Rule
Edited by ABDUL SHERIFF
& ED FERGUSON

*The History & Conservation of
Zanzibar Stone Town*
Edited by ABDUL SHERIFF

Pastimes & Politics
LAURA FAIR

*Ethnicity & Conflict in the Horn of
Africa*
Edited by KATSUYOSHI FUKUI &
JOHN MARKAKIS

*Conflict, Age & Power in North East
Africa*
Edited by EISEI KURIMOTO
& SIMON SIMONSE

*Property Rights & Political
Development in Ethiopia & Eritrea*
SANDRA FULLERTON JOIREMAN

Revolution & Religion in Ethiopia
ØYVIND M. EIDE

Brothers at War
TEKESTE NEGASH & KJETIL
TRONVOLL

From Guerrillas to Government
DAVID POOL

Mau Mau & Nationhood
Edited by E.S. ATIENO
ODHIAMBO & JOHN LONSDALE

*A History of Modern Ethiopia,
1855-1991* (2nd edn)
BAHRU ZEWDE

Pioneers of Change in Ethiopia
BAHRU ZEWDE

Remapping Ethiopia
Edited by W. JAMES,
D. DONHAM, E. KURIMOTO
& A. TRIULZI

*Southern Marches of Imperial
Ethiopia*
Edited by DONALD L. DONHAM &
WENDY JAMES

A Modern History of the Somali
(4th edn)
I.M. LEWIS

*Islands of Intensive Agriculture in
East Africa*
Edited by MATS WIDGREN
& JOHN E.G. SUTTON

Leaf of Allah
EZEKIEL GEBISSA

*Dhows & the Colonial Economy of
Zanzibar 1860-1970*
ERIK GILBERT

*African Womanhood in Colonial
Kenya*
TABITHA KANOGO

African Underclass
ANDREW BURTON

In Search of a Nation
Edited by GREGORY H. MADDOX &
JAMES L. GIBLIN

A History of the Excluded
JAMES L. GIBLIN

Black Poachers, White Hunters
EDWARD I. STEINHART

Ethnic Federalism
DAVID TURTON

Crisis & Decline in Bunyoro
SHANE DOYLE

*Emancipation without Abolition in
German East Africa*
JAN-GEORG DEUTSCH

*Women, Work & Domestic
Virtue in Uganda 1900-2003*
GRACE BANTEBYA KYOMUHENDO
& MARJORIE KENISTON
McINTOSH

Cultivating Success in Uganda
GRACE CARSWELL

*War in Pre-Colonial
Eastern Africa*
RICHARD REID

*Slavery in the Great Lakes Region of
East Africa*
Edited by HENRI MÉDARD
& SHANE DOYLE

The Benefits of Famine
DAVID KEEN

www.ingramcontent.com/pod-product-compliance
Lightning Source LLC
Chambersburg PA
CBHW051608230426
43668CB00013B/2032